The Spirit of Japanese Law

The Spirit of the Laws

Alan Watson, General Editor

The *Spirit of the Laws* series illuminates the nature of legal systems throughout the world. Titles in the series are concerned less with the rules of the law and more with the relationships of the laws in each system with religion and moral perspectives; the degree of complexity and abstraction; classifications; attitudes to possible sources of law; authority; and values enshrined in law. Topics covered in the series include Roman law, Chinese law, biblical law, Talmudic law, canon law, common law, Hindu law, Islamic law, Buddhist law, customary law, Japanese law, and international law.

THE SPIRIT OF
JAPANESE LAW

John Owen Haley

The University of Georgia Press
Athens & London

Paperback edition, 2006
© 1998 by the University of Georgia Press
Athens, Georgia 30602
All rights reserved
Designed by Walton Harris
Set in 9.5 on 14 Trump by G&S Typesetters, Inc.

Printed digitally in the United States of America

The Library of Congress has cataloged the
hardcover edition of this book as follows:

Library of Congress Cataloging-in-Publication Data

Haley, John Owen.
The spirit of Japanese law / John Owen Haley.
xx, 251 p. ; 24 cm. —(The spirit of the laws)
Includes bibliographical references (p. [213]–246)
and index.
ISBN 0-8203-2022-6 (alk. paper)
1. Law—Japan—Philosophy. 2. Law—Moral and ethical
aspects—Japan. 3. Justice, Administration of—Japan.
I. Title. II. Series: Spirit of the laws (Athens, Georgia)
KNX440 .H35 1998
349.52—dc21   98-17860

Paperback ISBN-13: 978-0-8203-2887-4
          ISBN-10: 0-8203-2887-1

British Library Cataloging-in-Publication Data available

www.ugapress.org

To Dan Fenno Henderson

CONTENTS

ACKNOWLEDGMENTS

Scholars form a very special sort of community. In all that we do we are peculiarly interdependent. We stand on others' shoulders to see more distant horizons. What we know and write reflects the ideas and research of past and present generations. What we say and profess has no meaning without the receptive listeners of present and future generations. Their reactions and responses make the efforts worthwhile. This book thus reflects what I have learned from others, especially my colleagues at the University of Washington—Don Clarke, Dan Foote, and Toshiko Takenaka. I also owe a special debt of gratitude to a small but growing band of friends in the field—Larry Beer, Frank Bennett, Vicki Beyer, Taimie Bryant, Harry First, Kōichirō Fujikura, Tony Freyer, Jean Grier, Masahito Inouye, David Johnson, Bob Leflar, Mark Levin, Percy Luney, Mitsuo Matsushita, Curtis Milhaupt, Setsuo Miyazawa, Minoru Nakatani, Kenneth Port, Mark Ramseyer, Dan Rosen, Arthur Rossett, Steve Salzberg, Alex Seita, Malcolm Smith, Veronica Taylor, Frank Upham, Michael Young—whose wisdom has been so generously shared. I remain equally indebted to Sharon Murata and Richard Torrance for their work as research assistants many years ago and more recently to Yana Hirata. Rob Britt of the University of Washington Gallagher Law Library provided invaluable help. Kristine M. Blakeslee of the University of Georgia Press saw this through. Nor could this book have been completed without the efforts of Kyle Morrison, Jane Fox, Vicki Mastoriodes, Jean Knight, and other members of the secretarial staff of the University of Washington School of Law.

INTRODUCTION

This book is about law and legal institutions in Japan today. Legal rules and the values that they express and that motivate those who participate as the primary actors within the legal system are its primary focus. The aim is to isolate and explain patterns and approaches that appear at least to give Japanese law identity and coherence. How law is made and enforced is secondary.[1] Noted rarely and only in passing are the great preponderance of Japanese legislation and judicial cases that deal with common issues in common ways. No attempt is made to cover even exceptional Japanese approaches to the myriad issues that Japan, like other industrial societies, has to face. By necessity mention is made of some aspects of the history, development, and scope of law in Japan. A general understanding of the values and domain of law is essential to an appreciation of the principal themes—implicit as well as explicit—of law in Japan. Considerably greater attention, however, needs to be paid to the primary participants in Japan's legal system—legal scholars, lawyers in practice, prosecutors, and above all judges. They are law's actors. They are the ones who make and enforce legal rules. Their role, history, and organizational context provide insight into their shared as well as institutional values. What is intended is neither a history of Japanese law and legal institutions nor a study of law and society in contemporary Japan. Rather, the subject, as entitled, is the spirit of Japanese law.

Law has many meanings. The law of the anthropologist can comprise nearly any norm, rule, or principle, any sanction and mechanism for enforcement that can be identified in society. Community norms, custom and convention, the judgments of the wise, the pronouncements of the sacred, and the commands of the ruler all come within its domain. The law of the lawyer is not as expansive. Its realm and reach are far more constrained. The law treated here is the law of lawyers. It is limited to the rules and principles, the remedies and sanctions, and the processes by which law is made. This limitation is not, however, arbitrary or insubstantial. To define law otherwise and more broadly would obscure much of what this book is about. The spirit of Japanese law is not simply the spirit of Japanese society. Except as reflected in the values and practices of those who make and enforce the legal rules—legislators and lawyers, prosecutors and police, jurists and judges—these values would not have particular or special application in the rules and principles of the state. We would not be able to distinguish differences that may have meaning and lead to insights with respect not only to the legal system, narrowly defined, but also to the broader society. With law like flowers we would miss the distinctions between species and thus the rich variety and complexity of what surrounds us.

To attempt such a study is also a daunting task. Much has been written in English on Japanese law. The works that describe particular areas of law seldom attempt, however, to explore deeper themes and values that underlie the diverse rules and principles that constitute the corpus of any particular field of law or that motivate the processes, institutions, and actors within the legal system. Closer to such an endeavor are those studies that deal with the interrelationships and reciprocal influences between the legal system and Japanese society. From them we learn how social organization and community controls, societal values, and social practices have helped to mold and in turn have been molded by legal rules and processes. We gain insight into the contribution of law to social change in Japan and elsewhere. Less attention, however, has been paid to the internal influences that guide and shape the development of legal rules and the patterns of their enforcement—how, for example, judicial administration or prosecutorial goals affect the rules and practices of the law.

Some would set aside cultural factors altogether or deny outright the significance of social distinctiveness, relying instead on a universal "rationality" of all actors, whether economic, political, or legal. They may argue that any quest for the "spirit" of law is a quixotic pursuit. Yet they too posit an institutional framework, processes, and legal rules that establish the parameters within which rational choices are made. Assume rational behavior and it becomes apparent that context determines outcomes. Thus the whys and hows that explain the parameters of rational behavior force acknowledgment of the central role of shared values, beliefs, and expectations—in other words, culture—in establishing the critical conditions for social actions. So too culturally determined constructs within a legal system channel rational behavior to its often distinctive consequences. Even so, distinctive culture does not inexorably equate with distinctive law. The question remains whether some fundamental themes, patterns, or values distinguish Japanese law in ways that determine the often distinctive outcomes of rational choice in Japan.

A few might further question whether meaningful inquiry is possible into values intrinsic to any legal system without inclusion of cultural perspectives and the relationship of society to law as either process or rule in the affairs of daily life. To have significance, what is described must relate to the essentials of Japanese experience in the family, the workplace, or the neighborhood. In these areas textbook legal rules seem remarkably remote and formal legal processes seem distant and unfamiliar. Any discussion of law even partially divorced from social realities will fail to address the primary issues that Japanese confront on a daily basis. Surely if there is indeed something coherent in Japanese law, it must touch routine patterns of life in Japan.

Many of these doubts and questions relate to concern over claims to Japanese exceptionalism. The literature in English on law in Japan often leaves the impression of legal institutions and rules, the courts and codes, transplanted from abroad but pruned to fit into a very different garden, that continue to grow and develop as a unique national system. Too frequently neglected is the continuing identity of Japanese law within the civil law tradition and the shared concern of Japanese who tend these transplants so that they conform to the patterns of growth and development of their origins. Japanese contract practices and company behavior may differ, but the rules of Japanese contract and company law are not distinctively Japanese in any significant respect. The apparent values of Japanese law remain on the whole the values in time and place of their predominately European origins.

Thus there would appear to be very little if anything distinctive or exceptional to the rules and processes of the Japanese legal system that might enable us to point to a "spirit" of law as distinguished from the society from which legal rules emerge. Whatever the underlying values and norms that may have been expressed in traditional Japanese law, the legal rules of contemporary Japan have been adapted from European and, to a lesser extent, American sources. There is little within Japanese law, some say, that is fundamentally peculiar to Japan.

Few of the rules on contemporary Japanese law may be uniquely Japanese. Nonetheless, Japan has not simply replicated the laws or institutions of any one foreign legal system. If only as a hybrid, the mix of legal rules and legal institutions gives the Japanese legal system a distinguishing cast. More significant, however, is the combination of a continuous process of selective adoption of foreign models and the application of these adopted rules in the Japanese cultural or institutional environment. As described below, the autonomy of Japanese legal reforms as well as the choice of European legal doctrine and their enforcement in Japan's social and institutional context ensure the distinctiveness of Japanese law and its spirit.

To argue that law in Japan has distinctive characteristics is not, however, to say that Japan is exceptional in its peculiarity. We often lose sight of the similarity of Japan's experience in adapting its law and legal institutions to the civil law tradition with all but the handful of countries that share a legal heritage shaped by British colonial rule and remain within the common law tradition. In East Asia, for example, only the national legal systems of Malaysia and Singapore are today outside the ambit of the civil law tradition. Some, like Indonesia, reflect the influence of European colonial rule, but others, like Thailand and China, share with Japan the experience of self-selected reception of European law. Whether continental European or British in more immediate origin, all contemporary legal and political orders reflect the profound influence of Roman law. Whether assimilated by invading tribes, implanted by settlers, imposed by colonial rulers, or used as models by indigenous reformers, in the course of two millennia the institutions of Roman law have become universal. Of course, they are not everywhere the same. Ideas and institutions, whatever their origin, acquire in diverse settings over time transforming gloss that differentiates them from those at their source. In the process of adaptation and transformation, repeated patterns and themes begin to emerge that are as relevant to law as to other facets of social life. The "spirit" of any particular legal order thus comprises the pervasive themes, patterns, or values that appear repeatedly within it and shape and reshape the rules and processes of law. Japan is therefore no different from all other nation-states in dealing with the problems of accommodating the ideas and institutions of transplanted law within perhaps an even more mutable culture.

To discern and explain these themes, patterns, or values in contemporary Japanese law is the more daunting challenge of this book. It is one thing to say that distinguishing features exist but quite another to identify accurately what they are or mean. Despite the marginal advantages of a broader and implicitly comparative perspective, outside observers have neither the full store of knowledge nor the sensitivity of those who experience the system from within. Nor can this be a matter of purely subjective judgment or intuitive guess. Even without empirical tests, for the lawyer at least, a confirming standard does exist. The quality of the argument is evidenced in the accuracy of its forecast. The value of such a study therefore depends upon whether it enables us to predict more accurately the future course of Japanese law.

Courts and judicial decisions are central in this endeavor. In Japan as in nearly all contemporary legal systems, however central the role of others—legal scholars, the practicing bar, or prosecutors—may appear, judges generally have the last official word. In applying legal rules made by others in individual cases, judges determine what the legal rule means as it applies in particular circumstances. However, judges do not always have the last word. So long as the parties themselves remain free to ignore the rules laid down by judges, they remain in control. Or, in the case of criminal justice, to the extent that the police or prosecutors are allowed to divert offenders onto other tracks for correction and thus to avoid adjudication, they define the rules. As in the case of most contract and other optional (or default) rules of private law, such freedom or diversion may itself be an explicit value of the legal system. It may also be a consequence of less intentional features. Excessive costs and other barriers can prevent meaningful access to the courts, and process rules can preclude the justiciability of significant claims. Even in such instances, however, judges have a major role. They remain the principal actors in determining the accessibility of the courts, the legitimacy of alternative channels, and the effectiveness of legal rules in shaping social behavior.

The role of judges in Japan deserves special emphasis. John Henry Wigmore, who witnessed the formation of Japan's contemporary legal system as a teacher and advisor in Japan in the late nineteenth century, noted the historical similarity between Japan and England in the preeminence of adjudication and judge-made law.[2] Contemporary Japanese scholarship on Japan's legal history echoes Wigmore's observations.[3] Today, too, Japanese courts play a central part in the process of creating and enforcing legal rules. The Japanese judiciary enjoys broad public trust. Japanese judges have an enviable record of honesty. Litigation has long been a forceful instrument of legal and political reform. The dynamics of law and social change in Japan can indeed be described in terms of the tensions between courts and their administrative rivals.[4]

To be able to predict what judges will do in future cases with any degree of certainty or probability, we must be able to identify collective aims and motives—not simply the justifications—judges have in reaching certain conclusions. Values are important. They are guideposts and references in forecasting what judges in a particular case are most likely to decide. Lawyers can and do routinely predict how judges will interpret and apply legal rules in most lawsuits. Such forecasting will usually be quite accurate to the extent that the rule is stated without ambiguity or ambivalence and the outcome of its application to a known set of facts can be predictably considered "fair" or "just" by the judge and, as perceived by the judge, the community at large. Add any uncertainty, as for example to the meaning of the language of the rule itself, the facts of the case, or the "justice" of the result, and prediction becomes a much more risky venture. This process of prediction is of course what much lawyering is all about— assessing the likely outcome of cases to be decided in the future by judges based on prior cases and an understanding of the various conventions and beliefs that influence judicial behavior. In the process lawyers routinely make educated guesses as to the values judges hold and their influence on judicial decisions.

As guideposts, the most important values are those that are shared. In other words, culture—defined as shared values as well as habits, expectations, and beliefs—also counts. In any legal process, culture has several facets. Narrowed to judicial behavior, culture includes the values and beliefs shared within each of the various communities to which a judge belongs from the broadest, even global, scope to the narrowest scope of status, class, or profession. Defined in this way, culture encompasses the values and beliefs of not only the national community at large but also the legal profession and the judiciary.

Legal values are only one of several elements of a legal culture, which includes understandings about law, the legal process, and the judicial role that combine as constituent components of the legal system itself. The spirit of law as values is a piece of the puzzle of law itself. The spirit of Japanese law is thus as integral to the formal system of Japanese justice as the rules of its codes.

Unfortunately, too often the word "culture" is used without much care and as a result it loses its usefulness as an element of analysis. More precisely defined, culture becomes a critical factor in understanding the nature, role, and dynamics of law in any society. Culture is, however, simply a descriptive label. It does not—and should not—imply a normative judgment as to whether the habit or belief is valid or invalid, good or bad, rational or irrational. Culture is also frequently misused as a fixed, immutable element of social reality. We need to keep in mind that culture is also mutable. It changes. The important question is thus not whether values, expectations, and habits change but how and why.

Finally, some readers about to begin a book on Japan may be tempted to conjure up something exotically unique, a conflict-free society in which law is rarely needed and has little significance. Others may tend to emphasize exceptional features of Japan as a state-directed industrial producer, so homogeneous and conformist that law has little place. A glance should suffice to show that the idea of Japan as a harmonious, homogeneous, and conformist society is false, but whatever kernels of truth may be found in these or similar views, they ignore most of the landscape. Japan today has much more in common with its western industrial peers than its own past. As previously noted, Japan's legal system is no more unique than the French or German or any other national legal system. To focus on features of Japanese law that contribute to its singular identity is not, to repeat, to deny the equally if not more pervasive characteristics it shares with other industrial democracies, particularly those within the civil law world.

The Spirit of Japanese Law

1 Law's Values

In Japan, as in any other country, some values and beliefs embodied in law are peculiar. They reflect the necessarily unique shared historical experience, habits, and values of Japanese society. Other values and beliefs, however, are less exceptional. In contemporary legal systems worldwide, most of law's values—albeit with different levels of emphasis and especially realization—are in fact universally shared. The legitimacy of legal rules and adherence to rule by law, judicial neutrality, and the independence of judges to decide individual cases free from personal gain or direct political intervention are among the most obvious. Others are common only within communities formed by particular legal traditions. Understandings on the sources of law differ, for example, between religious and secular legal traditions. Similarly, certainty and consistency are valued differently between the common law and civil law traditions. Japan thus tends to share the values and beliefs of the legal traditions to which it has past or present affinity. Important among them are fundamental assumptions and values common to all contemporary legal orders within the civil law tradition. These assumptions and values include a shared understanding of the nature of law itself.

JUDICIAL DECISIONS AS SOURCES OF LAW

Whatever the word "law" may mean in other contexts, within the institutional matrix of contemporary states law is today almost universally understood in positivist terms as, at least principally, an instrument of governmental control. Even the most fervent proponents of natural law are forced to admit that no legal rule or principle is truly realized without some form of positivist expression. Thus, in Japan, as elsewhere, law is defined as the rules and principles articulated by legally established institutions through formal processes also provided by law. As law these rules differ from both formal rules made and adhered to by institutions that do not exercise lawmaking authority as well as informal rules recognized and even enforced by the community, however binding or functionally equivalent to legal rules either may be.

Law has long been understood in Japan as an instrument of government control. Law comprises rules and principles intended as binding standards of conduct and behavior. All are today formally sourced in a legislated constitution, five basic codes, an ever increasing corpus of statutes as well as through statutory delegation of legislated power, the authority to regulate, cabinet orders, ministerial ordinances, and prefectural and other local government regulations. Whatever the primary source, however, legal rules and principles in codes and statute books remain mere words on paper until interpreted and applied in the context of actual cases and real-life situations.

Any system of law with a hierarchy of courts and concern for predictability inevitably develops a body of rules and principles articulated by judges in the course of adjudication as they interpret legislated rules, fill in gaps, and amplify the bare bones of codified or statutory language. Japanese scholars dispute the status of judicial decisions as a formal source of law.[1] Nonetheless, in Japan, as in all developed legal systems, judges adhere to prior decisions, particularly those of higher courts. Judicial decisions thus function in Japan, as elsewhere, in effect, if not in theory, as a secondary but significant source of law.

The emphasis in Japan on judicial precedent seems to be particularly strong. Predictability is not the sole concern. Notions of fairness that like cases require like outcomes and the mandate of a unitary system of national law underlie a special stress on consistency.[2] In one of the classic prewar studies of the role of precedent, Izutarō Suehiro (1888–1951) added a third impetus: the recognition of the imperfection of all legal rules over time and the related need for adapting legal rules to changing social conditions. In his words: "Legislation is the work of the human mind. It is impossible to make a perfect product that will meet all the exigencies of the changing world. Even if it be possible to have a law which fits perfectly all social conditions at a certain point of time, change in the society will immediately make it an imperfect product. Only judicial precedents can supply the contents to fill the original and subsequent gaps and so afford the people with criteria for their conduct."[3]

Hence, the 1890 Court Organization Law required the Great Court of Cassation (*Daishin'in*) to sit en banc when overruling a precedent.[4] The 1947 Court Law similarly precludes today petty bench decisions contrary to prior interpretations of the constitution and other laws and regulations.[5] The Code of Criminal Procedure provides as formal grounds for appeal on questions of law a lower court judgment at variance with judicial precedent as well as the absence of a judicial precedent on point.[6] Even without such formal recognition, however, Japanese judges themselves have long considered themselves bound by judicial precedent.[7] Since the early 1920s, the Japanese courts have selected for publication decisions of their highest court as "judicial precedents" (*hanrei*). Before 1923, the official compilation of judicial decisions by the Great Court of Cassation was simply entitled as a record of judgment (*hanketsuroku*).

Nor is adherence to precedent a modern innovation. Whether buttressed by some special cultural concern for continuity or deference to hierarchical authority or simply the manifestation of past practice, historically judicial lawmaking has been a characteristic phenomenon of law. In Japan as in England, which as previously mentioned Wigmore noted many years ago, much of traditional law was created in the context of adjudication by administrative officials. Today, in any event, whatever scholars may say, lawyers and the courts alike rely upon and cite judicial decisions as controlling authority.

As in other civil law systems, scholars too are among law's primary actors. They play a significant role in articulating the rationale and theory of legal rules. In Japan they have historically formed a connecting bridge for the introduction of ideas and institutions from abroad. In the seventh and eighth centuries a corps of official court scholars versed in T'ang law assisted in drafting and explicating Japan's first codes.[8] The tradition of Chinese learning continued into the eighteenth and mid-nineteenth centuries.[9] Scholars today continue this tradition of transmitting legal concepts and theory. They are also critics. In both roles they reinforce the importance of judicial decisions by challenging the underlying orientations and continuing to introduce reforms from outside sources. Once consensus among scholars is reached, scholarly opinion (*gakusetsu*) becomes an important source of law as well.

Some would add custom (*kanshū*) and reason (*jōri*) to the list of sources of law.[10] Custom is expressly acknowledged as a source of law, for example, in article 1 of the Japanese Commercial Code as well as article 2 of Japan's basic conflict of laws statute, the *Hōrei*.[11] Customary rules, however, only acquire the attributes of law indirectly when recognized by judges and to a lesser extent by scholars. A customary norm may appear to operate as a legal rule in the sense of its influence as an apparent, socially enforced, standard for behavior. Yet custom like culture is not immutable. Customary norms change. Nonconforming conduct is the catalyst and imitation, the driving force. Once articulated and enforced by a court or other formal law-enforcing institution, however, customary norms become fixed as legal rule. A rule thus created is no longer fettered by the vicissitudes of social change. Only when incorporated through legislation or adjudication are any of the three—scholarly opinion, custom, or reason—truly transformed into legal rules. In the end judges decide what scholarship, which custom, and how reason becomes law.

LAW AND MORALS

Japanese are not alone in taking for granted a definition of law and legal rules as instruments of governmental control and ordering. Few others today would disagree. Whatever its sources, ends, or formulations, law, in the words of Roscoe Pound, is a mechanism of "efficacious social engineering."[12] Law works because it binds. We are compelled to obey. By what force is seldom even questioned. Most presume the legitimacy of state-directed means of coercion through judges, sheriffs, bailiffs, prosecutors, and police or through some sort of internalized acceptance of the moral force of legal rules that we accept as compelling. Less often acknowledged are the social pressures of community, family, and peers whose approval we cherish and whose disapproval we try to avoid. Within legal traditions in which moral admonition to be law-abiding is strong, or conversely the legitimacy of legal rules is closely associated with their "justness," moral and related community pressures have significant bearing on compliance. Rarely is there a felt need to distinguish between sources of legitimacy or to question the moral underpinnings of legal rules. Until the legal mechanisms of social control fail, why we obey the law is seldom questioned. Even then the question of whether we should obey the law contains its own answer.

In the West as in other traditions in which the earliest conceptions of law and legal rules are identified as having deistic origin, legal and moral rules tend to fuse. The identity of moral and legal rules buttresses law's demand for compliance. It also establishes within the legal order the idea of legal as well as moral constraints on those who rule. Even with the development of the secular state, some notion of natural law norms persists, imparting restrictive values to the nature of legal rules even as purely secular expressions of governmental policy. The idea that law, by its nature, includes normative values that restrain those who make law or require them to enforce rules and principles they did not make themselves thus produces a fundamental tension in contemporary Western states. The conflict is posed in the question of whether we are obligated, as either a moral or legal proposition, to obey unjust laws.

Consider a fundamentally different set of conceptions about law and morality. In such an alternative legal order the separation of law and morals could mean shared acceptance of two independent, although perhaps related, spheres and sources of rules and principles. Both would command obedience, but one as a matter of moral obligation, the other as a legal duty. Some rules might overlap, for example, were the moral order to include the principle that those who hold political power are to be obeyed or were some legal rules to reflect moral precepts. The tensions of European natural law and positivism, which arise out of the gradual disassociation of what is sacred and what is secular, would not arise at least with the same poignancy. Moral rules would not require legal enforcement, nor would they be expected to be enforced necessarily by law. Similarly, unjust laws would legally command the same degree of compliance as just laws. Both would have the same degree of political legitimacy. In cases of conflict, inevitably questions would be asked regarding the actual extent of compliance. Which rules would in fact become more socially internalized? Which ones would the community be most likely to enforce? The answers seem self-evident. Without shared community acceptance—in other words, cultural conformity—legal rules are less likely to be obeyed without extensive means of coercive compulsion. In other words, to be effective without community acceptance, legal rules require effective formal enforcement. What then of Japan?

Within the broader East Asian tradition shaped under the direct or indirect influence of the civilization of imperial China, a separation of law and morality was fundamental. From the third century B.C., law in imperial China was understood as a secular instrument of state control. As a matter of policy as well as belief, many legal rules were designed to enforce moral (Confucianist) propositions. As law constituted an imperial command, obedience was a fundamental moral as well as political obligation. And the moral sphere provided the principal constraints of legitimacy on the exercise of imperial authority. However, as a vehicle of imperial authority, law itself had no deistic, religious, or other moral nexus. Greek, Roman, and later medieval Christian notions of "justice" as inclusive of both moral and legal meaning had no counterpart. What was moral or "righteous" remained separate and apart from what was legal. To be sure, righteous behavior could coincide with legal behavior on the part of ruler or ruled alike. Such coincidence, however, remained just that—a coincidental joining of the two.

Despite the enormous influence of imperial Chinese law on Japan, differences between Japan and China in the conceptions and separate roles of law and morality were substantial. Japan did not develop into a imperial state governed by a centralized officialdom selected by examination with legal rules designed to order and regulate the behavior of both ruled and ruler. The Chinese concept of the mandate from heaven was neither needed nor introduced. Japan's imperial institution became the centerpiece of its own official creation myth, transforming a tribal chieftain into a perpetual sinofied ruler. Japan thus did not recognize the restraints on arbitrary imperial power of the mandate from heaven. Nor did the Japanese indigenously develop or fully accept any belief system with universally applicable norms of behavior. The idea of a generalized, naturally ordained social hierarchy with corresponding moral obligations remained a relatively superficial veneer in Japanese social relationships. S. N. Eisenstadt makes this point a central theme in his observations on Japan.[13] Japan remained uniquely insulated from the intellectual and religious transformations that engulfed the Mediterranean, South Asia, and China two and a half millennia ago. Although Japan felt their influence, the universalist claims that became embedded in the cultures influenced by these civilizations did not take full root. Japan's indigenous legal order reflected the imposition of Chinese imperial institutions and concepts of law and governance not as a result of external pressures as in other parts of Asia but rather by indigenous rulers in a kinship-based society in which both deity and rule remained particularistic. Between the fifth and eighth centuries these rulers recast tribal Japanese communities only partially into what they designed as a variant of a sinofied imperial state. Their introduction of imperial Chinese law along with a written language, religion, technology, and the arts recreated Japanese civilization. For a millennium law was in effect defined in terms of imperial Chinese notions. Nevertheless Japanese particularism remained. Despite the universalistic mandates of Buddhism and Chinese ethical thought, primal religious and political practices were accommodated and remained strong. The emergence of a warrior class and warrior ruler followed patterns embedded in a tribal system. Moreover, as warrior governance acquired the forms of centralized bureaucratic rule, Japan's peasant villages acquired many of the characteristics of colonies governed indirectly through vicarious responsibility of local leaders by military conquerors from often distant barracks. Distance and indirect rule enabled Japan's villagers to preserve collective autonomy by outward deference to those in authority above them, despite internal deviance with respect to any externally imposed and unwanted rules they could safely ignore.

Although legal rules themselves may not have had moral force, they did reflect the legitimacy and values of those with political authority. Coupled with primal notions of the sacred and deference to the acts of an ancestral past, fundamental institutional continuity was also ensured. Imperial penal and administrative codes (*ritsuryō*) endured into the mid-nineteenth century. Similarly, edicts of the great warrior lords were honored and preserved as if sacrosanct texts. Thus in Japan, as in China, the great legal reforms of the country's earliest history remained in place, albeit narrowed in application and supplemented by warrior edict to near oblivion. The result is at least to some a paradox of deference with neglect. Legal rules and institutions remained intact from the distant past irrespective of extreme and often violent political change. Yet avoidance and noncompliance made many instrumentally irrelevant.

As noted above, in the evolution of Japanese governance, a substantial body of judicial precedent developed. However, the idea of law remained confined within the conceptual framework of the imperial Chinese tradition. As represented by the Chinese characters *ritsu* and *ryō* in the compound used to denote a legal code, law meant a set of penal proscriptions with appropriate penalties and administrative rules. Rules related to what jurists today classify as "private law"—such as contracts and property—of course did exist. Such rules, however, were found and enforced within an essentially administrative and penal legal order. No notion of "rights" with correlative "duties" was needed or could even develop. No concept of a corpus of private law comparable to the Roman law tradition could have existed in this system of administrative regulation. Any notion of a legal "right" divorced from bureaucratic institutions of enforcement or of the initiation and control over the mechanisms of law enforcement left to private parties would have been antithetical to the Chinese imperium. Thus, traditional Chinese law by its nature could not develop the idea of rights with correlative duties. Nor could legal scholarship emerge as an essentially autonomous order of legal concepts and principles. Law could only remain a set of duty-defining rules to be enforced by imperial or warrior officials.

LEARNING

Japan's contemporary legal system was constructed with little reference, however, to such foundations. A century ago, an elite group of Japanese reformers working closely with individual French and German advisors had all but completed a massive transformation of the Japanese legal system. Their efforts represented an almost complete break with the past. Past practices and legal precedents were compiled and consulted, but they were recast completely in modern Roman law categories and conceptualizations. In 1889, the Meiji emperor had granted his subjects a constitution. A year later a newly established parliament, elected under a new electoral law, was enacting statutes while administrative officials were beginning to write and implement related regulations. New civil, commercial, criminal, and related procedural law codes had been drafted, debated, redrafted, enacted, and promulgated. Newly established educational institutions had begun to educate and train a new corps of judges, prosecutors, and barristers and a new generation of legal scholars and government officials. A new system of land, commercial, and family registration had been established. A new legal language was being created and new legal concepts and theory were being introduced. New laws, institutions, and legal processes had begun to operate to fill in the gaps and deal with the new social and economic problems of the transformed imperial Japan as an emerging industrial and military power.

This second reception transformed Japan into a modern state. The introduction of western law inexorably produced new tensions. Behind the code system, its institutions, and its principles of legal ordering were a set of foundational norms and values related to the role of law and the liberal state in social ordering. These norms and values included the primacy of private law, exemplified by a civil code and the judicial process. Within private law, property and contract were the legal categories of central concern. The legal institutions, processes, and rules of this new political and legal order reflected those of their origin. The institutions and concepts introduced from western models themselves incorporated values and unstated premises defining law, the state, and the relationship of both to the individual and community. They incorporated nineteenth-century European ideals of a liberal political order in which the role of the state was defined primarily in terms of maintaining order and ensuring an environment in which the individual would be able to fulfill self-defined aims. Such values provoked direct and lasting challenges to a society in which legal rules, moral precepts, social patterns, and restraint of self tended in practice to reinforce community interests at the expense of individual pursuits. Out of these tensions, a distinctive legal system as well as a distinctive society evolved, and the gradual process of mutual adaptation of new rules, processes, and institutions to their social environment proceeded.

The paradox of deference and neglect also continued. The authority of the state and law expanded but its powers were on all fronts constrained. The literature on law and society in Japan, for example, is fulsome in its depiction of both the centrality of legal rules and Japanese tendency toward legalism in both a positive and negative sense as well as the "informality" of Japanese governance and the social irrelevance of legal rules and processes.

Other than perhaps the extent and success of the reforms, Japan's effort was hardly remarkable. Throughout the nineteenth century in Europe, the Americas, Africa, and Asia, laws and legal institutions were being recast. Japan's experience in legal reform was an almost universal phenomenon as part of the process of creating the modern nation-state. So too was Japan's choice of models. Except in those territories subject by settlement or conquest to British colonial rule, continental Europe provided the principal reference for legal reform. As a result today the legal systems of all but a handful of nation states share a basic institutional framework derived primarily from continental European origins. To borrow Mirjan Damaska's term, the "grammar" of the civil law tradition has become an international language.[14]

To say that Japan has borrowed law is therefore true but trite. What makes the Japanese experience exceptional is not its debt to a "foreign" tradition. The distinctive feature of Japan's experience is its autonomy. Foreign models were not imposed but truly self-selected. In Asia this distinction is shared only by China and Thailand, both of which were influenced by Japan's example. More significant, the process of autonomous borrowing was itself a reflection of a more fundamental characteristic—an emphasis on learning. This latter feature of Japan's legal reception is more basic and more important. The willingness and desire to learn from foreign models continues to be one of the dominant themes of Japanese life.

Nearly all of Japan's first generation of modern legal scholars studied in Europe or the United States. The pattern was quickly institutionalized and became routine. Yet, until recently, the opportunity to study and travel in the West was a privilege few Japanese could individually enjoy or afford. Japanese travel abroad today in numbers that only a few years ago seemed unimaginable. In fact until recently fewer Japanese per capita had ever been outside of Japan than the citizens of any other industrial country.[15] During most of the postwar era, institutional support was necessary. Even today, government grants, company overseas training programs, and law firm stipends for foreign study provide the bulk of support for the hundreds of young Japanese law students in the West. No country expends so much for learning abroad, especially about law.

The process of learning is not of course limited to law or to foreign study. Japanese industry—particularly the large, multiproduct trading firms—rivals national governments in its information-gathering networks. The Japanese are not only among the most literate and widely read people in the world, they are also among the best informed. Both the public and private media pour into Japan the latest data on every conceivable topic from all corners of the globe.

Learning is more than exposure. What the Japanese do with what they learn is crucial. In law as in other fields, the reception of ideas and institutions is an ongoing process with continuous adaptation and reform. The Japanese view social change as a perpetual aspect of life. Thus, as exemplified by Suehiro's quoted remarks on the need for judicial precedents, Japanese jurists seek to ensure that legal rules also keep pace with social, political, and economic change. There are nevertheless certain parameters to intentional change. Learning from others has all of the advantages of followership in allowing others to bear the risks of innovation and error. Learning from the West also presupposes an acceptance of the locus of leadership in Europe and the United States as the source of ideas. It reflects a decision to conform to patterns established or being tried in the West. In law these unstated premises lead to a notable caution with respect to legal reform. Rarely do the Japanese venture along untravelled paths. They tend either to reformulate past practices or to borrow. By the same token, European and American examples continue to influence both the targets and rhetoric of legal reform in Japan. The Japanese themselves choose their agenda for reform, but that agenda usually reflects what is happening in New York or London or Hamburg as much as circumstances in Tokyo.

AUTHORITY OF LEGAL RULES

Other themes emerge in an effort to identify the values embedded or expressed in Japanese law and legal institutions. Some are familiar. Contemporary Japan shares with its North American and European peers a wide spectrum of fundamental legal values. A commitment to the rule of law as a form of legalism is evident in Japan's adherence to constitutional government and procedural forms. Legal rules define the scope and limits of state authority and action. Even prewar proponents of notions of imperial authority acknowledged that the Meiji emperor's "gift" of a constitution in 1889 not only bound all officials of the state but also, as explicitly stated in its preamble, all future heirs to the throne.

The ramifications of a strong belief in the adherence to legal rules by state officials have come to include continuing concern for coherence and conformity within the legal system. The emphasis on doctrinal consistency in terms of the European origins of much of Japan's basic law and legal institutions helps to explain the continuing role

of scholarship and study abroad as well as judicial reluctance to reformulate or discard past understandings. Whatever the theoretical
role of judicial decisions as a source of law, however, deeply embedded values ensure the importance of judicial precedent in predicting
the rationale and results of future cases.

A shared acceptance of the legitimacy of legal constraints upon
state actors also contributes to informality. To say that informality
can result from the acceptance by officials that they must act strictly
within legally defined parameters may seem contradictory. The sense
of contradiction or paradox should vanish, however, once the statement is explained. First, the law itself must allow informality. To the
extent that statutes explicitly delegate broad discretionary authority
to officials or implicitly permit discretion by granting authority without prescribing procedures, the law permits informality. Second, the
relative rigidity of formal processes and procedures makes the flexibility and adaptability of informal actions even more attractive. So
long as state officials act within broadly defined areas of authority but
refrain from formal acts, the law often allows them a degree of otherwise denied discretion. Thus by relying upon directives that do not
bind either issuing officials or their recipients, state officials are often
able to avoid legalistic constraints.

COMMUNITY

Another cluster of values is common to a more widely shared East
Asian legal tradition. These values define state authority in broader
and often more intrusive terms but without coercive powers of corresponding reach. Until the introduction of Western ideas, the authority of those who ruled had no ideological boundaries. No notion existed of a separate "private" sphere of human activity into which
"public" authority could not legitimately intrude. Constraints on the
capacity of the state to act and to coerce—in other words, the limits
of power—did preclude full and effective exercise of that authority.
Those who ruled could not actually do fully what they could have
justifiably done. The limits of power should be distinguished, at least

conceptually, from the limits of authority. Traditional political rule in East Asia was restrained by the practical limits of power, not conceptual or ideological constraints on authority. As a result, social organizations in East Asia can be viewed in part as arrangements for avoiding or subverting control by those who ruled. Kinship ties, as well as various forms of collective protection, for example, were strengthened by desire for greater freedom from control by those who ruled. The legitimacy of control by those who rule together with the social mechanisms to escape that control account for deep tensions within the Japanese legal and political systems. The most important of these mechanisms also have strong normative support. Ancestor worship and reinforcing Confucianist familial values are, for example, common to all East Asian societies. They also have continuing influence.

Whatever their source, as beliefs and attitudes that have shaped Japan's particular historical experience, these and other norms are today Japanese values. Some can be viewed as contemporary expressions of past tensions and the product of cultural change that in turn underpin the present and will inexorably shape the future. Others, like ancient warriors who have emerged always victorious against past challengers, seem more permanent and unchanged. Embedded, therefore, in Japan's contemporary legal order are values rooted in mixed sources, some in conflict, others enduring. Of these none appears as dominant or enduring as Japan's communitarian orientation.

The communitarian emphasis of Japanese society is widely acknowledged. Although Japan is considerably less homogenous and cohesive than many Japanese and non-Japanese appear to appreciate, no one denies the strength of community. Japanese are commonly described as "group-oriented" and conformist. Missing in most accounts is a carefully considered definition of what community—at least for Japan—really means.

In Japan, it appears, all are enmeshed within a dense web of relationships. The individual appears subsumed by community and effectively constrained by its mechanisms of social control. Despite hierarchial form, however, these tend not to be one- or even two-sided, patron-client dependency relationships. The traditional village remains the paradigm. What fits best is the image of the village as the product of a mutual need for cooperative effort. Community in Japan thus seems best understood in terms of a sense of mutual interdependency and a shared sense of belonging. What anthropologist Takie Lebra labels "social relativism" is another way of putting it.[16] The dependency of each member on others as components of the collective whole works to ensure that all have a sense of place and common need for the contribution of others. From such interdependency and mutual need comes a belongingness, which can be both satisfying and controlling. Among the more positive consequences is the security that allows freedom to express personal views and to be different so long as community norms are not in question. Less positive features can be equally strong. To belong imparts security, but it also constrains.

Community should not be confused with association. The term "community" is often misused to label associations formed as individuals voluntarily join together for a variety of aims while remaining independent actors, as free to leave as they were to join. In associations, any significant degree of interdependence is rare and the relationships established tend to be superficial and relatively easy to rupture. Personal preferences and other interests intervene. As individuals the participants come and go. Its aims achieved, the group disbands.

As applied to Japan, community is very different. Community in Japan means much more than an association of otherwise independent persons. It does not have to have a single cause or function. Joining is not easy; nor is withdrawal. It has members, not participants, whose entry and exit are constrained by interdependencies and broadly shared interests that develop and are sustained by the group. Expectations of trust and moral obligation create formidable bonds.

Reciprocity is among the more significant manifestations of community in Japan. Whether by family or firm, friends or faction, Japan itself seems to be held together by reciprocal obligations that arise within commonplace, everyday, social interactions. As one Japanese law professor on the eve of departure to return to Tokyo after teaching in the United States for several months put it, "I will miss the freedom of my life in America. As soon as my plane lands at Narita, I will have to reopen my mental account book of social debts and credits. Almost everything you do in Japan involving others results in either a debt you must repay in the future or a credit you can count on collecting. And we are always striving to keep our accounts in balance."

The Japanese are socially oriented. They share, in Lebra's words, an "ethos" of sensitivity to social interaction and interpersonal relationships without a sense of absolutes, especially between right and wrong. Missing, as noted previously, is a sense of universal standards with the sort of clearly demarcated dichotomy between good and evil evident in almost all other cultures. Morality like identity is defined in terms of relationships, in contrast to universally applicable principles that subject the individual to an externally fixed standard of behavior or thought. This is not to say that Japanese do not recognize wrongs but that they instead tend to evaluate conduct in terms of relationships.

On the positive side, this tendency allows Japanese to emphasize compassion and tolerance. A recent comparative study of attitudes toward crime revealed little difference in Japanese and American demands for punishment in cases involving wrongdoing by strangers. In contrast though, the Japanese surveyed were much more forgiving of those with whom they had some personal or community connection.[17] The authors did not attempt, however, to investigate the dynamics of the process—the extent to which Japanese try hard in such situations to establish or discover relationships and thereby cease to be strangers. As Lebra points out, "[I]n order to attain an end—whether social or nonsocial—the creation, maintenance, or manipulation of a relevant social relationship is a foremost and indispensable means."[18]

Many observations on the interrelationships between law and community in Japan focus on the influence of the communitarian aspects of Japanese society on law. Few deal with the ways in which legal rules and their enforcement aid in confirming community or reinforcing the extralegal constraints that contribute to the role of community in contemporary Japan. Yet legal processes, legal actors, and legal rules continuously reinforce the communitarian controls of contemporary

Japan. The ways in which legal rules are made, enforced, interpreted, and applied not only reflect Japan's communitarian emphasis but also contribute to its endurance in face of inexorably eroding influences.

One element is reliance on consensus in the formation of legal rules. Lawmaking by consensus gives legislated legal rules an aura of fairness and an inherent legitimacy. By consensus legal rules acquire an intrinsic capacity to induce voluntary compliance. Consensus thus fosters public acceptance and obedience to legal rules. As a deeply shared process value instilled within the family, the school, and the workplace, consensus, in contrast to majoritarian decision-making, gives greater meaning to community membership. To become marginal in Japan means that one is left outside of the community itself.

The question of whose consensus governs remains. Even within the community not all necessarily participate. To have a voice, one must sit at the table. Conflicts over political influence in Japan are less about who has the authority to make the decision or who wins the majority to their side than simply having a seat. And as within all hierarchical social structures, the opinions and preferences of some matter more than those of others. Equality of legal status does not mean equality of influence. But that too can to some degree be a matter of consensus.

A second feature of Japan's communitarian orientation is the role of community in the process of law enforcement. In a society in which community controls represent the primary determinants of social behavior, it is not surprising that legal rules tend to be enforced more through community action than state coercion. Japan may not be distinctive in the fact of community involvement in enforcing legal norms, but few other industrial societies share so extensive a reliance on community in law enforcement. Judges as well as prosecutors and police actively involve the community in the law enforcement process. They expect that community action will not only prevent crime but will provide assistance in enforcing legal rules and correcting behavior. At every stage of the criminal process, diversion back into the community of offenders who confess, show remorse, and receive pardon from compensated victims is its most notable manifestation. The pattern is not, however, restricted to criminal law enforcement. It re-appears and repeats in nearly every area of legal ordering. Behavior that does not conform to community norms risks community sanctions.

Community is not necessarily benign. Nor are community norms necessarily legal norms. Individual identity and self-fulfillment do not always coincide with community interests and norms. For many Japanese the individualistic premises—and the emphasis on rights—of modern western law offer a liberating protection against the op-pressive aspects of Japan's communitarian emphasis. To the extent, however, that legal rights can be directed toward community rather than state constraints, they offer a means to a desired end. As Yōichi Higuchi puts it, society is the tyrant in Japan.[19] Only rights against community rather than the state can provide meaningful protection. The extent to which constitutional and other rights designed to limit the powers of the state can be transformed in Japan to empower the state to protect the individual from community is a prominent issue in law's domain in contemporary Japan. An emphasis on "rights" in the context of efforts for political and social change can best be un-derstood as a means for developing consensus rather than judge-made or majoritarian legal reform. Thus the language of rights in Japan be-longs less to the domain of law than to community attitudes and behavior.

Another manifestation of Japan's communitarian orientation in law is the use of legal rules to prevent unilateral expulsion from the com-munity. Judicial decisions that limit contested divorce, unilateral worker discharge, landlord termination of leases, or one-sided rupture of ongoing business relationships confirm community. The courts thereby empower, at least in a limited manner, those with greater de-pendency and weaker bargaining leverage without, however, impos-ing legal rules that create uniform results or determine the outcome of negotiated withdrawal. In effect, legal rules are used not to main-tain relationships but to prevent their termination without mutual consent and to restrain community exercise of its most coercive sanc-tion: to create outcasts. This theme is evident in judicially imposed rules, often despite legislated rules, related to the elemental units of community: the relationships between husband and wife, master and servant, landlord and tenant, and business patron and client.

A closely related theme is the converse refusal of the courts to impose rules that give the individual legal protection against the community. Courts may act to redress imbalances in bargaining power, but they also tend to defer to the autonomy of the community in ordering its internal affairs. At least as represented by its judges, the Japanese state seems peculiarly reluctant to intervene into the community to protect the individual. Thus unlike welfare capitalist states of western Europe or socialist regimes east or west, the Japanese state has not replaced community as a source of security nor has it stood against community as protector of individual interests. Instead, community remains a vital link between the state and the individual. Communities serve as conduits for state policies and mechanisms of social control as well as sources of security and protection of the individual from the ubiquitous authority and the potentially coercive power of the state.

AUTONOMY

These patterns of confirmation and reinforcement of community go hand in glove with an equally important, albeit less emphasized, value: a desire for freedom from the control of others or, in a word, autonomy. The controls of community in Japan in turn produce an impulse for autonomy. This impulse has become a prominent and pervasive social value in Japan. It is held by individuals as well as communities. Upon reflection it should not be surprising that in so communitarian a society as Japan, autonomy—individual or group—should be so highly valued. In a society in which security depends so much upon interdependent membership in a group, individual autonomy is rare. The Japanese judiciary, as described in detail in chapter 5, exemplifies the pervasive pattern of control exercised within nearly all large, bureaucratic organizations, public and private, in Japan. Although independence in adjudication is a legally and socially protected right, Japanese judges are subject to continuing oversight and assessment as they progress through their careers. They are not alone. Only a few members of Japanese society (most notably physicians and lawyers) are able to achieve some autonomy—the combination of security with freedom from dependency and control by others. Explicated here primarily in relation to the judiciary, the desire for freedom from control by others dominates much of Japanese social life. It too is a pivotal aspect of the spirit of Japanese law.

In the end, law in Japan remains a somewhat suspect but respected mechanism of state control in a communitarian society. It is an instrument used by those who govern to order society, but one viewed with suspicion by those who seek freedom from governmental power. Conversely those who seek greater freedom from communitarian constraints seek greater rights and criticize those within and without Japan who would contain legal controls as they apply to the community. As government has become increasingly subject to the political and legal controls intrinsic to democratic rule, law and the primary actors of the legal system have gained an increasing degree of community trust. Yet, law still remains a less preferred means of social control, one that by its nature always has the potential to override and ultimately replace more familiar and more accessible means of social ordering. By the same token, law in Japan has also served to strengthen communitarian bonds as well as to control or contain the role of the state. The spirit of Japanese law can thus be summarized as permissive with respect to the community's relation to both the individual and the state, expansive in defining official authority and discretion, controlling with respect to state power and state direction of individual activity, and in most respects empathetic in ensuring compensatory and reconciliatory approaches in private relationships.

2 Law's Domain

By law the state exerts its authority and coercive powers. Law expands as far as state authority may reach. But law also defines the modern state's authority and its powers. In this sense law determines and thereby regulates its own realm. The spirit of law is also the spirit of the state and its role in society as performed through the primary actors of the law—those who make and enforce legal rules. Thus, the law of the lawyer defines its own domain.

BORDERS

Law's domain may actually be more confined than its ostensible scope, especially in those societies in which order is maintained more by patron, kin, or community. Where the penetration of the formal instruments of governmental control is weak, law and the state may not have as effective a reach as their apparent domain would suggest. Strong communities, it is said, tend to develop within weak states.[1] The converse axiom would appear to apply to contemporary industrial states. They seem to be strong with correspondingly weak communities. The welfare state has gradually substituted for the intermediary communities that traditionally provided security and protection for the individual. In this respect too, Japan at least superficially appears to be unexceptional.

As an industrial state, the formal institutions and policies of welfare capitalism are evident. Yet for good or ill, governmental protection and state welfare in Japan appear to be far more limited. The social order seems to be maintained more by an array of informal mechanisms of social control. The disapproval of perceived misconduct—"shaming" if you will—by friends, neighbors, and colleagues in the workplace appears to operate quite effectively to channel social behavior in directions the community, but not necessarily the state, considers proper.[2] For Japan, in comparison to its industrial peers, there seems to be less law and fewer legal actors. Japan has fewer prosecutors—less than 2,200—and less crime; fewer judges—about 2,600—and less litigation. With only 15,000 or so practicing attorneys, Japanese society seems to be bereft of meaningful access to those whose function is to activate and keep in motion the machinery of the legal system. Even the number of administrative officials remains comparatively small. More remarkable, the number of nonmilitary government employees at the national level has gradually decreased since the mid-1960s.[3]

Scratch the surface of initial impressions that law in Japan has little significance and a deeper reality quickly appears. Legal rules effectually govern as many of the basic areas of Japanese life as they do in most contemporary industrial societies. Legislated rules, judicial precedents, and legal scholarship in combination create a rich corpus of sophisticated jurisprudence in all fields of law. Japan's legal literature is voluminous, even in English. Translations of all the codes and much legislation are available. English-language loose-leaf commentaries, monographs, and periodicals detail the rules and enforcement processes of Japanese governance and public administration, taxation, commercial transactions, corporate relations, trade and investment controls, securities regulation, banking, labor relations, criminal justice, land use regulation, and environmental law. More than one hundred and forty-five publishers in Japan each year turn out hundreds of books and journals devoted primarily to law and legal topics. Surveying the volume of legal publications in 1968, Richard Rabinowitz found that by 1960 at least 195 separate periodicals devoted to law were being published in Japan, many quarterly, some monthly, and at least one biweekly.[4] Today a widely used index to legal periodicals lists more than 1300 serials that regularly publish articles on law.[5] Japan may have fewer statutes, regulatory rules, and judicial decisions than some of its industrial peers, especially the United States, but legal rules cover as much of Japanese social life as they do that of any other state. Whether as state-approved norms or state-imposed sanctions, law matters, and its domain is large.

Legal rules are as significant in defining the role of the state and state institutions as they are in channeling private behavior. As Elise K. Tipton notes in assessing Japanese police behavior during the 1920s and 1930s, "Japanese legalism" requires "that there should be legal boundaries to the scope of official discretion" and necessitates "a legal basis for [official] action."[6] Hence Japan's two modern constitutions and the related statutes that establish Japan's governmental structure define both the authority and the powers of each of its parts. Whether official transgressions of these legal norms are sanctioned by courts or by internal mechanisms of the administrative and political system, legal rules matter. Law determines what officials may and may not do. The administrative powers of the state were then as now limited by the constitution and other law. Establishment laws (*setchi hō*) for each ministry define its general authority and powers. Unless expanded by special statute, basic legislation fixes the boundaries of the state's administrative competence. Since the Meiji Constitution (1889), Japan has adhered to principles that require a statutory basis for the exercise of administrative authority. The rights of subjects could not be infringed by administrative regulation, and crimes and criminal penalties could be created only by statute.

Judicial enforcement of these restraints was limited under the Meiji Constitution by an administrative court system with especially narrow jurisdiction. No appeals were permitted without express statutory authorization. Even then, only a single tribunal existed, and it was generally staffed by judges (councilors) with past ties to the imperial bureaucracy.[7] Nevertheless, the regular judiciary expanded its role in reviewing administrative actions through tort claims against the state as well as within the context of other civil and criminal actions.

The Japanese state is restrained less by legal rules, however, than as a result of various constraints on its coercive powers. From the moment the legal reforms of the late nineteenth century were completed, a process of gradual and varied containment of power began. The number of judges and prosecutors and, after 1934, even lawyers failed to keep pace with population increases. The postwar Occupa-

tion reforms continued the process as more effective electoral constraints ensured ultimate parliamentary control over administrative
powers. Typically, legislation enabling governmental intervention or
involvement in the economy or other areas of Japanese social life
would fail to include comparable enforcement powers. The result was
the necessity for negotiated agreement among those most directly affected with respect to basic public policies. In each instance, whether
ultimately subject to administrative or judicial enforcement, or simply left to community response, legal rules function as determinate
norms for private and public conduct. Law is thereby an essential element of social and political ordering.

REGISTRIES

When combined with both legal and community processes of enforcement, legal rules operate in Japan with considerable bite to channel
and direct private behavior. The registries provide perhaps the out-
standing example. There are three. The family registry (*koseki*) is administered by the ward (*ku*) or town (*shi*) offices of all local government authorities. The other two registries—the immovable property
registry (*fudōsan tōki*) and the commercial registry (*shōgyō tōki*)—
are maintained by branch offices of the Ministry of Justice. All registration procedures are governed by separate statutes and are subject
to Ministry of Justice regulations. Although the codes and special
statutes may provide the substantive rules governing registered legal
relationships, registration procedures are determinative in many instances in defining them. The most common means for securing the
rights of creditors, for example, involve the use of land as collateral
and registration as the enforcing mechanism.[8] Since 1978 a special
statute has governed such devices, but Japanese courts had long recognized them as effective alternatives to the security interests provided in the Civil Code.[9]

In a legal system in which the fundamentals of family identity and
status are the product of registration, Civil Code rules regarding family relationships from birth through death can be pervasively enforced.

In family law everyone is subjected equally to the process. No one can avoid it. In the process registration officials subject to the regulatory commands and legal interpretations of their administrative superiors become the principal fact finders and law appliers in lieu of judges guided by precedent and general principles of law.

The family registry also exemplifies the interaction between law and social control in Japan. The registry provides a record of family relationships and personal history, including divorce, illegitimate birth, and, in the case of felonies, criminal convictions. The required submission of certified copies of a person's registry entries by schools, employers, banks, and others in effect invites the stigma of having offended social norms governing personal status and behavior. The legal rules may be neutral or permissive, but registration enables disclosure and the resulting social control.[10]

Some may quarrel with any inclusion of such administrative rules and mechanisms of social control as law. They are, however, in both formal and functional terms no less law than the rules set out in a statute or the principles articulated in court decisions. That they differ in important respects, not the least of which is the breadth of discretionary enforcement generally allowed government officials in Japan, goes without saying. The administrative rules and mechanisms of administrative enforcement are nonetheless a large tract in Japanese law's domain.

REGULATORY CONTROLS

In common with other industrial states, in Japan too, the vast bulk of all legal rules are administrative. Administrative regulations are viewed by most observers of Japan as the primary mechanism of state control in Japan. In comparative terms, such observations may appear commonplace. In all contemporary industrial states, administrative regulation occupies the premier position in the hierarchy of legal controls. The primacy of private law is past. Since the first decades of this century, all societies have witnessed the expansion of administrative regulation and the rise—or resurgence—of the administrative state. The vast majority of all legal rules in all countries are made by administrative officials pursuant to broad delegations of legislative powers.

The expanding role of the twentieth-century state, especially in economic regulation, is evident in Japan as well. However, in comparison with other industrial states, Japan was quite tardy in enacting comprehensive economic regulation. Not until the eve of World War II were the variety of regulatory controls common in Europe and the United States by the end of World War I established in Japan. Except for the Ministry of Finance, the influence of governmental institutions responsible for administrative oversight of various areas of the economy was negligible in comparison to those bureaucracies that administered the rules governing public safety and order, the Home and Justice ministries in particular. The influence of the Home Ministry was especially great. Through its powers of assignment of prefectural governors, it virtually controlled local government in prewar Japan. It also had jurisdiction over the police and public construction. Dismantled under the Occupation, its responsibilities were divided among the newly established ministries of Construction, Labor, and Home Affairs as well as the National Police Agency and Tokyo (Metropolitan) Police Department.

Private law continued in prewar Japan to occupy a preeminent place as the primary mechanism for social ordering by law. Demands for social reforms, particularly legislation to deal with rural tenancy, labor relations, and other social and economic ills mounted with Japan's rapid industrialization. Legislative efforts affected significant economic interests. One of the causes encountered major political obstacles. Just as landholders dominated Japan's first parliaments, by the mid-1920s industrial and commercial interests had become politically preeminent. Social reformers from both the radical right and left laid the blame on corruption and alliances between business interests and politicians that they increasingly considered to be intrinsic to liberal parliamentary regimes. The influence of the *zaibatsu*, the conglomerate firms that dominated Japanese banking and international trade, was evident.[11] Extensive regulatory controls were not politically feasible until the 1930s, concomitant with the dissolution of party politics and the ascendancy of ultranationalist reformers in both civilian and military bureaucracies. On the other hand, more modest reforms revising private law rights were easier to achieve, as in the case of legislation on land and house leases. Whatever the cause, however, the assertion of private law rights whether in property, contract, or tort (delict) remained the primary means of legal redress. As social and economic conflict produced greater litigation, however, conservative reformers joined with the political elite to enact legislation that first allowed and later required "conciliation" (*chōtei*) in a widening variety of civil disputes.[12] Another, more draconian response was the enactment of the Peace Preservation Law and the use of criminal prosecution to prevent the spread of radical socialist activity.[13] The consequence was to place police, prosecutors, and judges, not the civil bureaucracy and economic planners, at the center.

By the late 1930s an expanding war in China and military mobilization had led to the imposition of the most extensive economic controls in a century. Even then, however, the Japanese pattern did not include the broad direct wartime controls familiar in the United States and Europe. Instead, Japan relied upon a system of less direct intervention through mandatory industry control organizations, designed less for a regulatory aim to constrain industry behavior than to achieve as great a degree of self-sufficiency as possible. The complex structure of control associations and cooperatives created vehicles for Japan's economic communities to interact with government. Japanese economic regulation thus left the participants, as noted below, a considerable degree of influence and autonomy. Japanese industry preserved as a result broad scope for self-regulation. The wartime consequence was that Japan was never able to mobilize fully. Nonetheless, the structure proved to be quite resilient and enduring.

Japan's postwar economic structure in nearly all areas reflects what Yukio Noguchi refers to as the "1940 System" of wartime controls as enhanced in several crucial aspects by the Occupation economic reforms and legislation intended to foster Japan's postwar economic recovery and growth.[14] The characteristic legal rules of postwar Japan were largely the product of war and its aftermath. These rules govern economic activities. They are administered by what may best be labeled the "managerial" rather than "regulatory" bureaucracies of the Ministry of International Trade and Industry (MITI); the Ministry of Agriculture, Forestry, and Fisheries; and other ministries with broad jurisdictional grants covering broadly defined areas of economic activity. In effect, economic law replaced social law. With the abolition of the Home Ministry and the introduction of more inclusive constitutional guarantees to protect the freedom of political and intellectual activity, a substantive shift occurred in law's domain in postwar Japan.

Parallel changes also occurred as both civil and criminal law ceased to be the primary means for ordering economic behavior. Economic bureaucracies now replaced judges as the pivotal actors in dealing with economic and social conflict. So long as the public agreed that economic recovery and growth remained the nation's highest priority, judges would play a secondary role as officials in Japan's economic ministries became the principal mediators of social conflict.

With these changes law's domain also narrowed. Legal rules seemed almost irrelevant in Japan's postwar "managerial" system. Informality characterized the interaction between government officials and industry in formulating and implementing policies to promote economic growth and deal with the inexorable conflicts such growth produced.[15] The Japanese economy became ordered more through long-term business relationships, collective pricing and production arrangements, and continuous negotiation with government officials than by legal directives and controls.[16] To be sure, a formal structure of licensing and legal approval requirements constituted the framework within which such informal processes operated, but within that structure, legal rules could be ignored or bent. Take, for example, Japan's foreign investment, trade, and currency controls. The approval requirements of two statutes enacted during the Occupation as emergency legislation—the Foreign Investment Law and the Foreign Exchange and Trade Control Law—were used as the principal instruments of Japan's postwar economic policies.[17] Not only were there hardly any cases under either law, but it appears that the Japanese government never formally denied an application for foreign investment approval. Rather, disappointed applicants simply complied with requests that they withdraw their applications. The informality of enforcement, however, should not be confused with the relevancy of the rules. The leverage provided by these statutes, supplemented by permissive cartel legislation, enabled government officials to pursue a policy of export promotion and import substitution quite effectively for more than a decade.

Informality should not be viewed as either an exceptional or an intrinsic feature of Japanese law or even regulatory controls. In a recent comparative study of antitrust enforcement in Japan and the United States, for example, Harry First contrasts the predominantly "legalistic regulatory culture" of the United States with what he calls the "bureaucratic regulatory culture" of Japan:

> A legalistic regulatory culture is one focused on protecting the law's beneficiaries from identified harmful acts. Its core concern is victimization and it works by prohibitory rules. Such regulation is individual case oriented, fact-bound, and backward-looking. The decision-making model is a trial, with its requirement that evidence be presented and a judgment be logically justified.
>
> A bureaucratic regulatory culture is focused on how the economy should be structured and run. Its core concern is economic welfare and works by guidance. This type of regulation is group-oriented, theory-based, and forward-looking. The decision-making model is consensual. Rigorous justification for particular decisions is not only unnecessary but may be unwise.[18]

First's description of both "cultures" fits a wider spectrum of legal activity. Especially apt is his emphasis on the role of law in legalistic regulatory cultures to protect identified beneficiaries rather than a more overarching concern for social structure and how society runs. Overlooked in the comparison, however, is the similarity between the actual enforcement processes in the two systems. The Japanese antitrust enforcement authorities, like their U.S. counterparts, function under a statute that proscribes certain conduct and sets out penalties for any violation. Enforcement of this statute in Japan is as "backward-looking" as U.S. law. The procedures for enforcement are also similar. Investigations are initiated within the agency or by outside complaint. If evidence of a violation is found and the respondent does not admit to the violation, the formal process continues with further investigation and formal evidentiary hearings conducted by a designated hearing examiner. Resort to informal action is common only when the respondent admits the violation and negotiates an informal resolution or when the investigation yields insufficient evidence to sustain a formal finding that a violation was committed and both sides wish to compromise. Administrative enforcement proceedings in the United States do not differ in any significant way, except that the investigatory powers of U.S. enforcement agencies are much more extensive and coercive and the sanctions—including treble damage actions and attorney fees—tend to be greater. On the other hand, American government agencies, organized as highly socialized career bureaucracies with the same sorts of promotional objectives and managerial authority as most Japanese economic ministries, also tend without externally imposed requirements to function in ways that resemble First's "bureaucratic" model of informality.[19] In other words, informality in Japan is more a product of institutional structure than some enduring cultural trait or preference. It can be explained best by the relative autonomy of individual Japanese ministries, their predominantly promotional goals, a strong reluctance on the part of the Diet to give, and as a result officials to seek, greater formal powers, and the endurance of past patterns and modes of political and bureaucratic interaction with industry.

CONTINUING INFLUENCE OF EUROPEAN LAW

Much of Japanese law continues to be influenced by external, particularly European, models. Aided by scholars, Japanese lawmakers—legislators, administrative officials, as well as judges—continue to look to European and American law. The influence of United States examples is often overstated. The codes and basic structure of Japanese law remain European in origin, and European developments remain important. Even in constitutional law and other areas where American models were used, however, European example is also influential. The various amendments to Japan's Antimonopoly and Fair Trade Law exemplify this tendency.[20] Although proposed as part of U.S. occupation policy and drafted with U.S. legislation as the model, since 1949 the influence of German law has prevailed. Among the principal features of the 1953 amendment was the introduction of two broad exemptions. One was allowance with approval for "recession cartels" (*fukyō karuteru*). The other permitted, also with approval, "rationalization cartels" (*gōrika karuteru*). Both reflected the influence of the West German government's 1952 draft (*Regierungsentwurf*) of the 1957 Law Against Restraints of Competition, which, as a compromise with those who opposed any complete ban, introduced "structural crisis cartels" (*Strukturkrisenkartelle*) and "rationalization cartels" (*Rationalisierungskartelle*).[21] Similarly, the 1952 Export Transactions Law (amended a year later as the Export and Import Transactions Law) also followed the West German example in exempting export cartels.[22] A more recent example is Japan's new 1994 Products Liability Law, which, despite two decades of gestation, did not become law until after the European Union had adopted a similar set of rules, which were closely tracked in the Japanese statute.[23] The extent to which Japanese lawmakers seek to ensure Japanese conformity with international standards and the prevailing legal norms of its Organization for Economic Cooperation and Development (OECD) peers can be explained at least in part by its communitarian bias. Japan seems compelled to remain in step with the norms adopted within the "communities" of states in which it identifies itself as a member.

The continuing influence of European law is especially notable with respect to Japanese emphasis on doctrinal development and consistency. The development of administrative law doctrine is a salient example. Japanese administrative law was built upon the barest of constitutional and statutory bones. The 1889 Meiji Constitution provided for an administrative court and restricted the ordinary courts to the adjudication of civil and criminal cases. The statute establishing Japan's single Administrative Court added little except to fill out in greater detail the structure and jurisdiction of the institution. Drawing from French and German scholarship, Japanese scholars and judges filled out layer by layer an impressive corpus of administrative law. They introduced the definitions and distinctions of public and private law and the concept of "administrative acts" (*gyōsei kōi*). In so doing, they constrained the already limited reach of the Administrative Court and further limited whatever effectiveness it might have had for redressing administrative misconduct. On the other hand, these doctrinal constraints enabled the ordinary courts, in both civil and criminal actions, to play a more expansive role in policing official negligence and misbehavior.

Despite the abolition of the Administrative Court and the invitation to an expanded common law definition of "judicial power" under the American-inspired postwar constitution, however, Japanese jurists did not abandon prewar doctrine. Rather prewar concepts continued to apply with full restrictive force. Armed, however, with additional constitutional and statutory authority, which significantly expand the availability of civil damage relief to cover nearly any injury-causing error by administrative officials, Japan's courts today have the broadest possible mandate to review all forms of government activity.[24] Once again constraints on available measures of remedial relief should not be confused with the scope of the courts' authority to review governmental action.

LITIGATION

Whether managerial or regulatory, administrative law is not the sole source of legal rules over economic activity in Japan or other contemporary legal systems. The largely optional (default) provisions for contracts and companies of Japan's civil and commercial codes are equally significant in establishing rules that govern without the need for negotiation over each and every transaction or inclusion in every contract document. Some, particularly the rules of company law, may be effectively enforced through the registry requirements, as indicated above, but most are formally enforced, if at all, in lawsuits upon petition by aggrieved claimants.

The role of litigation in Japan has been a disputed topic. One fact does stand out. Japanese litigation rates are consistently lower than all comparable industrial states. Christian Wollschläger's comparison of Japanese and European litigation rates over the past century is the most recent and exhaustive study undertaken to date. He finds more litigation per capita in Japan than in Europe during the late nineteenth century. During this century, however, a "wide distance" separates Japan from Germany and other European systems. He concludes that "Japanese avoidance of litigation is firmly established in its legal culture."[25]

Suffice it to say that Japanese do litigate when they have something to gain. Japanese, like people everywhere, make rational choices to maximize economic gain and personal interests. Japanese entrepreneurs in the nineteenth century were not slow to appreciate and utilize the advantages of new legal forms that enabled them to create banks and limited liability companies.[26] Nor did landowners at the turn of the last century neglect to take full advantage of the legal regime for the protection of property under Japan's new Civil Code. Today no one should be surprised that as the number of practicing trial lawyers in Japan increases, filing fees are reduced, and other constraints on litigation are eased, the number of lawsuits being filed per capita is increasing. It is equally unremarkable that Japanese file suit in the United States against other Japanese because of broader discovery, higher damage awards, or other perceived benefits of U.S. law.[27]

Economic gain, however, is not the sole motivating aim. Emotional needs, reflected in the wish to belong and to maintain relationships, to receive respect and status, or simply to seek revenge, are surely as forceful. Indeed the desire for compensation or greater wealth may simply be symptomatic reflections of more basic psychological concerns. Because litigation between individuals will nearly always be the consequence or cause of a rupture of relationship, few sue friends or family. Lawsuits begin with a grievance and thus, to the extent that social organization and established patterns of social behavior reduce the sense of grievance or enable potential litigants to resolve any dispute without rupturing their relationship, litigation is less likely. As described in greater detail with respect to crime, by means of apology and reintegration, Japanese appear to be able not only to maintain relationships and community, but also to create curative relationships that reduce both the sense of grievance and desire for retribution.

What should be kept in mind is that litigation is less a process of dispute resolution than a means of law enforcement. To stress resolving disputes over enforcing legal rules as the aim is in itself telling of an attitude toward the importance of law and legal rules in social ordering. As explained in greater detail below, the emphasis by Japanese judges on the settlement of disputes reflects a value judgment about law and its proper domain. Even in the case of tort litigation, code-established principles as defined by Japanese judges into relatively clear and certain particularized rules of proper conduct and care are effectively enforced, albeit more through negotiated settlement than litigation.[28]

Litigation in Japan also serves as a tool for reform. Frank Upham made the point a decade ago.[29] Protracted litigation was instrumental in inducing legislative action to cure the industrial pollution, to reduce the hazards of toxic chemicals, to correct inequalities in employment of women, and, as described in more detail in chapter 8, to realize the political and social ideals of the postwar constitution. In these and other instances, lawsuits have served a consensus-building purpose. The weakness of judicial enforcement in Japan enables us better to see and to understand a more universal phenomenon—the role of the judiciary in articulating norms that both reflect and foster consensus. Coercive power is not necessary. Especially in a society in which consensus is valued, law can induce social change by its persuasive force.

CONSENSUS AND COMMUNITY NORMS

In some respects, legal rules, especially statutory rules, seem even more relevant in Japan than in many other societies. To a great extent, this impression may be the result of the processes for making law and the values of those responsible. As Tom Tyler's valuable study of Chicago shows, people obey the law more because of its legitimacy than its coercive potential.[30] To the extent that legislators and bureaucrats, judges and prosecutors—those who make and apply legal rules—act in ways that conform to the community's shared values regarding both the content and processes of law, their decisions are more likely to induce compliance and support. Ronald Dore makes a similar point with respect to Japan. What makes Japan work so well as a cooperative society in which legal rules do count, Dore argues, is their "morally compelling force which reduces the impulse to deviate and bring sanctions into play."[31] The capacity of Japan's legal actors to establish legal rules and processes that do reflect community values is therefore critical to their relevance and a significant factor in explaining Japan's success.

Legislation involves an often arduous and time-consuming process of developing consensus. Indeed, some regard this aspect of the Japanese legislative process as its distinguishing characteristic.[32] Consensus requires participation in the lawmaking process of all interested parties. Although most statutes are actually drafted within the ministry with principal jurisdiction over the subject matter, all other interested bureaucracies become involved. Typically, media attention provides the catalyst for a political response. A special deliberative committee, which will usually include the principal scholars as well as government officials with expertise on the topic, will be formed. As they reach consensus, they become, in effect, a project team for drafting the legislation. Usually, the drafting process begins at the ministry-division level. As drafts are completed, the bill will proceed upwards in the ministerial hierarchy with continuous discussions and negotiations with other concerned ministries and members of the special committee. The final drafts are reviewed by the Cabinet Legislation Bureau, which functions more to ensure technical accuracy and clarity than to deal with issues of policy. At this point the bill undergoes final evaluations within the majority or coalition parties' review boards and interministerial meetings. A decision by the cabinet to submit the bill to the Diet completes the process. Within the Diet, the bill will be considered by the appropriate parliamentary committee in each house. Consensus usually overrides majoritarian politics and ensures a significant role for Diet committees.

The need for consensus also explains why Japan has so many advisory groups and ad hoc policy groups outside of the formal legislative process. Often chaired by eminent legal scholars, the most active of these may work for decades before the necessary political consensus is reached. The recently enacted Administrative Procedure Law, for example, had been first proposed in 1952, and the final statute was based on a widely circulated draft completed a decade earlier.[33]

Consensus, as a requirement for lawmaking, does not mean unanimity. What is required is assent by those who participate in the process. Thus, participation becomes critical. Because the assent of those who participate is generally necessary, much political maneuvering and conflict in Japan thus involves, as noted previously, getting a seat. Once there, meaningful participation in the process is assured. In other words, political effort is directed less at winning over a majority and more at gaining access to the process. As a result, controversial reforms rarely succeed and much legislation fails to reflect the interests, desires, or propensities of many Japanese.

Once enacted as legislation, legal rules acquire as a result of at least the perception of consensus an exceptional legitimating influence. Even the most initially controversial legal rules, if enacted after a long period of discussion and debate, can be viewed as an expression of national community agreement. In statutory form, they acquire a legitimacy that legislation in more majoritarian lawmaking systems seldom acquires. The legislative process itself provides an explanation for why in Japan people obey the law. The perceptions of the process ensure the sense of fairness and legitimacy that Tom Tyler and Ronald Dore see as essential.

As explained in greater detail below, this tendency also affects the role of judicial lawmaking. Judicial decisions, as a result, are less capable of inducing voluntary community compliance and are thereby confined more to the process of building consensus. Although, for instance, the new Products Liability Law did not expand in any significant way the prevailing judge-made rules on manufacturers' liability for defective products that threaten public health and safety, enterprises throughout Japan responded immediately to ensure compliance and limit any potential liability.[34] This pattern is not new. One of the best examples is the case of the limitation of landlord rights by judicial decision in the first decade of the century. Judges refused to apply either code principles or contractual rules that allowed landlords to terminate lease agreements or effectively to determine their duration. Judges used various devices to avoid the ostensible code or contract provisions. By 1921, consensus was reached and the Land Lease Law and House Lease Law were enacted, effecting the same result.[35] More subtle is the restraint that legislation places on judicial lawmaking. The courts were quite willing to ignore general code rules in order to protect tenants, but legislation that addresses the issue directly is far less likely to be transformed. Hence the courts have not reinterpreted the 1991 Land Lease and House Lease Law, which was intended to alleviate the principal economic effects of the prior protenancy regime.[36]

The emphasis on consensus also evidences a profound concern for community over the interests of both the individual and the state. Unless community interests are also at stake, even the most acute need for legal reform to protect individual or state interests is insufficient to overcome the requirements for consensus. As a result, the discourse of legal reform in Japan tends to echo the communitarian bias. Appeals made to advance individual and state concern are worded as community needs. In some instances where, as noted, rights are asserted in an effort to promote social reform, upon close examination the beneficiary is the community, not the individual. While legislation manifestly intended to further individual or state interests becomes especially suspect, similar rules are accepted if understood to foster the narrowest economic interests or, more importantly, the autonomy of any single community within Japan.

What distinguishes Japanese economic regulation is less its form than its use of these requirements to restrict entry and to provide leverage in the oversight of economic activity. Although, as noted above, many of Japan's regulatory laws can be explained historically as products of wartime and immediate postwar conditions, they reflect—and thus can be understood politically—the economic interests of established enterprise "communities" and organizations as much if not more than any conceivable public interest as the Japanese economy recovered and grew in the early postwar years.

Beginning with the 1927 Banking Law, for example, licensing was used to create Japan's tightly closed and segmented financial services industry.[37] The 1942 Food Control Law created a multilayered distribution structure of regional and local cooperatives and government purchasing agencies.[38] Despite the repeal of the 1942 law under 1994 reform legislation, the basic structure created during the war remains intact.[39] Licensing, combined with direct government control through public corporations and agencies, established monopoly power in transportation and telecommunications. Legal rules are less significant in these areas in which the state acts with managerial rather than regulatory oversight. Policies are made and implemented through a variety of channels, many informal, with administrative officials participating as active players rather than regulators of private conduct in the decisions that affect an industry as a whole and the economy in general.

COMMUNITY CONTROLS

However important legal rules or principles may be as a reflection of community norms for proper conduct or a means for creating community consensus in Japan, the enforcement of law—the sanctioning process—is largely left to the community.[40] Law as a means of coercive state control is less used and less significant in the everyday affairs of most Japanese than it is for the citizens of other highly developed industrial states. Administrative regulation in Japan may be extensive, but it is considerably less coercive. Political accountability during the postwar period has at least operated to limit the coercive powers granted to administrative organs. Seldom are administrative officials empowered to order compliance with regulatory edicts. Japan has remarkably few record keeping requirements. Political pressures have prevented the state from enacting tax collections measures to ensure thorough tax identification numbers for all bank accounts, the most basic means of surveillance of financial assets. Few Japanese regulations take the form of prohibitions and prosecution typical of many U.S. regulatory statutes. Those that do, such as the Japan Antimonopoly and Fair Trade Law, as enacted tend to reflect American influence. Constitutional restraints have also long curtailed the authority of the legislature to delegate its criminal lawmaking powers and more recently even criminal intent seems to have become an element for criminal prosecution of economic crimes in Japan.[41] To the nonlawyer such legal constraints may seem minor, but they nonetheless reflect a profound difference in the degree of effective administrative coercion and control in Japan relative to the United States. The weakness of formal enforcement in Japan contributes to the need for consensus in lawmaking. Without assent to the rules, their voluntary enforcement would not be possible. Without the means of effective coercion, those responsible for their implementation must out of necessity involve those affected in their formation.

3 Law's Actors I

In Japan self-help is widespread, but professional assistance still is often needed. A variety of actors play specialized roles in meeting such need within Japan's contemporary legal system. They include legal scholars, attorneys, scriveners, prosecutors, police, judges, notaries, tax agents, patent agents, government officials, even company employees. Many are licensed legal professionals. Others are government officials or business managers whose functions at some point in their career may include law-related technical tasks. Two—police and scriveners—have a ubiquitous presence throughout the country. Because of the pervasive role of registration, judicial scriveners play an extremely important role in the lives of all Japanese. Many communities have no lawyers, but no town is without a judicial scrivener or the police.[1] Three of these categories of legal professionals—attorneys, prosecutors, and judges—share an elite status as legal apprentices and graduates of a two-year legal training center to which less than 3 percent of all applicants are admitted. Their number is small, as noted, and they tend to be concentrated in Japan's major urban centers, primarily Tokyo and Osaka. Except for police, nearly all of Japan's legal actors hold an undergraduate degree in law from one of Japan's several hundred public and private faculties of law.

EDUCATION AND TRAINING

Measured by numbers Japan is one of the most educated societies in law in the world. As in most other countries, especially continental Europe and Latin America, enrollments in law faculties is large. For most of the century, more students in Japan have studied law than any other subject, including any of the natural sciences, engineering, or business. Today Japan's law students outnumber the students of any other faculty except for engineering and economics. More than 150,000 university and college students in Japan study law, nearly four times as many as in the United States. As in nearly all countries except the United States, legal education in Japan remains an undergraduate curriculum without a narrow professional or vocational purpose. To produce lawyers is not the primary aim. This contrast with the United States (and Canada) is pronounced. Law students are educated as generalists. Efforts are made, however, to introduce some elements of American legal education by those scholars who have studied and taught in the United States.[2] Within nearly all law faculties, many innovative courses and teaching methods can be found. With the American experience in mind, several universities have introduced in their graduate programs professional training programs in law designed for mid-career business managers and others who may be seeking a career change. Nonetheless, neither the students nor their teachers view legal education at the undergraduate level in terms of training for a legal career. Those who intend to attempt the entrance examination required for qualification as a lawyer, prosecutor, or judge usually spend as much time outside of class preparing for the national entrance examination as they do in class or preparing for university exams. The notion that the elite law graduates who enter government service are "technocrats" in any meaningful sense of the word is false. Even to say that those graduates of the University of Tokyo who aim for elite bureaucratic careers have honed their skills in the technical science of government through the study of administrative and constitutional law exaggerates the nature and purpose of such courses as well as the realities of undergraduate legal education in Japan.

Most law faculties include political science. Some combine law with economics and a few with literature. The curriculum in law is systematically structured for academic purposes into categories for basic subjects, such as legal history, jurisprudence, and foreign law, as well accepted classifications of private and public law. Despite the efforts that faculty may devote to such schema, students are rarely required to take courses or examinations in sequence. Lectures and an enormous volume of books and journals written for law students do expose them to the codes and their underlying principles, the basic theories and rules of law. Students rarely have even the opportunity, however, to study more than one or two advanced topics of commercial and regulatory law. Moreover, they enjoy a wide freedom of choice in what to study—or indeed whether to study at all. Undergraduate education in Japan is not demanding. Legal education is more significant for those who hold the lectern than those who receive a diploma.

Entry into, rather than graduation from, the university is the career-determining event. In Japan the process of sorting students out for particular career specialties in law as other fields occurs less within a university than among all universities. The image of an elevator is an apt metaphor to describe the process. Some elite public and private universities take their graduates to the upper floors; some stop at lower levels. In law the University of Tokyo continues to rank the highest. Its graduates dominate the legal professions, higher level government offices, even corporate managerial positions. For most of the postwar period, more than two-thirds of all Supreme Court justices, a plurality of all lawyers, and roughly 80 percent of all ministerial bureau directors have been Tokyo law graduates. Closely ranked with Tokyo are the handful of national universities—notably Kyoto, but also Hokkaido, Kyushu, Nagoya, Osaka, and Tohoku, all of which were established as "imperial universities" during the first two decades of the century—as well as a cluster of private universities, concentrated in Tokyo, such as Waseda, Keio, Chuo, and Meiji. Graduates of institutions at the other end of the hierarchy, with few exceptions, seem relegated to careers with less status if not pay. As a result, as noted, the examinations that matter most and demand the greatest time and effort in preparation are those separately administered by each university and college for undergraduate admission.

The examination system today begins as early as preschool to select those admitted into the stratified university system. Because those who are admitted to university-managed preschools or kindergartens are not required to pass as demanding an entrance examination for admission into the next level, getting into the institution at the lowest level is sometimes thought to give the student a significant subsequent advantage. Also, because compulsory education ends at the end of the ninth grade, entrance examinations are also required for public high schools. The university entrance examination remains, however, the crucial career-directing event in the lives of most Japanese. The examination system has produced a thriving business in entrance examination preparatory schools or *juku*, for students at all levels. Such schools assist students preparing for their initial entrance exams as well as those who, not succeeding at their university of choice, prefer to try again rather than enter a less preferred university. An added complication is the scheduling of individual university entrance examinations. Each institution gives a separate examination on-site, often charging a less than modest fee. Until the mid-1980s all of the national universities, which are considered the most elite, administered their examinations on the same day. The applicants had to choose which exam to take.

Demanding, extremely selective entrance examinations ensure a kind of meritocracy. Despite occasional private university scandals—nearly all involving favored treatment for the offspring of a substantial donor to one of Japan's elite private medical faculties—entry into Japan's elite national university law faculties is based solely on the applicant's performance on the examination. Universities take impressive measures to safeguard the security and secrecy of their examinations. Except with respect to access to preparatory education, neither family status, wealth, or political influence is a factor in admissions. The examination requirement for entry to public and private high schools reduces even further the advantages of status and social influence. In this environment merit tends to be defined in terms of performance on examinations. What counts, however, is the student's ability to absorb and retain a large store of information on all required subjects. Thus success requires prodigious memorization with the associated discipline and self-denial. Indeed, the more difficult and selective the examination, the more elite in terms of merit the institution and its graduates seem to be viewed.

Because the national legal examination (*shihō shiken*) required for entry into the Legal Training and Research Institute (*Shihō Kenshū Jo*) is today Japan's most selective, not only are those who are admitted treated with notable deference, the schools from which they graduate share their glory. The informational bulletin on the law faculty of one prominent private college in Tokyo, for example, includes prideful reference to the recent increase in the number of its graduates who were admitted to the Institute. As a result of the system of preferred admissions within the institution, the influence of the success of these graduates extends to the college's preschool. Again, the University of Tokyo leads the pack. Not only do its graduates outnumber the successful applicants from any other university, typically more than half will succeed before graduation on their first attempt. Whether this results from the exposure to faculty most likely to draft and grade the examination, the test-taking skills of Tokyo graduates, or some other measure of the quality of education remains a matter for conjecture.

The elite in law in Japan are thus those who gain admission as legal apprentices to the Legal Training and Research Institute. Established initially as a professional training program for judges and procurators, the Institute, which is administered by the judiciary, comprises a two-year apprenticeship required for all career judges, procurators, and with minor exceptions, practicing attorneys. Admission is based on a series of three examinations—two written tests and one oral interview. The maximum number of those admitted to become legal apprentices (*shūshūsei*) is fixed by government regulation. The number today is seven hundred, an increase from five hundred in the late 1980s. The number rose to one thousand in 1998, and efforts are being made to increase the number to fifteen hundred by the turn of the century. Legal apprentices receive a rather substantial government stipend. Thus the two-year term is likely to be reduced to a year and a half by 1999.

The difficulty of the national legal examination, like university entrance examinations in Japan, is not new. Shūsei Tokuda, one of Japan's most popular prewar novelists, describes the travail of his eldest half brother's failed attempt in 1885 to pass the qualifying examination to become a lawyer: "Even now, Hitoshi was moved to tears when he remembered how assiduously Ken'ichi had studied for his examination to become a lawyer. A red blanket over his shoulders, Ken'ichi would sit up all night at his desk while the rest of the family slept."[3]

After spending four months in the Institute's facility on the outskirts of Tokyo, each apprentice is assigned to a district court, a local procurator's office, and a designated law firm in one of Japan's forty-seven prefectural capitals. At the end of a sixteen-month apprenticeship, apprentices return to Tokyo for a final four- to six-month training period. The program emphasizes trial practice. Under the supervision of a faculty of judges, prosecutors, and a few practicing lawyers, the legal apprentices learn how to draft judicial judgments, indictments, and complaints.

Even graduate university education, which tends to be narrowly devoted to a single field, offers nothing akin to the multifaceted professional study of law that exists in American law schools. Those in graduate programs tend to be divided into two groups—those who are preparing or waiting for an academic career and those who wish to maintain university affiliation while studying for a second or third attempt to gain admission to the Legal Research and Training Institute. Recognizing this dichotomy, several universities have begun to offer two separate graduate program tracks, only one of which requires a research paper for the degree. The graduate degree remains secondary, however, to the first, undergraduate degree in law. Because the undergraduate degree is sufficient for entry into all legal careers, including teaching positions, pursuit of a graduate degree inevitably carries with it a degree of stigma of initial failure. The best and brightest do not need the graduate degree.

Except for those who study abroad or on their own, the education of the Japanese lawyer remains limited to the relatively superficial introduction to the basic rules and principles of the codes, with perhaps a seminar or two on some specialized field, as an undergraduate and during the Institute's training for trial practice. Other than the rare graduate of a faculty other than law who manages to gain admission to the Institute, Japanese lawyers (as well as law graduates generally) will have little systematic exposure to other disciplines. Despite some general education requirements during the first two years of their university experience, their knowledge of history, economics, math, science, and the humanities in general will have been more a product of self-education and their secondary education than their undergraduate experience. Few will have even studied many of the most relevant specialized fields of regulatory or commercial law in any depth. Except for their training in trial practice at the Institute, most remain generalists. Status depends on merit in Japan, but within the system of legal education, merit is based more on the selection for entry than the knowledge acquired for exit.

Even apart from the entrance examination system, the market for education is immense in Japan. The Japanese are among the most literate people in the world and devour literature of all sorts. Self-improvement is a major industry. Law may not lead the list, but it is one of the most studied fields. Sold to the general public each year is a vast array of literature on law. The number and variety of legal manuals and guides on every conceivable topic of interest to the average person is vast. They range from comic books on constitutional rights to handbooks on consumer protection. The general public is also kept well-informed about law by the media. Because so many Japanese in every career field have a basic legal education, basic information about law is widely diffused. Numbers determine the market for legal literature. Because law students outnumber lawyers ten to one, most books on law are written and published for undergraduate student readers and their teachers. Japan's professional legal literature tends to be concentrated in a handful of periodicals, which include the text and commentary on most significant court decisions at all levels. Significant court cases are reported widely and well. New legislation is explained with detail and care. The general public in Japan knows a lot about the law.

SCHOLARS

Legal scholars play two separate but closely related roles in the life of law and its development in Japan. As the principal architects of Japan's codes and conduits for the reception of German legal science in their interpretation, Japan's academic jurists were responsible for the conceptual infrastructure of Japanese law. The pattern of studying abroad and introducing upon return new theories and approaches has continued for more than a century. Between 1875 and 1908, for example, the number of students sent abroad by the Japanese government to study law (forty-three) exceeded those in every other field except engineering (eighty-seven), medicine (eighty-five) and physics (fifty-three).[4] In few other countries is the study of comparative and foreign law as pervasive. Translations of even quite mundane foreign writing on law often receive both commercial gain and scholarly acclaim. Younger scholars are encouraged to spend two to three years abroad within a few years after they have begun to teach. Their mentors will often select the country, if not the school, contributing to a hierarchy of promise and achievement among their protégés and foreign institutions by recommending who should study where. Although Germany continues to be a favored destination, especially for those specializing in civil and criminal law and procedure, the United States has become the host country of choice for the largest number of Japanese scholars in all fields. Each year America's elite law schools, ranked as perceived from Japan, receive dozens of petitions from Japanese scholars for places as visiting scholars if not advanced degree candidates. As a consequence of these disparate influences, Japanese law faculties in recent years have introduced a variety of innovations in teaching methods and fields of study that reflect an equal variety of foreign sources.

Japanese legal scholars self-consciously seek to learn from abroad in order to continue the development of Japanese law. For them the study of foreign law does not represent principally either an effort to discover universal truth or individual enlightenment. The aims may include both knowledge for its own sake as well as personal career gain, but on the whole the pattern reflects an unquestioned assumption that they are Japan's principal conduits for foreign knowledge and learning and continuing renewal and reform. Continuous contact with developments in continental European law, especially German legal developments, is crucial. Japanese scholars understand that Japan's participation within the civil law tradition has, in a broad sense, constitutional overtones. Japanese law is bound by categories, concepts, and principles deemed to be fundamental to the Tradition. Law thus cannot be purely an instrument of policy. Fundamental principles, a language, and a "grammar" channel and constrain its expression and application. Legal reform and change thus require accommodation and ideally European, particularly German, antecedents.

Legal scholars in Japan are even more self-aware of their related role as critics. Foreign law is studied out of the belief that appropriate models for change and reform can be found abroad. To some extent this attitude simply reflects past experience and the previously mentioned concern that Japan remain in conformity with its peers and the civil law tradition. However, many scholars think of themselves as reformers required by their career to function as catalysts for change. The Japanese sensitivity to the opinions of others in defining their own standards of conduct—another manifestation of Japan's communitarian emphasis—makes foreign opinions on Japan exceptionally influential. Scholars are among the principal intermediaries for foreign views. They can be quite selective, however, choosing to draw attention to criticisms of practices they themselves wish to see reformed. The study of foreign law is only one facet of this role. Critical evaluation of the law and active participation in efforts to legislate reforms are equally important aspects of the scholar's role. Worth noting is the particular stress Japanese legal scholars place on legal constraints on state action. With few exceptions, Japanese constitutional law scholars are highly critical of what they view as a conservative passivity on the part of senior judges and Supreme Court justices. Their criticism creates a tension that fosters at least gradual change.

Many younger Japanese scholars also find in the American experience attractive models for emulation. In a society bound by community controls, freedom from social constraints and emphasis on state-protected rights are especially appealing. As a result these scholars are critical of both American scholars who object to the extreme of American "legalism" as well as those who see elements of a beneficial community focus in Japanese patterns.[5] For American scholars not to find fault with those aspects of Japanese law that Japanese critics desire to reform is particularly unnerving.

Japanese legal scholarship also continues to evidence Japan's intellectual debt to continental European jurisprudence, particularly German legal science. Zentarō Kitagawa's seminal studies of Japanese reception of German legal theory document the transformation of Japanese civil law during the late Meiji (1868–1912) and Taishō (1912–1926) eras.[6] One legacy of this early Japanese scholarship is a continuing emphasis on coherent conceptual underpinnings for the rules and principles of law. Japan owes an enormous debt to the first generation of scholars who helped build the foundations of contemporary Japanese law. Exemplary of these early scholars is Ei'ichi Makino (1878–1970). Makino was a professor of criminal law and jurisprudence in the Tokyo Imperial University Faculty of Law. The author of more than one hundred books, he was instrumental, as noted subsequently, in the introduction of both the abuse of rights and good faith principles. He played a major role in the prewar development of Japanese criminal law as an advocate of a rehabilitative and more communitarian approach. Unfortunately none of his works have been translated into English, and outside of Japan he remains unknown. Yet, his works evidence extraordinary originality, breadth, and sensitivity to the most basic concerns of law.[7] His 1922 essay on the "relevance" (gutai-teki datōsei) of law, which some credit as the seminal study of the good faith principle, was a study of Japanese case law, not European theory.[8] Nevertheless, he incorporated what he learned in Europe, especially the time spent under the tutelage of Franz von Liszt (1851–1919), into his scholarship and into Japanese legal practice.

Theory, as Masami Itō notes, is the Japanese scholar's central concern.[9] Japan's legal scholars tend thus to evaluate judicial decisions more in view of their particular theoretical predilections and less with respect to the contextual concerns that by necessity motivate the judges who write them. A consensus of scholarly opinion—tsūsetsu—regarding any point of Japanese legal interpretation is usually sufficient to put to rest any further contention or controversy. The concerns and emphases of contemporary legal scholarship in Japan signal the directions the legal developments are taking. The influence of legal scholars in Japan is also a matter of numbers. They outnumber all other legal professionals by a large margin. In sheer volume their published output is immense. Few individuals today, however, wield the sort of overriding influence that was evident among their forbears in the formative years of modern Japanese law.

Internally Japanese law faculties retain the characteristics of most Japanese communities. Despite increasing mobility among younger faculty—caused in part by expansion of elite national and private law faculties, such as the University of Tokyo, Waseda, and Keio, autonomy remains an unspoken premise. Detailed regulatory requirements emanating in large part from the Ministry of Education, which has general powers of oversight and, with respect to national universities, resources, are pervasive. Yet, whatever their formal authority, faculties in Japan still retain notable control over their internal affairs. Like in the Tokugawa village, the interplay between regulation and faculty autonomy is complex, but a significant degree of autonomy is preserved. Community pressure—bullying, if you will—is the primary means for maintaining norms of conduct. It would be unthinkable, one is told, for a junior faculty to appeal outside of the faculty to hold it accountable to rules established for the university at large.

ATTORNEYS

Upon completion of the Institute's training program, legal apprentices enter one of the three principal legal professions. As detailed below, the personnel office of the Supreme Court appoints from sixty to eighty graduates each year as assistant judges. The Ministry of Justice similarly seeks to fill forty to fifty assistant procurator posts. Only a few—less than 2 percent—seek other careers. Thus the number of Institute graduates in Japan's elite ministries, business enterprises, and law faculties is minuscule. All graduates are qualified to become practicing lawyers (bengoshi), and the vast majority begin legal practice in one of Japan's many two- or three-lawyer offices. Few return to join the bar association in the prefectural capitals where they apprenticed. Most remain in Tokyo, joining one of the district's three bar associations, or move to Osaka or another large urban center.

Professional learning begins once the sorting process ends. As in the largest business enterprises and government bureaucracies, most specialized professional education takes place on the job. For the vast majority of attorneys this means learning how to litigate cases. A few will have joined one of the larger law offices in Tokyo that engage in a variation of the commercial and business practice common in the United States and larger commercial centers in Europe and Latin America. This select group of commercial or *shōgai* lawyers—about 5 percent of the total population of attorneys—advise business clients on a wide range of financial, intellectual property, and corporate matters, usually related to international transactions. Some will join one of the more politically active offices that tend to specialize in labor relations. The number of lawsuits and consequent development of labor law attests to their influence. Most in any event will learn to be trial lawyers working under a senior mentor, trying to build a base of clients who are willing to pay monthly retainer fees. As they succeed, they will establish their own offices and, as they become established, bring in one or two younger lawyers to mentor. Chie Nakane uses the example of lawyers to illustrate what she views as a predominate pattern of autonomous artisanship in Japan's "vertical" social organization.[10]

Legal scholars are not the only law reformers in Japan. The bar contributes significantly to a continuous emphasis on both social and legal reform. The influence in Japan of lawyers who are active in "progressive"—that is, left-liberal—reform efforts is remarkable. Progressive-reform lawyers dominate the national Federation of Bar Associations as well as many local bar associations. They can claim a long tradition. For more than a century, lawyers have led many of Japan's most significant reform movements. Many were involved in radical politics. Lawyers such as Tetsu Katayama (1887–1978), Japan's first Socialist prime minister (1948), were active in the prewar labor and rural tenant rights movements as well as the founding of Japan's Socialist Party. Lawyers were also prominent in Japan's Communist Party. Many were prosecuted and imprisoned under the prewar Peace Preservation Law to become leaders in the party in postwar Japan. More representative, however, of the prewar attorney reformers were individual lawyers like Tatsuji Fuse (1880–1953), Takuzo Hanai (1886–1931), and Rikisaburō Imamura (1866–1954) who, despite significant differences in their personalities and ideological leanings, all gained national prominence for their work as criminal defense lawyers representing the accused in the most famous criminal trials of the era from the 1907 Ashio mine pollution riot cases and the 1910 Shūsui Kotoku high treason trial to the 1935–37 Teijin scandal trials. Their dedication to the principles of rule by law and procedural process enshrined in Japan's new codes helped to ensure that Japan's legal order did not become the meaningless veneer of an unrestrained authoritarian state. Others, such as Ichirō Kiyose (1884–1967) and Toshimichi Hara (1867–1944), who in 1927 became the first lawyer in Japan to occupy the post of Minister of Justice, represented an elite corps of liberal reformers within the mainstream of Japanese politics. Hara, for example, along with Hanai, who was also active in electoral politics, and Kiyose, was among the principal architects of Japan's short-lived jury system (enacted in 1923, effective in 1928 but lapsed by the end of the war). These leaders of the Japanese bar reflected the easy entry of Japanese attorneys into active political careers and the ability of lawyers to combine professional and political activities. Many worked to expand democracy but remained fearful of the threat of social revolution. Hara, for example, was also a strong supporter of the Peace Preservation Law. These and other lawyers moved easily between professional and political careers. Tōru Hoshi (1850–1901) was one of Japan's first lawyer-politicians. In the late 1870s Hoshi became the first Japanese to be admitted to practice as an English barrister and one of Japan's first licensed lawyers, having drafted the regulations for the new profession of advocates himself. Others include Ichirō Hatoyama (1883–1959), who first entered politics in 1911 and served as liberal party prime minister from 1954 to 1956. By the mid 1930s lawyers had become the most numerous single occupational grouping in the Diet. At least in hindsight, Japan's first generation of lawyers is remarkable for their rise to national prominence as lawyers. Few attorneys since the Pacific War have achieved similar individual acclaim or status. Nonetheless, their professional ideals continue to resonate. The mission of the Japanese lawyer today, in the words of the Preamble to the 1987 Code of Attorney Ethics, is "the protection of fundamental human rights and the realization of social justice."[11]

Within the Diet since the war, about 5 percent of all members have been lawyers. More than half were members of one of the new moderate-conservative parties formed in 1992 and 1993 as a result of defections from the ruling Liberal Democratic Party.[12] Also, a significant number of lawyer parliamentarians during the postwar period have been Communist Party members. The Communist Party, in fact, has supported lawyers in cities throughout the country. The high proportion of politically active lawyers on the left influences many aspects of the legal system. One consequence is a reformist cast within the profession and an often sharply critical stance toward the government and established institutions—other than the profession itself.

A more tactical difference distinguishes the activities of politically active reform lawyers today. The primary professional role of progressive prewar attorneys like Fuse, Hanai, and Imamura was criminal and some civil defense. Their reputations rested on their efforts as counsel representing individuals being criminally prosecuted by the state or, in the case of the tenant-farmers' reform effort, defending tenants in civil suits brought by landlords seeking to enforce their property and contract rights. Today progressive lawyers are more likely to initiate litigation as plaintiff attorneys. Civil litigation, rather than criminal defense, has become the reformist lawyer's primary instrument of social change. Nearly all issues of social concern in postwar Japan, from defense policy to pollution, have involved civil suits brought by plaintiffs seeking to promote reform. Big business may have replaced landlords, but the state remains as a principal antagonist. One result, as Frank Upham argues, is conflict over the role of the courts between those who resist and those who promote change.[13] However constrained access to the courts may be, litigation continues to be a favored tool, and the courts have the last word.

Progressive reform is hardly the overriding concern of most lawyers in contemporary Japan. Despite the influence on the bar of its most progressive members, most lawyers in Japan today are considerably more preoccupied with mundane matters of financial security and social respect. In this respect the Japanese bar is hardly exceptional. A second more distinctive element of the ethos of the attorney in Japan is an emphasis on autonomy. A deeply felt desire for independence or freedom from control by others motivates nearly all lawyers in Japan. Almost every lawyer in Japan will attribute to this aim the personal decision to become an attorney and thus the costs and risks required to qualify. As might be expected in as socially dense and constrained a society as Japan, concern for autonomy and independence is a widely shared fixture of Japanese culture. Within the legal profession it is, along with concern for financial security and social status, among the most important factors in the choice of lawyering as a profession and has become a primary canon of professional ethics. To quote again from the Code of Attorney Ethics, the second sentence of the Preamble states: "In order to achieve their mission, attorneys shall preserve their professional freedom and independence and maintain the highest degree of autonomy." The statute regulating the practice of law prohibits any lawyer without permission of the bar to become an employee of any business or other organization and few lawyers tolerate direction by others.[14]

In this respect the individual lawyer—and judicial scrivener—stand apart from those who choose to become either procurators or judges, both of which involve careers within a highly disciplined and controlling bureaucracy. They all share, however, concern for the autonomy of the group—the procuracy, the judiciary, and the bar.

A prominent theme in the history of the bar in Japan was the effort to gain autonomy for the profession as a whole. The bar long sought juridical status for bar associations both to restrict the right to represent parties in court and to act as intermediaries to licensed attorneys. These were among the earliest and most ardent demands of the profession. In 1912 legislation was introduced in the House of Representatives not only to recognize the corporate status of bar associations but also to give them responsibility for all disciplinary action against their members. The bill also included provisions on the duties and responsibilities of attorneys with sanctions against those engaged in illegal representation. The bill failed, but similar demands were made in response to the government's proposal for reform in the early 1930s.[15] Not until the 1949 Attorney Law were all of these proposals finally enacted into law. Nobuyoshi Toshitani traces similar efforts by judicial scriveners to achieve recognition of their status as an autonomous profession with, not coincidentally, higher incomes.[16]

Sensitivity to social status is another significant but gradually fading concern among Japanese lawyers. The perception endures, if not the actual memory, of widespread public disdain for the profession in prewar Japan. Japan is hardly unique in the paradox of concomitant high social esteem for individual lawyers as eminent and respected jurists with correspondingly low regard for the profession as a whole. One needs only compare the status of Thomas More with the public attitudes toward lawyers in general at least as depicted by Shakespeare in sixteenth-century England. Shūsei Tokuda's widely read 1905 novel *Shokazoku* (The minor aristocrat) exemplified the popular view. In it appears a young lawyer named Umebara, who is unable to find employment because of the glut of law graduates. Umebara, in the words of Richard Torrance, Shūsei's biographer, "is definitely a villain" who persuades Ocho, the mistress of an aristocrat named Akioka, to extort money from the aristocrat's wife. Ocho commits suicide as a consequence, and Umebara then persuades Ocho's brother to revenge his sister's death by killing Akioka's wife.[17]

To the extent that newspapers shaped public attitudes in Japan during the 1920s and 1930s, there is ample evidence of the low esteem of the profession. In article after article, lawyers were portrayed in the worse possible light. Readers of the Tokyo Asahi newspaper (*Tōkyō Asahi Shinbun*), for example, were regularly informed about lawyers strangling their daughters or otherwise attempting to kill their children, running amuck on trains, stripped naked and fighting with farmers, being shot while breaking into a neighbor's home while in a drunken stupor, running away with an indentured geisha, being involved with a gang of con artists, and even stealing court documents.[18] Reports of lawyers defrauding clients were commonplace.[19] Even the most prominent, if not prosecuted for direct involvement in clandestine political activity, were subject to arrest and public stigma for bribery, theft, and other infractions of the law.[20] Lawyers were also the victims of increasing incidents of private violence in the early 1930s.[21]

Incomes also suffered. The number of lawyers increased dramatically in the 1920s, and complaints of unauthorized practice and pettifogging increased throughout the period. The profession thus strongly supported prohibition of practice by nonlawyers and welcomed the increasingly restrictive requirements on entry. The 1949 statute thus represented a major achievement for the Japanese bar. Lawyers were accorded the same status as prosecutors and judges in terms of their educational qualifications, entry was limited to the handful of apprentices provided under the national budget, and the bar associations gained near complete autonomy in regulating the activities of their members.

A "unified" profession of lawyers, prosecutors, and judges with respect to entry and training has not meant increased mobility among lawyers, prosecutors, and judges. Instead the three professions have become obdurately segmented. With very rare exceptions, lawyers do not become judges or prosecutors; judges and prosecutors enter practice only upon retirement, although not infrequently prosecutors but seldom judges will make the change at mid-career. The contrast with prewar patterns is notable. From accounts of the careers of many of Japan's best-known jurists, movement between the procuracy and the judiciary and into politics appears to have been much more fluid. The procuracy and the judiciary were less divided into separate careers or professions. Both initially had aspects of functional offices into which those qualified within the Ministry of Justice could move. At least in the formative years of the profession, the careers of many of Japan's most influential jurists were marked by such mobility.

Makoto Egi (1858–1925), for example, entered the Tokyo Metropolitan Police Bureau after graduating from the Law College of Tokyo University in 1884, two years before it became the Imperial University. He transferred to the Justice Ministry in 1885 and was appointed as a procurator. Four years later he moved to the Agriculture and Commerce Ministry as secretary to the Minister. After the enactment of Japan's first 1893 Attorney Law, he resigned from his official post to enter practice.[22] He quickly became one of the leaders of the profession. He actively participated as a member of several of the most important government law reform committees, such as the Code

Investigation Committee (*Hōten Chōsa Kai*) and the Temporary Legal System Deliberation Committee (*Rinji Hōsei Shingikai*). In 1914 Egi was elected president of the Tokyo Bar Association.

Ichirō Hatoyama's father, Kazuo Hatoyama (1856–1911), began his career upon return from the United States, where he had studied law at both Columbia and Yale (1875–80), as an instructor in the Tokyo University Law College. In 1882 he was elected to the Tokyo Metropolitan Assembly. Two years later he returned to full-time teaching at Tokyo University. A year later he joined the Ministry of Foreign Affairs. In 1886 he left government service to begin his career as a lawyer and reenter politics. In 1889 he successfully passed the examination to be qualified as an advocate (*daigen'nin*) under the regulations for advocates and began to practice law in 1892. He was promptly elected as president of the Advocates' Association (*Daigen'nin Kumiai*). He was subsequently elected president of the association and its successor, the Tokyo Bar Association. Hatoyama's national political career also commenced in 1892. He lost in his first bid for a seat in the newly established Diet in 1890 but succeeded in the election to the Second Diet two years later. He became Speaker in 1896 and remained a member of the House of Representatives until his death in 1911.

Within the Ministry of Justice a similar pattern remained evident into the 1930s. Kazuo Hatoyama's son-in-law, Kisaburō Suzuki, exemplifies the mobility between judicial and procuratorial offices as well as the involvement of former Ministry of Justice officials in the political life of prewar Japan. Suzuki began his career in the Justice Ministry in 1891 as a judge. In 1907 he was promoted to Chief Judge of the Tokyo District Court. He then left judicial office to become a procurator and in 1912 was appointed procurator of Japan's highest court, the Great Court of Cassation, on which he later served as a justice. By 1921 he had advanced to become Procurator-General. He resigned from the government to enter politics and served as Minister of Justice in 1924. He later became Home Minister (1928) and president of the Seiyūkai, one of prewar Japan's two principal political parties.

The lives of Japan's first lawyers, like Egi and Kazuo Hatoyama, and political leaders, like Ichirō Hatoyama and Suzuki, are exceptional because the patterns they set did not continue. Rather, the careers of those trained in law became increasingly fixed into segmented paths with virtually no mobility in or out of the rigidly defined and largely autonomous procuratorial and judicial career bureaucracies and, except for retiring prosecutors and an even smaller number of judges, the bar.

PROCURATORS

The procuracy is today the smallest and most troubled of the three principal careers in law in Japan. Three related values—the quest for the truth, absolute political neutrality, and public trust—reflect its highest ideals. Political corruption has seriously challenged all three. Before proceeding further, an introduction to the office and its organization is necessary.

The Procurator's Office is organized like other government agencies as a tightly knit career bureaucracy. Administered centrally as an independent agency within the Ministry of Justice, the procuracy maintains separate offices for each judicial district in Japan (fifty district court offices and 452 local offices corresponding to branch courts), each high court (eight), and the Supreme Court. Initially but only briefly, the primary responsibilities of the procuracy included supervision of judges.[23] From its inception in 1872 as the agency for those responsible for state prosecution, the highest office has been the Procurator-General. Like nearly all other public and private organizations in Japan, personnel decisions—appointment assignment and promotion—are made by a central personnel office.

Japan's public prosecutors begin their careers, as previously described, upon completion of legal apprenticeship in the Legal Training and Research Institute. Most remain in the agency until retirement. Concern over recruitment, morale, and retention, however, was instrumental in the Ministry of Justice's strong support for increasing the number of legal apprentices in the Institute. Under a system of personnel transfers between the Ministry of Justice and the Supreme Court, about a dozen prosecutors and judges are exchanged each year.

Such assignments are temporary. The judges typically are assigned to administrative and civil cases in which the state is a party. Otherwise there is no lateral entry. Some scholars and lawyers, including the Federation of Bar Associations, express concerns that this pattern echoes the mobility of the prewar system and that the distinctive roles and functions of the judicial office may be compromised along with scrupulous protection of civil liberties.[24]

Japan in 1993 had only 2,092 prosecutors (1,173 full and 919 assistant prosecutors). Their total caseload exceeds three million criminal violations involving more than four hundred thousand offenders and approximately eighty thousand criminal prosecutions a year, in addition to representation of the national government in all civil and administrative litigation. In the most thorough empirical study of the Japanese procuracy in any language, David Johnson argues that despite these case totals, individual prosecutors are not overworked.[25] He points out that more than 80 percent of all criminal violations involve routine traffic offenses, most of which can be processed expeditiously by assistants after routine police investigation through summary proceedings that do not require prosecutorial participation.

The procuracy shares with other Japanese bureaucracies a strong sense of elite status and mission. Like other state officials, procurators perceive themselves and justify their authority as representatives of the public interest. Unlike even the most influential of the economic ministries, however, Japanese procurators enjoy powers that correspond with their authority. To them is delegated control over the most coercive of all state controls—the prosecution of criminal offenders.

Prosecutorial discretion is an essential feature of Japan's system of criminal justice. Without the authority to determine whether to initiate a public prosecution, the procuracy would indeed be reduced to a less autonomous agency of functionaries in the system. The importance of this authority, manifested in the power to suspend prosecution (*kiso yūyo*), is widely viewed by prosecutors themselves and outside observers alike as a unique feature of the Japanese system and an indispensable tool of prosecutorial authority.[26]

Important legal, political, and social constraints on the exercise of prosecutorial discretion do exist. Since the early 1930s by statute the state must pay compensation to those falsely accused of a crime, and since the Occupation a citizen board of inquest has authority to review prosecutorial decisions whether or not to prosecute a case.[27] Whether either significantly influences the decisions prosecutors make is doubtful.[28] The more decisive controls are internal.

Johnson lists four: a regularly consulted and often mechanically followed manual of guidelines and standards for charging offenders and recommending penalties, a system of hierarchical consultation and approval (kessai) by at least one and often two or more supervisors in all cases except minor traffic offenses, annual audits (kensa) of case dispositions aimed particularly at instances in which no charge is made, and finally personnel review for job posting and individual career advancement. These controls are intended to ensure consistency and to prevent error. Johnson argues that they are important and effective. Discretion is less of a prerogative of individual prosecutors than of the agency as a whole. His research also substantiates the view that within the procuracy considerable effort is made to prevent prosecution of any case that might result in acquittal. To lose a case is a cause for disgrace. Consistent postwar conviction rates of more than 99 percent attest to the efficacy of such controls in preventing the prosecution of suspects until prosecutors are assured that the accused is guilty and that they have marshalled sufficient evidence to withstand judicial scrutiny and persuade the judges of the certainty of the defendant's guilt.

As Johnson observes, prosecutors worldwide face two risks in the prosecution of any case. The first is that they will fail to prosecute a person who then commits another offense. The second is that prosecution proceeds but a presumptively innocent defendant is acquitted. For American prosecutors, the first poses the greater professional costs and thus they tend to err in favor of prosecution at the risk of acquittal. For the Japanese prosecutors, acquittal has more career costs and thus they tend not to prosecute if uncertain of success. Even more "unforgivable," within the procuracy, Johnson states, is to prosecute someone who is innocent. What Johnson refers to as the "cardinal objectives" of Japanese prosecutors—ascertaining the truth and making an accurate decision to charge—go hand in glove with these efforts. It would be misleading to stress the self-interest of prosecutors in avoiding mistakes over their professional objectives and values. They are mutually reinforcing. As a result the procuracy consciously makes its own determination—a preliminary adjudication—of guilt. This pattern reflects the prosecutor's prewar role.

The position of the procurator in prewar Japan was modelled on the *Procureur* in French law. The office of procurator was equal in rank to that of judge. The French system includes an intervening screening process before any person can be brought to trial under the supervision of an examining judge (*juge d'instruction*). Prewar Japanese procurators participated with the examining judge in this dispositive "preliminary investigation" of cases reported by the judicial police, who handled the initial investigation under procuratorial oversight. Prosecutors were responsible for presenting a complete dossier on the case to the examining judge, who had the authority to conduct a full investigation, including the interrogation of witnesses, to determine whether the evidence warranted indictment and public trial. Critics argue, however, that the judges routinely let the dossier control.[29] The proceeding was conducted *in camera*. The secrecy of the proceeding was even more strongly condemned by American authorities responsible for postwar reforms.[30] Organized under the Ministry of Justice, the procuracy was also subject to the politically appointed minister's decisions to initiate prosecution. Like the prewar bar, the procuracy sought greater autonomy from such political control.

The Occupation reforms attempted to recast the procurator along American patterns. Eliminated were the "preliminary investigation" and with it the office of "examining judge." The role of the judge was reformed toward that of an umpire in an adversarial trial with the procurator acquiring more adversarial functions. Hence some consider it more appropriate to use the American term, public prosecutor, for the office today. The influence—or at least the function—of past practice remains, however, within the procuracy as its members view their role more as representatives of the public interest whose duties include a painstakingly thorough preliminary determination of guilt.

The postwar reforms also gave the procuracy much of the institutional autonomy—but not, it should be emphasized, the individual autonomy—the procuracy had long sought. The Procurators Office Law sets out the "principle of prosecutor independence" (*kensatsukan dokuritsu no gensoku*) by conferring the authority to decide on particular cases in the Procurator General. The present insulation of prosecutorial decisions from the politically appointed Minister of Justice is similar to a pattern proposed in 1927 by Toshimichi Hara while Minister of Justice in the Tanaka Cabinet.[31] Only once in postwar Japan, as noted below, has a Minister of Justice intervened. The resulting outcry from the public and the procuracy was sufficient to prevent any repetition. Nevertheless, indirect political pressures are evident, whether in the form of informal ministerial intervention or anticipatory concern over the political implications of decisions whether to prosecute or both.

One manifestation of the procuracy's concern for as much insulation as possible from political intervention is the emphasis on neutrality (*fuhen futō*) and strict fairness (*gensei kōhei*) as defining principles of prosecutorial conduct. The 1935–37 Teijin case is recalled repeatedly as the exemplary prosecution.

The Teijin affair began in 1927 when, as the result of the bankruptcy of the Suzuki Shōten, the Bank of Taiwan acquired 220,000 shares of stock of the Teikoku Jinzō Kenski company the bank held as collateral for a loan. A purchasing syndicate comprised mainly of members of the *Banchōkai*, a group of businessmen connected with an effort to unify Japan's prewar political parties to oppose the rising influence of the military, negotiated with the bank to purchase the stock. They agreed on a price of 125 yen based on the market value of fifty yen per share as of May 30, 1934, and, with the legally required approval of the Bank of Japan, one hundred thousand shares were transferred. The value of the shares quadrupled within six months. The media charged corruption. In 1935 criminal charges were brought against Bank of Taiwan officials and members of the syndicate for breach of trust and against prominent officials in the Finance Ministry and the Bank of Japan for bribery. The trials lasted for nearly two years, finally coming to an end in 1937. All were acquitted. Nonetheless, the trials confirmed public views, buttressed by results of earlier prosecutions, of the intrinsic corruption of Japan's political and business elite and the role of the procuracy as an agency that, free from such fouling influence, was worthy of the public trust.

The earliest and to some the most significant prosecutions were the 1909 sugar bribery cases and the 1915 Siemens case. The sugar bribery cases involved twenty-five current and former Diet members who were found guilty of accepting bribes in return for tax concessions for Japan's leading sugar producer. The Siemens case was the first scandal to bring down a cabinet. It involved the bribery of naval officers to secure a contract to provide the electrical equipment for a naval vessel being built for the Japanese by a British shipbuilding firm. The scandal broke when the *Asahi Shinbun* reported allegations of bribery from evidence presented in a related trial in Berlin. Three officers were convicted, a pending measure to increase the Imperial Navy's budget was defeated in the Diet, and the cabinet headed by Admiral Gombei Yamamoto resigned. Procurator-General Kiichirō Hiranuma (1867–1952) who had led the prosecution in 1909, however, expressed his reluctance to prosecute the naval officers involved for fear that it would sully the reputation of the emperor's navy.

Japan's contemporary procuracy was forged out of these and similar bribery scandals during the first three decades of the century. Hiranuma was the master craftsman of this effort. Like his junior colleague and ally, Kisaburō Suzuki, Hiranuma had begun his career in the Justice Ministry. He joined the Ministry in 1888 as a junior procurator, rapidly advancing to become Procurator-General in 1912. In 1921 he resigned to serve briefly as Chief Justice of the Great Court of Cassation. By 1922 he had reached the pinnacle of his career as a government official as Vice Minister of Justice. Late in 1923 he entered politics with appointment as Justice Minister. From 1926 to 1936 he served as Vice President and then from 1936 to 1939 as President of the Imperial Privy Council. He became Prime Minister in 1939. Although most historians emphasize Hiranuma's antiliberal and ultranationalist views and his influence on Japan's aggressive militarism, as Richard Yasko persuasively argues, Hiranuma was the driving force in the creation of Japan's procuracy as one of Japan's most professional and powerful bureaucracies.[32]

Hiranuma began his career as protégé of Kunitomi Yokota (1850–1923), Hiranuma's predecessor as Procurator-General as well as Chief Justice of the Great Court of Cassation. Yokota had promoted Hiranuma to assist in establishing a professional and politically autonomous procuracy. Hiranuma, joined by Suzuki, soon attracted a large following of Justice Ministry officials, mostly career procurators, who were to share Hiranuma's vision of an independent procuracy purged of all outside loyalties, with extensive authority, power, and political influence. The means to this end included the selective resort to prosecution of leading political figures for bribery. Hiranuma's willingness to prosecute the politicians involved in the Siemens scandal but reluctance to prosecute any officers of the Imperial Navy is indicative of his deep disdain for Japan's emerging liberal political order through which, he believed, private interests determined policy through corrupt politicians and their supporters. The sugar bribery cases were thus the first and the Teijin case simply the final episode in a series of prosecutions that could be viewed as serving to enforce standards of honesty and good government and purging the procuracy and other government bureaucracies of political influence. By exposing what Hiranuma and his supporters saw as the stench of party politics and the corresponding purity of the procuracy as the guardian agency of national virtue, the procuracy was promoting the public interest and the welfare of Japan as a nation.

Hiranuma's antiliberal views may best be understood as a virulent version of more traditional attitudes with respect to what is meant by the public welfare. Defined under the influence of imperial Chinese ideologies, notions of public versus private in Japan were traditionally viewed in terms of a dichotomy between broader community (public) versus narrower selfish (private) interests. Thus state officials in modern Japan have tended to view the public interest as a concern for the collective welfare rather than the sum of the interests of the individual or other discrete components. Implicit in this dichotomy is a rejection of claims that the private sector may have an equivalent justification or that general welfare can be defined as the amalgam of self-regarding conduct.

The rejection of self-interest as a justification of authority has important consequences. The strength of this view and its effective enforcement within the procuracy as well as other relatively closed, centrally controlled government bureaucracies help to explain Japan's remarkable record in preventing official corruption. Concern for authority and the realization that corruption would undermine the public trust on which authority rests act as powerful preventative agents. And—perhaps the most positive legacy of Hiranuma's efforts—the Japanese procuracy has an enviable record of prevention of at least the more venal forms of corruption. However, its record for political neutrality and independence during the first three decades of postwar politics in Japan has not been blemish-free.

Two bribery scandals prior to 1976 were the catalyst for cabinet resignation and change of government. Both, however, left lingering doubts with respect to the political neutrality of the postwar procuracy. The first was the 1948 Shōwa Denkō case, which forced the resignation of the Ashida Cabinet. It involved allegations that Shōwa Denkō executives had bribed officials and influential political leaders to obtain low-interest loans through the Reconstruction Finance Bank. Prosecutors indicted sixty-four individuals, only two of whom were ultimately convicted by the Tokyo District Court in 1962. Two of those indicted—Takeo Fukuda (1905–95) and Kakuei Tanaka (1918–93)—were later to become prime minister.

The second case was the 1954 shipbuilding bribery scandal, which resulted in the collapse of the second Yoshida Cabinet as a protective maneuver and perhaps influenced the merger of the two dominant parties into a single Liberal Democratic Party (LDP) the following year. The scandal broke in January that year as members of the opposition Democratic Party accused the Liberal Party of involvement in bribes and kickbacks from Hitachi Shipbuilding & Engineering Company in return for government contracts and subsidies. More than seventy-one persons were implicated, including Hayato Ikeda (1899–1965) and Eisaku Satō (1901–75), both of whom were also to become prime minister. Because Satō, then Secretary-General of the Liberal Party, was a member of the Diet in session, approval by the Minister of Justice for his arrest was necessary. Under instructions from Prime Minister Yoshida, the minister refused the prosecutors' request and further investigation into the scandal was prevented. Public protest over this "exercise of supervision" (*shikiken hatsudo*) brought down the government. As noted above, this was the last instance of direct and open political intervention in the postwar period.

In light of these two cases, particularly the 1954 Shipbuilding case and the apparent passivity of the procuracy in the face of widely known instances of similar political graft, the political independence and trustworthiness of the procuracy were subject to increasing doubts. With the exception of Toshiki Kaifu, every Japanese prime minister who served between 1954 and 1993 was implicated in at least one major bribery scandal of the postwar period. As Japan prospered, the amounts involved reached a magnitude that was difficult to ignore. "Money-power politics" (*kinken seiji*) denoted the era. Widely believed to have been directly involved in nearly every major political bribery case of the period, Prime Minister Tanaka was viewed by many as its leading star. Aroused by reports of massive corruption during Tanaka's two years as prime minister, public pressure finally forced Tanaka to resign on December 9, 1974. Less than two years later the Lockheed scandal began what many prosecutors hoped would be the turning point.

The scandal broke in the United States in February 1976 with revelations by executives of the Lockheed Aircraft Company that payments had been made to politicians and government officials in several countries, including Japan, in order to secure contracts for the purchase of civilian and military aircraft manufactured by Lockheed. With evidence obtained with the assistance of United States Department of Justice lawyers, twelve businessmen and three politicians, including Tanaka, were indicted. All were convicted, including, on October 12, 1983, Tanaka, the last defendant. Tanaka promptly appealed (*kōso*) and the appellate trial commenced. Nearly a decade later, before the final decision was handed down, Tanaka died. Tanaka's arrest in the wake of the Lockheed bribery revelations was widely praised as an example of the procuracy's political independence regained.

The principle of strict neutrality today requires the procuracy to avoid any partisan political activity. Yet paradoxically it often justifies if not compels the procuracy to play a pivotal role for change at critical intervals of Japanese political life as much today as in the past. Decisions by the procuracy to investigate and prosecute leading political figures accused of receiving payments for political favors continue to deepen public distrust of politicians while reinforcing confidence in career officials. So long as public perceptions of a corrupt-free officialdom persist, the procuracy can be expected to remain a potential catalyst for political reform and potent agency of state authority.

In this respect, the 1976 Lockheed scandal, subsequent trial, and first instance conviction of Kakuei Tanaka was the exemplary postwar case. The failure of the procuracy to act in similar fashion in the series of subsequent scandals involving other members of Tanaka's political faction as well as three prime ministers (Nakasone, Takeshita, and Miyazawa), strengthened doubts.

In the midst of prolonged media coverage of payments to LDP leaders by an express package carrier, Tokyo Sagawa Kyūbin, one of the political kingmakers of the party, Shin Kanemaru, was alleged to have received large political contributions, a portion of which he had kept for himself. The allegation was confirmed by investigation into his personal affairs, including a search of his home. The result was a preliminary decision to charge Kanemaru with a minor violation with a minuscule fine. The media outcry was immediate. In the midst of the tumult, on September 29, 1992, the Chief Prosecutor for the Sapporo High Court, Michio Satō, wrote for the *Asahi Shinbun* an impassioned reminder of the procuracy's first principles of absolute neutrality and independence.[33] For a senior prosecutor to criticize so strongly and publicly so politically sensitive a decision by the agency was itself sufficient to attract wide attention. The essay hit the mark. Kanemaru was subsequently indicted for offenses that carried substantial penalties.

Although no one suggests any contemporary counterpart to the political motives that drove Hiranuma and Suzuki in the prewar bribery cases, the procuracy's role in the Lockheed case and the series of political scandals of the early 1990s has had some similar effects. Not only have these cases led to political reform, ultimately contributing to the breakup of the LDP, the end of nearly four decades of unbroken LDP rule, and the most comprehensive electoral reform since the Occupation. They also have solidified the political autonomy of the procuracy and its public reputation as an independent and trustworthy agency of state authority and power. As Michio Satō pointed out in his 1992 *Asahi Shinbun* essay, without that public trust, the Japanese procuracy would lose its most valued assets: its autonomy and its discretion.

An ethos that Daniel H. Foote labels as benevolent paternalism is an equally strong attribute of the Japanese prosecutorial and police establishments.[34] What Foote and others observe from the outside, David Johnson confirms from surveys of opinions from within the procuracy. Take, for example, his survey of the goals or objectives that prosecutors consider to be the most important in their work. More than 10 percent of all prosecutors in Japan responded. In order of priority (and percentage), their primary goals were to discover the truth (99.6 percent), to make "proper" charge decisions (97.9 percent), to invoke offender remorse (92.7 percent), to rehabilitate and reintegrate offenders (91.5 percent), to protect the public (91.1 percent), to treat like cases alike (90.7 percent), to respect the rights of suspects (83.9 percent), to reduce the crime rate (83.8 percent), and to give offenders the punishment they deserve (82.5 percent). More than two-thirds (67.6 percent) answered that repairing relations between offenders and victims was a goal, a slightly higher percentage than those who listed efficient disposition of cases (65.5 percent) and twice as many as those who considered maintaining the reputation of the procuracy (36.6 percent). Less than a quarter (21.9 percent) replied that maximizing punishment was a prosecutorial aim and less than 10 percent responded that prosecuting and convicting as many cases as possible was an objective. Johnson also inquired about the disparate factors prosecutors consider in suspending prosecution of convictable offenders. He found again by rank and percentage (in parentheses) that the seriousness of the offense, measured by the harm done, and the likelihood of reoffending were the two primary considerations (each 90.1 percent) followed by the repentance of the suspect (80.3 percent), the motive for the act (76.4 percent), whether the offender had compensated the victim (76 percent), the victim's views on the appropriateness of punishment (70.8 percent), and the offender's prior record (70.1 percent).

The legally prescribed punishment ranked ninth (44.6 percent) and cooperation of the suspect with police and prosecutors ranked sixteenth (9.9 percent).[35] Some may be tempted to dismiss such responses to an American student's survey as intended to confirm an official line (*tatemae*) that may not accord with reality (*honne*). However, Johnson's evidence on the effectiveness of institutional controls to ensure that individual prosecutors internalize agency values and adhere to institutional standards is persuasive that these replies are accurate.

Suspension of prosecution provides prosecutors with the institutional means to realize such values. Foote quotes Hiranuma in promoting the use of suspension of prosecution *in order* to prevent crime.[36] By treating offenders who could be corrected leniently, Hiranuma perceived that crime could be reduced. Once convicted and punished, offenders were more likely to repeat offending. Hiranuma appreciated the difficulty those labeled as criminals had in reintegrating back into their communities. Thus reduction of the number of those with prior convictions itself was thought to have a positive effect on crime prevention and control.

For this process of crime prevention to work, the prosecutor must be able to distinguish those offenders who are correctable and thus can be treated leniently from those considered to be incorrigible who thus should be separated from the community for the sake of public safety. Because Japanese prosecutors are taught to consider the individual aspects of each case and believe in consistent treatment of like cases, not like crimes, many of the responses to Johnson's survey overlap.[37] A "proper" disposition is one that is consistent with agency guidelines, and the likelihood of a repeat offense is determined in large part by the attitudes of the offender in showing remorse and acknowledging accountability, the compensated victim in expressing pardon, and the family and other members of the offender's particular community in accepting responsibility for reintegrative support and control. In the one case, the prosecutors may "cry with the offender" and the victim and rely on community support and correction.[38] In the other, they may view incarceration or the death penalty as the only alternative.

4 Crime and Community

The potential dissonance between law and social behavior is perhaps greater in the area of criminal law than any other. Crimes represent the particular sorts of conduct those who make legal rules consider not only deviant in terms of their preferred norms but also warrant the most powerful public statement of condemnation and coercive sanction. Not all wrongs are crimes and not all crimes reflect social wrongs, at least in terms of the prevailing views of the community at large. Some patterns cross the disparate zones of culture and time. On the one hand, those who make criminal law—whether monarchs, parliamentarians, or judges—tend to allow for themselves greater immunity from legal norms than for others.[1] On the other hand, communities, left to their own devices, tend not to enforce—nullify, if you will—the legal rules they consider unfair or too harsh, or simply do not like. In these respects, Japan exemplifies universal practices. How it does so, however, is distinctive.

THE FORMAL PROCESS

From the apprehension of offenders to the determination of guilt and application of prescribed penalties, each stage in the formal criminal process in Japan is governed in theory as well as practice by the substantive and procedural rules of the constitution, codes, and special statutes. As with so many other fields of law, Japan's Criminal Code and Code of Criminal Procedure reflect the influence of continental European, particularly German, law and legal institutions with the addition of American-inspired constitutional protections and assorted adversarial features for criminal trials.[2] Despite several failed attempts at revision, successfully resisted even during the war by a lack of consensus within the law-related bureaucracies and more recently the progressive legal community, the 1907 (effective from 1908) Criminal Code remains in effect with relatively minor amendment.[3] Two scholars, Kansaburō Katsumoto (1866–1923) and Asatarō Okada (1868–1936), who had studied in Germany under Franz von Liszt (1851–1919) at the turn of the century, are credited with having introduced German subjectivism and ideas of causality into Japan and the Code.[4] As a result, the Criminal Code gives judges wide latitude in applying penalties.

The Criminal Code was considered by those responsible for the Occupation reforms to be compatible in nearly all respects with the new postwar constitution. Alfred C. Oppler (1893–1982), the former German administrative law judge who headed the division responsible for legal reforms under the Supreme Commander for the Allied Powers (SCAP), described the 1907 Code as a "relatively advanced piece of legislation" that required little modification to remain compatible with the principles of Japan's postwar constitution.[5] Only deletion of the *lèse majesté* provisions was considered necessary out of belief, at the time, that the principle of equality under the law mandated that even heads of state and government should not receive greater protection than ordinary citizens.[6]

In contrast, Japan's postwar constitution introduced most of the procedural protections of American constitutional law. The 1922 Code of Criminal Procedure was thoroughly revised to conform to the new constitutional requirements and enacted as a new code. The revisions gave the parties more initiative in criminal trials and enhanced the procedural rights of the accused and role of defense counsel. As a result, Japanese criminal procedure is a hybrid of continental and American law. Nevertheless, Japan continues to adhere to procedures that are generally more akin to continental practice. From an American perspective, the new code did not immediately transform defense counsel into vigorous advocates for the accused. Gradually, however, the adversarial features of the system have become more pronounced. Many criminal defense counsel today are by Japanese standards quite assertive in the interests of their clients. Others avoid confrontation and continue to balance the interests of those they represent with concern for their relationships with procurators and judges.[7] Some lawyers will withdraw from a case if convinced of their client's guilt. The preponderance of trials in which the accused has admitted guilt also reduces assertive confrontation. More determinative, however, are the intrinsic elements of Japan's trial process. The lack of a jury and any lay participation means that career judges are responsible for determining both facts and law. Their sense of this responsibility and the corollary concern for finding the truth preclude their acting more as umpires to ensure the fairness of the process but not necessarily the accuracy of the outcome, characteristic of a more complete adversarial proceeding.

The Japanese also continue to adhere to the fundamental principles of continental jurisprudence. Beccaria's twin principles that crimes and punishments can only be established by statutory law (*nulum crimen sine lege* and *nulla poena sine legeu*) were enforced during modern Japan's most authoritarian era and continue to apply with constitutional emphasis today.[8] As a result, Japan combines the substantive protections of European law with the procedural protections of American constitutional law.

DISCRETION AND DIVERSION

Discretion is the fulcrum of Japan's formal system of criminal justice. Whether exercised by the police in handling minor offenses, procurators under their formal authority to suspend prosecution, or judges pursuant to code provisions empowering them to reduce or suspend sanctions altogether, discretion enables Japan's criminal justice authorities to deal with crime and criminals in ways that work remarkably well.

At each stage in the process Japanese criminal justice authorities routinely exercise discretionary authority to divert offenders back into the community. Statistics tell something of the story. In 1994, for example, the Japanese police cleared 58.1 percent of all criminal code offenses. They referred more than 90 percent of the officially identified suspects to public procurators. Most of the offenders (68 percent) had committed a criminal traffic violation. Excluding these, almost 75 percent, however, were released without arrest or, it appears, further police formal process although reported. Arrested but released were an additional 2 percent of the offenders. Twenty-five percent of the identified criminal code offenders were arrested and referred for prosecution. Less than half of these were subjected to detention.[9]

The police use their discretionary authority under article 193 of the Code of Criminal Procedure for minor cases (*bizai shobun*) to resolve many cases without any report to the prosecutors. B. J. George cites statistics between 1975 and 1980 in concluding that an average ratio of 17.6 percent of non-traffic Criminal Code offenses were disposed of in this manner.[10] Assaults, thefts, fraud, embezzlement, and gambling were the most common. George's calculation may be too low. Minoru Shikita, former procurator and director of the United Nations Asia and Far East Institute for the Prevention of Crime and Treatment of Offenders (UNAFEI), estimates that in the early 1980s the Tokyo Metropolitan District police failed to report about 40 percent of all referable cases.[11] David Johnson repeats Shikita's estimate.[12] Whatever the correct number, less than a quarter of all cleared non-traffic offenders are arrested, referred to the prosecutor, and placed in detention before trial. An equal proportion are released without further process.

Procurators prosecute only about 5 percent of all prosecutable cases in ordinary criminal proceedings. As indicated previously, they permit the majority (53 percent in 1992), to be adjudicated in uncontested, summary proceedings (*ryakushiki tetsuzuki*) based on documentary evidence and handled by prosecutorial assistants (*jimukan*) with limited prosecutorial participation.[13] Most of these cases involve routine traffic violations, but some do not. For example, the initial disposition that caused public outcry in the Shin Kanemaru case was a summary proceeding. Procurators control the choice. The Code of Criminal Procedure provides that procurators may request that a case be adjudicated pursuant to simplified proceedings by summary courts (*kan'i saibansho*).[14] However, the accused must also agree in writing. The maximum penal fine for code offenses subject to summary proceedings is 500,000 yen (or U.S.$5,000 to $6,250 at prevailing exchange rates).[15] Most summary proceedings involve routine criminal traffic offenses. Summary proceedings are not available for more serious offenses for which a fine is not a statutory option. Consequently, cases involving homicide, rape, fraud, burglary, robbery, and extortion are not subject to summary proceedings.[16]

In all cases procurators, as described previously, have discretionary authority to suspend prosecution of any offender, even for crimes for which summary proceedings are not available. They routinely exercise this authority in 30–35 percent of all non-traffic Criminal Code violations by convictable offenders. The numbers vary by the crime committed. Procurators exercised this authority in 1994, for example, to suspend 5.1 percent of prosecutable homicide cases, 5.4 percent of robbery prosecutions, 7.3 percent of stimulant drug offenses, and 12.9 percent of all prosecutions for rape. In contrast, prosecution was suspended in 36.6 percent of all extortion cases, 49.8 percent of election law violations, and 82.1 percent of embezzlement cases.[17]

Nearly all suspects reported by the police are in fact determined by procurators not to be convictable. Losing a case is as significant a loss of face for police detectives as it is for the procurators. They tend as a result to continue investigation until convinced of the guilt and certainty of conviction.[18] Less than 3 percent of all police-identified suspects are generally released for insufficient evidence or similar grounds.[19] Similar reasons explain why those who are prosecuted are nearly always convicted. As noted previously, conviction rates in Japan hover consistently around 99.5 percent. Yet the courts seem equally lenient.

Judicial discretion, as noted, is an ingrained feature of the 1907 Criminal Code. Article 25 authorizes judges to suspend execution for one to five years in cases involving sentences of imprisonment of not more than three years or fines not exceeding 500,000 yen (approximately U.S.$5,000 to $6,250) for offenders who have not previously been sentenced to imprisonment or if five years has elapsed since their release. Because judges also have discretion to impose sentences within prescribed statutory ranges, so long as the statutorily prescribed range of penalties for a crime permits judges to sentence an offender to no more than five years imprisonment or no more than a 500,000 yen fine, they are able first to hand down a sentence that satisfies the requirements of article 25 and then to suspend it altogether. The effect of this provision is thus to allow judges to suspend sentences except for only a few of the most serious offenses (for example, arson of an inhabited building). In 1953 amendments permitted supervision during the period of suspension and revocation in the case of repeated criminal activity. Unless revoked, however, the sentence loses effect after the period of suspension ends. In addition, Articles 66–72 permit judges to reduce sentences under a variety of circumstances, including "extenuating circumstances" (*hanzai no jōjo ni shakuryō subeki mono*). For most cases the code limits reduction to one-half of the term of incarceration or amount of the fine. The maximum reduction for the death penalty is imprisonment for ten years.[20]

Few convicted offenders in Japan are subjected to more than a minor fine. In summary proceedings, as noted, the maximum penalty is about U.S.$2,500 at prevailing exchange rates. In practice, however, most offenders pay much less. Of the 1,150,696 defendants in summary proceedings concluded in 1992, only 0.5 percent were fined the maximum. Nearly 90 percent were fined less than U.S.$1,000. Two out of three were fined less than $500.[21]

When judges do impose incarceration, the terms tend to be short. Few convicted offenders sentenced to imprisonment serve more than one-year terms. Judges also exercise discretion and regularly suspend sentences for nearly two-thirds of all defendants they find to be guilty. The more serious the crime, however, the lower the proportion. In 1992, for example, sentences were suspended for nearly 25 percent of those convicted of homicide, 34 percent for larceny, 26 percent for robbery, 37 percent for arson, and 13 percent for rape. Those whose sentences are not suspended are seldom subjected to prison terms of more than a year. Only about 45 percent of all imprisoned offenders actually serve a full term. More than 50 percent are paroled before the expiration of their sentences.[22]

In summary, in 1992 more than nine hundred thousand offenders were identified by the police for having committed a non-traffic criminal offense. Of these suspects less than a fifth were prosecuted at all and of these only 6 percent in formal trial proceedings for which the penalty could be more than a fine. Nearly all of those prosecuted were convicted (99.99 percent) but less than half (40 percent) of the 6 percent were imprisoned and only 4 percent received prison terms of five years or more. Only half of these are likely to serve the maximum. In other words, less than 0.1 percent of all offenders in Japan actually spend five years or more in prison and less than 2.5 percent are incarcerated at all.

CONFESSION, REPENTANCE, AND ABSOLUTION

The decisions by police, procurators, and judges on how to exercise their discretion in treating offenders—that is, whether to report, prosecute, sentence, or parole—are based on a number of factors. Some are similar to those in other criminal justice systems: the gravity of the offense, the circumstances and nature of the crime, the age and prior record of the offender. In Japan, however, several additional factors rarely taken formally into account elsewhere—at least in the West—are determinative. As described in the preceding chapter, not only the attitude of the offender in acknowledging guilt, expressing remorse, and accepting accountability by compensating the victim but also the responses of the victim in expressing willingness to pardon and the community to correct are critical to the prosecutorial decision whether to divert an offender out of the formal system and back into his or her community. Police and judges apply similar criteria.

Minoru Shikita describes the pattern with respect to the police: "[T]he police, with the general accord of the chief public prosecutor of a district, need not refer all cases formally to the prosecution, but may report cases in consolidated form monthly, provided the offenses are minor property offenses, the suspects have shown repentance, restitution has been made, and victims forgive the suspects." The police, Shikita notes, invariably recommend a lenient disposition even in the cases referred to public prosecutors, if a suspect has shown sincere repentance about his or her alleged crime and the transgression against a social norm is not particularly serious.[23]

Japanese judges also stress the defendant's acknowledgment of guilt and sincerity in displaying remorse, evidenced in part by compensation of the victim and the victim's forgiving response, in deciding whether to suspend sentence. Expressions of remorse with reparation and apology to the victim are essential.[24] Victims in turn are expected to express pardon.

Most suspects confess. Eighty to ninety-five percent do so by most estimates.[25] Suspects not only confess, but they together with family and friends also seek letters from any victims addressed to the prosecutor or judge that acknowledge reparation and express the victims' view that no further penalty should be imposed. Such letters are so customary that most Japanese attorneys can accurately calculate the amounts usually required. No formal, institutionalized program for such restitution and pardon exists to facilitate the process. Japan does not have organized victim assistance organizations or either volunteer or government-supported victim-offender mediation programs. The process of reparation and pardon operates informally as a social response to crime buttressed by widely shared values and expectations. Victims have no formal standing. Yet as described by University of Tokyo Law Professor Atsushi Yamaguchi: "The lack of provisions for victim restitution does not mean that it has virtually no role to play in the Japanese criminal justice system. Rather, victim restitution is considered to be one of the crucial factors affecting the decisions of prosecutors, the criminal courts and the parole boards, not to mention the informal disposition by the police."[26]

Direct reparation of victims as a precondition for diversion enables offenders and their families to express their accountability to those they have harmed who thereby participate in the process without controlling it. The possibility of diversion in turn gives the offender an incentive to make amends and thereby also gives the victim the opportunity and inclination to pardon. Victims do not assume, however, the role of adversary or prosecutor, nor are they enabled to use the formal process vindictively for revenge. The authorities remain in charge. The victim must defer to the authorities' decision.

The offender's community also participates in the process of discretionary diversion. Friends and families of both victim and offender, their neighbors, fellow workers, employers, the other members of their respective communities in most instances of crime everywhere become involved in the process. In a very real sense they are also victims of the crime. In Japan, however, such participation tends to be more intense and more direct. Those identified with the offender as members of the community share the responsibility. They too are expected to show remorse and their willingness to make amends.

The community serves also as an agent of future control. The process works best if the community voices its disapproval, holds the offender accountable, and sees to it that the victim is compensated; but the community also acts collectively as the primary agent for offender restoration and control. Japanese criminal justice authorities appreciate the benefits of the community's response and thus encourage and rely heavily on community participation—both through formally organized programs and informal family, firm, and neighborhood ties. They count on community support for their efforts and, above all, the corrected offender. And the authorities support, use, and organize these efforts. Oregon Judge Robert Thornton notes: "The most significant difference between crime prevention in America and in Japan is in its organizational structure. Although citizen participation in both systems is purely voluntary, the American system is in reality a nonsystem compared to its Japanese counterpart, which is vastly more structured—a mammoth pyramid, to be exact, that begins at the neighborhood level and climbs step by step through the district, municipality, prefecture, and finally joins its forces at the national headquarters in Tokyo."[27]

All share an overriding aim: to control crime. The emphasis is correction, not punishment. Determination of guilt is of course necessary. Neither crime control nor correction results when innocent suspects are convicted. Law enforcement officials at all levels tend to share this objective. Thus, their roles are not confined to the formal tasks of apprehending, prosecuting, and adjudicating. Rather, once personally convinced that a suspect is an offender, their concern for evidentiary proof of guilt shifts to concern over the suspect's attitude and prospects for rehabilitation and reintegration into society, including acceptance of authority.

The focus is the offender, not the crime. Law enforcement authorities in Japan do not respond in terms of abstract notions of "just deserts" or of "debts to society" that require a particular penalty. The Criminal Code and related statutes do of course set out more severe penalties for more serious crimes. Equal treatment of offenders is also a constitutional norm. However, harsher penalties are imposed primarily for deterrence. Potentially dangerous offenders are incarcerated in order to prevent future criminal activity. Neither the law nor its enforcers, however, insist on a penalty that fits the offense or equal treatment of different offenders for like offenses. Equal treatment of offenders does not mean equal treatment of offenses. The Japanese police, procurators, and judges make the offender, the victim, and the community their principal concern and use their discretion to ensure the system serves a correctional goal.

CORRECTION AS LENIENCY

The leniency of the Japanese criminal justice system depends upon the responses of the offender, the victim, and the community. Apology and pardon are preconditions. The system is not, however, lenient by design. Apology and pardon are required for a more lenient response in effect because they are prerequisites for correction. Leniency itself functions also as a means to correction. Only when the correctional process has begun as evidenced by apology and pardon does the system respond with forgiving leniency to allow in effect the process to continue. Japanese law enforcement is not therefore always lenient.

Whether correction is likely depends upon the sincerity of confession and remorse. Because confession and repentance provoke leniency, and most offenders do confess, law enforcement authorities also generally expect offenders to confess and to behave with remorseful submission to their authority. Some suspects whom the authorities believe to be guilty do fail to admit guilt. In such cases the choice is clear: either the authorities are wrong and the suspect is not guilty, or they are right and the suspect is recalcitrant, unrepentant, and therefore not yet correctable. The authorities' responses to this dilemma are predictable. As they become increasingly convinced that the suspect is guilty, the greater at least the likelihood of harsh and possibly abusive measures as well as more intense investigatory efforts to prove guilt.[28] Despite occasional accusations, from all credible accounts, the actual incidence of abuse in Japan is extremely low.[29]

Confession alone does not convict. The absence of a guilty plea in civil law systems like Japan means that a trial based on additional evidence of guilt is always necessary. Even summary proceedings require an evidentiary hearing to determine, first, that a crime has been committed and, second, the culpability of the accused. Japan does not today have either a jury system or lay participation as in Germany. The judges in all trials have the duty to clarify evidence and, as the finders of fact, be convinced of the guilt and thus the reliability of any confession of the accused.[30]

Confessions do have evidentiary value. Police and prosecutors emphasize the importance of confessions because they lead to subsequent revelations by the accused that enable them to obtain other evidence of guilt more easily. The accuracy of the confession is critical. False confessions cause delay and impede the investigation.[31] In cases where the accused confesses and does not offer a defense, the judges are, however, less likely to scrutinize the collaborative evidence as vigorously as they would in a contested trial. Moreover, the potential of greater leniency for those who confess operates as an incentive to admit guilt. Again, community acceptance of shared responsibility for the offender's actions functions as a powerful disincentive for false confessions.

Not all Japanese approve. Many—including scholars, lawyers, prosecutors, and judges—object. The most controversial instance of such objection took place in 1948. The incident involved the first and last attempt by the Diet to intervene directly in what the Supreme Court viewed as a matter of judicial autonomy and is described more fully in that connection in the next chapter. Suffice it to note here that the concern of Diet members that judges had shown excessive leniency to suspects and offenders in several criminal cases led to a formal inquiry by the Judicial Affairs Committee of the House of Councilors. The initial investigation, which commenced in May 1948, was expanded in October to include both judicial and prosecutorial decisions. The principal cause was the Urawa case.

Mitsuko Urawa was the thirty-year-old mother of three daughters, ages eight, four, and two. She worked in a tea house in the Asakusa entertainment district. Her husband was a chronic gambler, who had sold or pawned what few possessions the family had. With the encouragement of her brother-in-law, she moved out of her home, taking the daughters with her. In despair and hopelessness after a failed attempt to restore contact with her husband, the district court determined, she poisoned her daughters. She did not immediately attempt suicide but later contacted the police and confessed. She then tried unsuccessfully to poison herself. She was convicted and sentenced to three years of imprisonment with labor. The court thereupon suspended her sentence. The procurators decided not to appeal and promptly released her. Such leniency, the legislators charged, reflected the remnants of "feudal" attitudes unfit for a democracy. The law and its sanctions, they asserted, should be applied fully and strictly.[32]

The Japanese criminal justice system is not easy on all offenders. Leniency is extended to those who confess, demonstrate remorse, accept their accountability by compensation to any victims, and, most important, not only receive pardon from those they have harmed but also expressions of future support and control from family and other members of the offender's community. Nor should such leniency be viewed out of context as an end in itself. We use the label to describe responses by criminal justice authorities to what they perceive as symptoms of correction. Moreover, these responses also involve the community and a set of often quite severe community sanctions and controls. The example of a bright young scholar serves to illustrate the point. Involved in a traffic accident that resulted in the death of a pedestrian, the police and prosecutors were by most international standards quite lenient. The scholar expressed remorse and made the socially expected, not insubstantial, payments to the family of the deceased. The family's expression of pardon was duly obtained. A summary proceeding was allowed and a relatively small fine was levied. It was evident that the scholar had learned his lesson and repeated occurrence of the behavior that caused the accident was unlikely. Nevertheless, his faculty asked him to resign his tenured position. His conduct had tainted the group. Until that stigma wore off, he could not return to teaching. During the interim, friends and colleagues aided him in obtaining a position with a law firm that presumably paid him as much if not more than he was making as a professor. Several years later he rejoined his faculty, but his career remained blemished. Reintegration into the community does not mean total redemption. Japanese society can be quite unforgiving.

Law enforcement authorities know what happens to remorseful offenders. They can anticipate the sort of vicarious community accountability that ensures both support and continued surveillance and control. They look for the symptoms that the process of correction has begun. If found, they respond in ways that will reinforce rather than diminish their efficacy. Penalties may have to be applied in any case because of the seriousness of the offense—its harm to the community—but the penalty is often more of a statement of that seriousness than an instrument of coercive correction. In other instances and other crimes—particularly the case of drug offenses—the commission of crime itself evidences to the authorities that the offender is beyond the normal means of correction and must be treated harshly. David Johnson quotes one procurator's attitude toward drug offenses on point: "We don't try to rehabilitate them. You can't. Nobody can. Drug users are dangerous criminals, threats to the public order, and they ought to be treated as such."[33]

Leniency also stops at the prison door. Japan's prisons are run with the discipline of a boot camp. The Miyagi prison in Sendai is the most severe. It houses the largest percentage of men serving life sentences. The interior is sparse. It includes a relatively large number of single cells. The remaining cells are small, with just enough room for eight men to sleep side-by-side on rolled out Japanese bedding (futon). The prison also has large workrooms where inmates under sentences requiring work (chōeki) are kept busy most of the day, a communal dining area, and, of course, a large communal bath. Outside are well-tended grounds with flowers and meticulously pruned trees and shrubs. Young guards are ever present. Prisoners have no privacy. At the approach of the warden and his guests—on this visit a group of Japanese graduate students in criminal law with their professor and an American visiting professor—the prisoners automatically and with military precision moved aside, turning rigidly to face the wall, hands tightly clenched behind their backs, even before the guard finishes barking out the order. As the warden entered each workroom, the guards came promptly to attention and, while saluting, shouted out the number of prisoners present and accounted for. In contrast with the discipline of prison life, security, at least by American standards, seemed quite lax. The prison itself is a aged structure, parts of which date from the mid-nineteenth century, as evidenced by the red brick facade. The visitors were not required to undergo any search, even one as routine as the electronic searches common in nearly all international airports. They were, however, asked to leave all cigarettes behind. Smoking is not allowed, and the warden expressed concern over any temptation.

The severity of Japanese prisons has recently become a topic of renewed controversy within the country and abroad. Some progressive lawyers decry the denial of privacy and other civil rights that prisoners in most other industrial countries appear to enjoy. They have invited foreign observers to evaluate Japanese conditions and sponsored an international human rights report.[34] The controversial Human Rights Watch Prison Project report, *Prison Conditions in Japan*, includes the most commonly expressed accusations. Instances of physical abuse by guards, the extreme rigidity of the system, the lack of any conception of prisoners' rights, and limitations on prisoner's communication with the outside head the list. Ministry of Justice officials and many reputable scholars contest these views. Even the critics concede that Japanese prisons do not suffer from the most common problems found in prisons in other countries. They are not overcrowded. Incidents of escape are extraordinarily rare. Japanese prisoners do not have access to drugs. There is little violence among inmates. Few are idle. Prisoners sentenced to imprisonment without a work requirement (*kinko*) it is said, often want to work voluntarily to avoid remaining in a small cell all day.[35] Nevertheless, in March 1996 two British prison specialists found the discipline "disturbing." Japanese prisons, they concluded, fail in functioning to rehabilitate offenders to enable them to be reintegrated into society.[36] The warden of Miyagi prison would probably agree. In a conversation with the author, he said, "Most of our prisoners are repeat offenders. They will be released when they have served their time, but most will be back. It's sad." The Miyagi prison, like its American counterparts, warehouses offenders.

The Miyagi prison may be the exception. It is a Class B prison for the most serious offenders, nearly all of whom have served repeated sentences and many of whom were members of Japan's gangster underworld (*yakuza*). Offenders sentenced to Japan's Class A prisons, most of whom are also repeat offenders but whose prior records suggest more promise for correction, have considerably lower rates of recidivism.[37]

Ministry of Justice studies of recidivism bear out the conclusion that Japanese prisons are generally not expected to rehabilitate. A 1980 study—the most recent—showed that recidivism, defined as another criminal conviction within three years, increased with the severity of the initial action taken, and remained less than 50 percent in all cases except for incarceration. Committing another criminal offense within the three-year period were only 11.5 percent of those offenders whose prosecution was suspended and were therefore released without penalty, 16.3 percent of those who were fined (presumably most traffic offenders), 21.5 percent of those prosecuted and convicted but whose sentences were suspended, 35.4 percent of those whose sentences were suspended but were placed on probation, 44.5 percent of those who were released on parole without serving their complete sentence, and 57.2 percent of those who were released after serving their complete sentence.[38] What these figures also show, however, is that the exercise of discretion at all stages of the criminal justice process to divert offenders is based on a remarkably accurate prediction of the likelihood of their committing another offense or that leniency itself fosters correction or a combination of both.

APOLOGY AND COMMUNITY

Apology works. Confession of wrongdoing and acceptance of responsibility toward those harmed begins the process of correction. It also restores—and creates—relationship. In a seminal article on apology in Japanese and American law and culture, anthropologist Hiroshi Wagatsuma and academic lawyer Arthur Rosett note the use of apology in Japan "as an indication of an individual's wish to maintain or restore a positive relationship with another person who has been harmed by the individual's acts." "The external act of apology," they note, "becomes significant as an act of self-denigration and submission" in which "the relational elements" of Japanese culture are given expression as a "commitment to a positively harmonious relationship in the future in which the mutual obligations of the social hierarchy will be observed."[39] Apology serves as an act of acknowledgment of wrongdoing and submission as well as an expression of a wish to maintain relationships and to abide henceforth by community norms. In cases of crime among acquaintances within communities, such observations make a lot of sense. In Japan, however, reporting of crime or other wrongs to outside law enforcement authorities may be remarkably infrequent. Japanese companies, we are told, commonly do not report employees who have broken the law, even in cases such as fraud and embezzlement. In the words of Thomas Rohlen, "such cases are usually hushed up."[40] This tendency is evident in recent incidents involving multimillion dollar bank and trading company losses as a result of employee wrongdoing as well as misconduct by Ministry of Health and Welfare officials in regulating Japan's blood banks.[41] These observations are quite consistent with the findings of Lee Hamilton and Joseph Sanders that as victims of wrongs, Japanese generally tend to be less retributive and more willing to accept compensation to put an end to the matter than Americans. "[A]cross everyday life, accident, and crime vignettes, Japanese respondents are at least as willing as Americans to advocate that *something* should happen to perpetrators, but they had systematically different ideas about what that 'something' should be. Judging an array of everyday life situations, the model sanction chosen by Japanese was some form of restitution; sanctions chosen by the Americans predominately served to isolate or punish the individual perpetrator."[42]

In a recent paper Takie Lebra contrasts the use and meaning of apology in Japan with the conclusions reached by several recent studies, including the monograph by Nicholas Tavuchis, *Mea Culpa*.[43] While accepting the view that some characteristics of apology have universal, transcultural application, Lebra emphasizes the particularity of the Japanese context. She finds in the notion of "self" and the relationship between apology and empathy an element that appears to be peculiar at least in emphasis to the Japanese. Thus apology is used in Japan in contexts that often appear unusual and difficult to explain to anyone unfamiliar with Japan. In the Japanese context, Lebra notes, "empathy is a main ingredient of both apology and guilt." Apology is an expression of personal sensitivity and sharing of injury and pain.

Lebra also observes that "empathetic apology" is usually not unilateral. She illustrates the point with the example of a father who apologized for his son's misbehavior, reported in a letter to the editor of the *Asahi Shinbun*.

> The boy was a troublemaker in school who intimidated his classmates and extorted money from them. His father, who was a former school principal, went to see the son's homeroom teacher in response to the latter's request. When he was told of his son's robbery, "he apologized with a deep bow, saying, 'I am very sorry.' Watching his father thus apologizing on his behalf, the offender was moved to tears. This was a turning point for him that changed his way of life completely." The message is that the father's surrogate apology aroused empathetic guilt in the culpable son, which turned out to be a breakthrough for the son much more effective than direct scolding and punishment.[44]

What of strangers? In *Everyday Justice*, Hamilton and Sanders emphasize the similarities between Japanese and American responses to wrongs committed by strangers.[45] Japanese and Americans, they

found, were equally apt to seek punitive measures against wrongdo-
ers they did not know. Hamilton and Sanders and their Japanese col-
laborators did not, however, attempt to investigate the dynamics of
Japanese behavior in the context of wrongs that are committed by
strangers. Apology and victim reparation create relationship. Through
intermediaries and introductions—typically, some mutual acquain-
tance known to both the offender and the victim through family or
workplace—the offender ceases to be a "stranger" and becomes a person with some connection, however tenuous, to someone the victim
knows. In this sense, apology reverses the process of estrangement
that wrongs in other societies seem to cause—making strangers out
of friends—and serves as catalyst for a less punitive and more repara-
tive and pardon-prone response. If so, then the emphasis on discretion
and diversion in the Japanese criminal justice process fosters community and profoundly reinforces the social mechanisms of correction and control.

A more universal consequence of apology is thus a reduction of
grievance toward the wrongdoer and creation of relationship. Japanese judges often remark that lawsuits rarely occur in cases where the
party responsible for injury to another has expressed empathetic concern—along with payment of consolation money. Risk management
teams in major hospitals have learned to respond similarly in cases
where medical intervention has caused harm. Apologies with expressions of sympathy and concern and a reduction if not cancellation of
any hospital charges are viewed as essential responses.[46]

Apology is also an act of submission and corrective control. As expressed by Tavuchis, "When we apologize, we are in the morally un-
settling position of seeking unconditional pardon precisely in the
context of our being categorically unworthy. . . . Responding to the
call for an apology and the process this sets into motion can be as
painful and devastating as, if not worse than, any form of physical retribution."[47] The consequences Tavuchis describes help to explain
both the demand for and resistance to public apology to the community at large in instances of major ideological conflict. For example,
in a major toxic drug case, negotiations over settlement reached an

impasse because, it was privately said, although willing to pay the amount of damages sought, the Japanese corporate defendant resisted the demand for an apology.

Each of these facets illustrates the dynamic effect of apology as catalyst in a complex process of social change. With apology, injury is acknowledged and empathy expressed; relationships are maintained and created; grievances are reduced and those involved cease to be strangers; submission is established and correction begins. What makes Japan different is that the formal processes of law enforcement foster and reinforce rather than discourage and repel its use.

LEGAL RULES AND COMMUNITY STANDARDS

Legal rules establish standards for the community. They have rhetorical value and, even when not enforced rigorously if at all, have persuasive effect. In some instances, the legislated rules in Japan as in other countries reflect influences that may have little relationship to community preferences or behavior. The criminalization of prostitution, for example, is sometimes explained as having been enacted because of foreign moral concerns and influence. Such rules can be understood as setting a national standard that Japanese at least believed at the time reflected the standards of the international community or at least industrial democracies. In this sense, Japan acts as a member of a community of nations as defined in light of Japanese cultural patterns. In other words, Japan enacts such rules because it is a member of a community that expects each member to have such rules. This fact does not mean that they are either effectively enforced or followed. Whatever the cause or reason, some rules, however, are made and indeed enforced to establish national standards despite community tolerance of the proscribed conduct. The case of parent-child suicide (oya-ko shinjū) is one of the most poignant examples. Marcia Goodman concludes from interviews that prosecutors rarely suspend such cases.[48] Taimie Bryant, however, cites a Japanese research report indicating that suspended prosecution in maternal infanticide cases is no less frequent than the average (30 to 40 percent) for all Criminal

Code offenses.[49] In any event, as in the case of Mitsuko Urawa, if prosecuted, conviction is almost certain, but sentences tend to be light
and seldom do the courts actually enforce even a mild sanction.

In such cases, the values of the prosecutors and the judges reflect
accurately broader community attitudes. As Bryant explains, Japanese generally empathize with the mother and tolerate without con-
doning the action.[50] In effect the legal rules—even when enforced—
have only persuasive effect so long as the ultimate sanctions of social
stigma are left to the community. The question remains, as Bryant
observes, whether harsher penalties would reduce the social legitimacy of the behavior or whether the result would be a lessening of
the trust and legitimacy of the law and those who enforce it.

5 Law's Actors II

Within the law's domain, judges rule—even in Japan. Judges are the law's primary actors. Who they are and how they understand themselves and their role, their recruitment, socialization, and organization are crucial to an understanding of law in any system. In Japan all of these factors combine to produce the most corruption-free, cohesive, as well as cautiously conservative yet reform-provoking judiciaries in the world. Judges are Japan's most frequent agents of legal change but only at a carefully managed and gradual pace in keeping with their sense of community values and their felt need for a consistent and widely accepted corpus of articulated legal rules and principles.

To many, such assertions—except the honesty of Japan's judges—may seem misguided if not outrageously wrong. The Japanese judiciary has long been viewed in the English-language literature on government in Japan as by far the least influential, much less dangerous, branch. Any emphasis on the importance of judges thus runs counter to received wisdom on either the dominance of administrative officials in Japan over the processes for making and enforcing legal rules or the role of legislators as their principals.[1] A few might even place scholars ahead of judges for their role in articulating the theoretical underpinnings of legal rules in civil law systems generally and in Japan in particular. Generally neglected, however, is the judiciary's ultimate authority and capacity—regardless of whether judges themselves exercise or even recognize it—to establish the parameters of its powers. Whether made or enforced by bureaucrats, legislators, or scholars, legal rules mean only so much and reach only so far as judges allow. Judges give life to legal theories that scholars can only profess and promote. That Japan's bureaucrats exercise broad discretion or that scholars have influence can be viewed as a product of decisions made by judges, not by bureaucrats nor by scholars themselves. Even the seemingly broad legislative freedom of the Japanese Diet is the result of judicial interpretation of the constitutional parameters of legislative authority and parallel judicial self-restraint in permitting effective challenge. Like the imperial institution in prewar Japan, the judiciary in contemporary Japan has become a central legitimating organ of government, but unlike the emperor, Japan's judges cannot avoid responsibility—the praise or the blame—for what they allow.

Japan's postwar jurisprudence—especially the constitutional rules and principles that define the allocation and scope of lawmaking and law-enforcing authority—rests on fundamental understandings shared by Japan's judges regarding their role and their powers. The postwar constitution vests the "entire judicial power" in the courts and expressly grants judges the authority for judicial review. Thus despite the provisions of article 41 establishing the Diet as the "highest organ of state power," described by Dan Henderson as creating a system of "double supremacy," only the Supreme Court of Japan has the ultimate authority to define the extent of its own competence.[2] The Supreme Court, not the Diet, is legally empowered under the constitution to determine the extent of both judicial and legislative authority and to resolve whatever conflict may arise between the two. The constitution and the laws and regulations issued under the constitution as well as the extent of the coercive powers of all organs of government—formal and informal—are thereby made subject to the courts. The law is what judges say it is. Judges thereby have the last word on what legislators, administrative officials, prosecutors, judges themselves, and even the electorate may or may not legitimately do.

Japanese judges also share what they commonly refer to as "the legal mind." As described below, this phrase refers to a belief in the constraints of legal reasoning and doctrine that bind them. They understand that common canons of statutory and constitutional interpretation govern their decisions. Although seldom made explicit in the stated reasons for their judgments, established principles and theories of the judicial function as well as the nature and scope of legal rules are accepted and thereby control what judges do. They, no less than their continental European counterparts, defer to legal doctrines developed and refined by a millennium of scholarly reasoning as well as particular legislated rules interpreted in the context of accepted methods to construe meaning in their application.[3] National differences do exist, but among its peers Japan is considerably less exceptional than the United States in departures from commonly accepted norms of judicial behavior.

Judicial decisions in Japan do not ostensibly deviate from these norms. Japanese judicial decisions can thus be analyzed in ways familiar to lawyers from a variety of national systems. By reconstituting the reality of the Japanese experience within the conceptual framework of western—equally so Japanese—juristic thought, we can evaluate as a matter of accepted principles the conclusions reached, for example, in constitutional cases by the fifteen judges sitting *en banc* in deciding the legal validity of constitutional claims. (Indeed, it can be argued, we have no alternative to some sort of imposed logic or mode of analysis. The very nature of discourse precludes us from dealing with external worlds except in terms of profoundly culture-bound ways of organizing ideas and thought.)

Judges in any career judiciary are also subject to bureaucratic constraints that simply do not exist in common law systems. As career government officials, they do not enjoy the degree of individual autonomy nor the overtly policy-making role of common law judges. Historically, the judiciary, along with the procuracy, constituted a highly specialized, elite corps of government officials responsible for the administration of justice and enforcement of legislated rules. Although in article 76 the postwar constitution mandates independence of all judges "in the exercise of their conscience [*ryōshin*]," no career judge in Japan has the freedom from hierarchical control enjoyed by common law judges.[4] Japan is again not exceptional with respect to the existence of such controls. But the degree to which the senior judges of Japan's judicial bureaucracy are able to monitor and impose constraints on individual judges is notable. Also, without powers taken for granted in common law systems—such as equity and contempt—Japan's judges depend far more on public confidence in their nonpartisan professionalism and expertise than their common law counterparts.

The constraints of a centrally organized bureaucracy should not be overstated. Judges in Japan do enjoy considerable individual as well as collective autonomy. The balance between constraint and freedom is quite delicate. To paraphrase the response of a senior judge to questions posed by the author about why he decided to become a judge and what have been the most satisfying aspects of his career: "What I and other judges appreciate most is our freedom. No one interferes with our decisions. We decide the cases before us on our own. This freedom is very satisfying."

Japan's judges decide cases without juries. They function under the burden of ultimate responsibility for determinations of fact and law in every case they decide. This point deserves emphasis. Unlike judges in common law jurisdictions—even those that have abandoned jury trials—Japanese judges do not function with an umpire's ethos. They are the finders of the facts in all litigated cases. They are subject to a legally enforceable duty to clarify facts and to find the truth.[5] They and the state are legally accountable for all negligent errors.

They are also subject to the predominant values of the civil law tradition, which include an emphasis on legal certainty and consistency in the application of law. The result is greater caution and passivity in the exercise of judicial authority than their common law counterparts.[6]

ORGANIZATION AND HIERARCHY

Japan's judiciary is today organized as a largely autonomous national bureaucracy. Japanese judges generally spend a professional life of thirty to forty years within a nationwide or unitary court structure that they themselves as judges administer. As in the case of the procuracy as well as nearly all ministries and other government and private organizations in Japan, entry is confined to the initial career appointment. Lateral entry is extraordinarily rare. And assignments and promotions are administered by a central personnel office. Thus judges, like almost all other government and corporate employees, begin their professional lives usually in their mid to late twenties. After initial appointment upon graduation from the court-administered

Legal Training and Research Institute, Japanese judges first spend ten years as assistant judges before they can be appointed as full judges for ten-year terms. Reappointment is routine, and more than half continue to serve until they reach retirement age at sixty-five. (Mandatory retirement for both Supreme Court justices and summary court judges is age seventy.)

The selection of assistant judges begins with entry to the Legal Training and Research Institute on the basis of what is regarded, as described previously, as Japan's most competitive national examination. Although formally appointed by the cabinet from a list of nominees presented by the Supreme Court, the selection is actually made by the central personnel bureau of the Supreme Court, which prepares the list.[7] Assistant judges are formally appointed, as noted, to ten-year terms. At the end of ten years, they are eligible for appointment as full judges, again for another term of ten years. Nearly all are promoted, and only two or three have ever been denied reappointment as a full judge at the end of the second term. The most controversial, and not coincidentally the last, incident of such denial occurred in 1970 and is described below. In each instance of a judge being denied reappointment, the personnel office of the Supreme Court made the decision not to include the judge on the list presented to the cabinet for reappointment.

The structure of the system of courts in which Japan's judges serve has four levels. At the bottom tier are 453 summary courts (kan'i saibansho), staffed, since the consolidation measures of 1990, by 806 summary court judges. Summary court judges do not have full qualification as regular judges. They are formally nominated for cabinet appointment by a special selection committee comprising all Supreme Court justices, the Chief Judge of the Tokyo High Court, the Deputy Procurator-General, representatives of the bar, and others "with special knowledge and experience."[8] Most summary court judges are in fact well known to the judiciary. The majority are individuals who previously served as administrative secretaries or clerks within the court system or career judges and procurators who have reached their respective mandatory retirement ages (sixty-five, as noted, for judges; sixty-three for procurators) and seek to serve as summary court judges until they reach the mandatory retirement age for that position (seventy). Summary courts handle civil cases involving claims of 900,000 yen (approximately U.S.$9,000) or less and minor criminal offenses for which the penalty is limited to a fine or brief imprisonment (in the case of minor theft), including the summary proceedings described previously. Summary court adjudication requires only a single judge.

The principal court of first instance is the district court (*chihō saibansho*). As of April 1997, there were more than fifty district courts with an additional 203 branches. Except for minor cases, which account for 70 to 80 percent of all adjudications, trials require a three-judge panel. There is no jury. Sitting alone or as a panel, judges decide all issues of fact and law, and must for all judgments write a complete statement of both. The district courts also have an appellate function with respect to civil judgments and rulings from summary courts. Criminal judgments are appealed directly to a high court. Because the first (*kōso*) appeal under Japanese procedure can involve a *de novo* trial of the facts, the district courts are in effect trial courts in all cases.

Paralleling the district courts are an equal number of family courts (*katei saibansho*) with jurisdiction over domestic relations, succession, and juvenile offenses. Unlike other courts in Japan, the principal actors of the family courts are not judges or other legal professionals but rather lay conciliators (*chotei'in*) appointed by the Supreme Court secretariat. Most are socially prominent members of the community. Many are law graduates. Some are distinguished scholars. They serve over many years, longer than the judges assigned to the court. Except for more serious juvenile offenses and contested issues in domestic relations and succession cases, family court proceedings are in effect discussions between the conciliators and the parties intended to produce settlement.

Above the district courts are Japan's eight high courts (*kōtō saibansho*), located from northeast to southwest in Sapporo, Sendai, Tokyo, Nagoya, Osaka, Takamatsu, Hiroshima, and Fukuoka, with six branches in Akita, Kanazawa, Okayama, Matsue, Miyazaki, and Naha. The high courts are appellate courts for either *kōso* appeals from district court judgments, criminal judgments from summary courts, or, in civil cases tried initially in summary courts, second (*jōkoku*) appeals limited to issues of law.

With 764 separate summary, district, family, and high courts, including branch courts, in addition to the more than one hundred judges assigned each year to the administrative offices of the Supreme Court, Japan's 1,393 career judges and 685 assistant judges are spread very thinly throughout the nation. Some of the branch court positions are not filled, but no district court has fewer than six judges. The number assigned to each court varies in relationship to the district caseload. Not surprisingly, the Tokyo District Court is the largest with 243 judges (in 1990), a third of whom are assigned to the criminal division and two-thirds to the civil division. The Osaka District Court is the next largest in terms of the number of judges with 146. The Oita District Court in Kyushu, along with Tottori in the southwestern part of Honshu, have had the highest litigation rates per capita since the early 1900s. Consequently, these courts have nearly twice the number of judges relative to the district's population as the courts in districts with significantly less litigation per capita, particularly the Tohoku region, northern Honshu. For example, the Oita District Court in 1990 had fourteen judges in a district of 1.24 million persons. The Sendai District Court in comparison had nineteen judges in a district of 2.25 million persons. The Tottori District Court had seven judges in a district of 616,000 persons, while the Fukushima District Court also had seven judges for a district of 2.1 million persons. Similarly, the number of judges assigned to branch district courts varies from twenty-three for the Hachioji branch of the Tokyo District Court to the thirty-five branch district courts without a permanently assigned judge and the seventy-seven branches with only one judge.[9]

At the apex of the judicial hierarchy is Japan's Supreme Court (*Saikō saibansho*). Fifteen justices appointed by the cabinet constitute the court. Except for constitutional cases they rarely decide cases *en banc*. Most are decided by one of the three petty benches, each with five justices, into which the court is divided. Japanese law does not currently provide for discretionary appeals, thus all cases originating in a district court have been subject to *jōkoku* appeal to the Supreme Court. The new Code of Civil Procedure, which becomes effective in

1998, allows the Court (as well as high courts adjudicating *jōkoku* appeals) to dismiss cases without a full hearing where from the record an appeal is unfounded.

The caseload of Japanese Supreme Court justices is staggering by most standards. Without discretionary appeals, Japan's justices receive and decide more than four thousand civil, administrative, and criminal cases each year, either *en banc* or as a petty bench.[10] This number means that each justice is generally responsible for reviewing about 1,300 cases annually. Although procedures for summary disposition have been introduced, the number of appeals the court must decide remains a major problem that reduces the quality of its decisions.

The caseload for lower court judges is similar. On average, Japanese district court judges (including assistant judges) have total caseloads of more than 1,100 civil, administrative, and criminal cases per district court judge per year. In 1995 judges disposed of ninety-eight ordinary lawsuits each.[11] Three-quarters of all cases are civil suits adjudicated by three-judge panels, thus judges assigned to civil cases actually deal with an even greater caseload. No summary judgment procedures exist. Furthermore, all lawsuits filed are either settled or pursued through trial to judgment. All judgments must include both the judges' findings of fact and application of law. Under such circumstances, judicial management and the efficient disposition of cases are given considerable priority over other matters, including the appropriate direction of a particular legal doctrine or nationwide uniformity of judgments in like cases. Such issues, along with the social consequences of the court's interpretation of particular legal rules and principles, are, of course, considered by judges, but these are rarely more than minor concerns.

AUTONOMY

Despite formal accountability and the potential for political intervention, Japanese courts today enjoy in fact almost complete autonomy from any direct political intrusion both with respect to individual cases as well as the composition of the judiciary.[12] Cabinet appointment of the Supreme Court justices and the career judges who staff all lower courts but one does give political leaders in power the potential to influence directly the ideological composition of the judiciary and thus the course of judge-made and interpreted legal rules. Indeed by lodging the authority to appoint judges and justices with the cabinet, as detailed below, the postwar constitution was intentionally designed to achieve a degree of political accountability. At least for the Americans who contributed to the drafting of the postwar constitution, judicial independence did not mean judicial autonomy. Under the constitution individual judges were to be bound by their "conscience" as well as the law in each case they adjudicated. Direct political control over the appointment of Supreme Court justices and lower court career judges was also intentionally provided. However, the political branches of government have long ignored the courts and the judge-administrators of the system have worked hard to preserve that judicial autonomy.

Japan's modern judiciary originated as a remarkably autonomous elite bureaucracy within the civil law tradition. By the late nineteenth century in Japan, judicial independence in terms of a separation of powers, insulation from intervention in the adjudication of particular cases, and the personal security of judges had been largely secured by constitution and statute. The Meiji Constitution provided (in article 57) that the courts exercised their authority "in the name of the emperor" (*tennō no na ni oite*). Many readers may pass over such language with at least a subconscious sense that the phrase has merely hortatory significance. In fact, however, the phrase is to be taken seriously. These are law words, terms with technical and enforceable meaning. To less explicit allusions to actions in the "emperor's name" a half century ago can be traced the political foundations of Japan's inexorable march to war and devastating defeat. Like the military's plea that the "supreme command" of the emperor precluded legislative or executive civilian control, the exclusive reservation of the authority to act in the emperor's name insulated the courts from any direct political intervention in the adjudication of cases by either legislative or administrative organs. The inscription "in the name of the emperor" was placed prominently in all courtrooms. It served as a meaningful reminder to imperial officials and subjects alike that the emperor's judges were not subject to political direction.

The security of judges was also guaranteed under express provisions of article 58 of Japan's first comprehensive court law, enacted pursuant to the constitution in 1890, which established the structure of Japan's contemporary career judiciary. Judges were to be appointed by the emperor with life tenure. Unless physically or mentally unable to carry out their duties or by virtue of a criminal conviction or disciplinary sanction, no judges could against their will be removed to a different office or court, nor could they be suspended or dismissed or have their salary reduced.[13] These protections were not perfect. The authority over appointment was delegated to the Minister of Justice in 1921, and judges were made subject to mandatory retirement from active judicial service at age 63 (65 for the Chief Justice of the Great Court of Cassation).[14] As individuals, judges were free to accept assignment to a different office. They could join the procuracy. And they could be persuaded to resign. Legal protections did, however, give judges a significant degree of formal security.

Judicial independence meant more than protection against outside political intervention. Of equal importance were statutory requirements to prevent political activity by judges. The political neutrality and professional integrity of the career judiciary was a critical aspect of judicial independence as understood by the makers of Japan's modern state. The 1890 Court Organization Law prohibited judges "on the active list of the judicial service" from engaging in the following activities:

1. To interest themselves publicly in political affairs.
2. To become members of any political party or association or of any local, municipal, or district assembly.
3. To occupy any public office to which a salary is attached or which has for its object pecuniary gain.
4. To carry on any commercial business or to do any other business prohibited by administrative ordinance. (article 72)

By the end of the nineteenth century, all judges and procurators in Japan were selected by examination. The 1890 Court Organization Law provided that judges and procurators had to pass two successive tests. Between the two tests, a three-year period of practical training in the courts was required (article 58). Graduates of an imperial university were exempted from the first but not the second examination (article 65). Imperial university professors were eligible after three years without examination (article 65). By 1900 Japan's judiciary comprised 1244 career judges, nearly all of whom had been selected through this process.

In practice the independence of Japan's prewar judiciary from direct political control does not appear to be in doubt.[15] Throughout the 1920s and 1930s, judges, like other government officials, were subject to the pressures of Japan's increasingly strident ideological forces. Some held moderate to extreme progressive views. A few judges as well as procurators were in fact prosecuted under the Peace Preservation Law or forced to resign because of suspected communist views.[16] Others shared prevailing conservative nationalist views.[17] Most presumably kept their ideological predispositions private and avoided both extremes.

Quite separate from the ideological conflict engulfing Japan was the budgetary crisis resulting from the Great Depression. In Japan the depression reached its peak between 1930 and 1933. By 1934 Japan had begun to recover. In the early 1930s governments under both political parties—the *Minseitō* Hamaguchi (1929–31) and Watatsuki (1931) and the *Seiyūkai* Inukai (1931–32) cabinets—were embroiled in a prolonged controversy over the effect on the judiciary of measures designed to reduce costs generally.[18] Because the tenure and salary of judges, but not procurators, was secured under the 1890 Court Organization Law, judges' salaries could not be reduced without amending the statute. Procurators, who like other government officials, were required to take a pay cut, objected to what they argued was unfair, discriminatory treatment of judges. In the end, the judges were pressured to take "voluntary" pay cuts. All three cabinets also reduced the number of courts, particularly the ward courts (*ku saibansho*), which in the prewar system functioned as the court of first instance for most cases.[19] Early in 1931 with the advent of the Inukai Cabinet, Kisaburō Suzuki, the newly appointed Justice Minister, initiated "administrative adjustments" (*gyōsei seiri*) as a result of which a number of judges resigned, ostensibly the consequence of the salary reductions.[20] If political motives were also a factor, they were surely intended to purge the judiciary of any partisan political influence.[21] Suzuki, like Hiranuma, sought to create an elite bureaucracy within the Ministry of Justice that would be assertive in its independence from what he considered sordid party politics.[22] In any event, the record shows no significant change in the direction of the courts and their development of the law toward a more statist or militarist stance. Richard Mitchell's exhaustive studies of censorship, thought-control, and political repression in prewar Japan confirm former Chief Justice Hattori's observation that judicial independence remained intact and judges were considered the most trustworthy of all government officials.[23]

Inasmuch as the pool of qualified judges was limited by the examination system—in 1936 there were still only 1391 career judges—whatever informal pressures might have persuaded particular judges to resign or retire early could not lead to any massive change in the composition of the judiciary. The examination imposed severe limits on the pool of judges from which politically acceptable candidates could be chosen. Nonetheless, judges were not totally insulated from politics.

The commanding political presence of both Kiichirō Hiranuma and Kisaburō Suzuki throughout the prewar period was a telling reminder of the nexus between politics and justice officials—procurators and judges.[24] Their ardently antiliberal nationalist views were unquestionably felt within both the procuracy and judiciary.[25] Their careers indicate, however, less the intrusion of politicians on career justice officials than the reverse. Such activities may help to explain why the *Seiyūkai*'s political rivals in the *Minseitō* were among the most vocal critics of the Ministry of Justice's administrative control over the judiciary.[26]

Others also voiced concern over Ministry of Justice dominance of the judiciary. The Japanese bar was especially active in seeking a change.[27] The close identification of judges with the procuracy was considered an unjust obstacle for defense attorneys, and they were galled by their inferior status relative to both procurator and judge.[28]

For the judiciary the problem of the prewar scheme was status, lack of full autonomy, and a career separation of judicial and procuratorial offices. Even judges at the highest level as members of the Great Court of Cassation were inferior in status to the Minister of Justice.[29] The administrative authority of the Ministry of Justice also meant that the procuracy had an often determinative voice in the assignment of judges, including appointment of the Chief Justice of Japan's highest court, and also could claim equality of status.[30] Since judges were equals within the ministry bureaucracy, it should be emphasized, they did exercise a significant degree of influence over the administration of justice in general and predominant influence over the administration of the courts. Nonetheless, conflicts were bound to occur and when they did, the potential for procuratorial influence was unavoidable. Thus it is not surprising that among the postwar reforms desired by the judiciary itself was to gain as much institutional autonomy as possible.

Japanese concerns over judicial independence echoed within the small group of Japan specialists assembled in the United States Department of State in the early war years to begin preparations for a military occupation of a defeated Japan.[31] Judicial reforms were hardly their first priority, but proposals to transfer administrative control over the judiciary from the Ministry of Justice do appear in their early planning documents. It was in fact one of the first and most concrete reforms of the legal system suggested in the course of presurrender planning. The first mention of any need for judicial reforms in available presurrender planning documents appears to be a May 9, 1944, revision of a preliminary memo on "Japan: Abolition of Militarism and Strengthening Democratic Processes," dated five days earlier and drafted by Hugh Borton. The revised version recommended change in the process for appointing judges by the Ministry of Justice.[32] In July 1944 the planning group had prepared a separate memo on the judicial reforms. Entitled "Japan: Treatment of Courts in Japan during Military Government," the document commended the high professional standards of Japanese judges who received appointment, in the words of the memo, "after rigorous qualifying examinations." The memo suggested no reforms in the existing system except the elimination of the Administrative Court and some provision to ensure the "independence of judges" from the Ministry of Justice.[33]

The wartime American proposal to protect judicial independence by transferring administrative authority from the Ministry of Justice was implemented by the Occupation authorities. The constitutional revisions proposed initially by the committee headed by Minister of State Jōji Matsumoto (1877–1954), which the Supreme Commander for the Allied Powers (SCAP) rejected outright, included only one reform related to the courts: the abolition of the Administrative Court and transfer to the regular judiciary of competence to adjudicate direct appeals from administrative decisions. In the end this change would be enthusiastically endorsed by the Occupation authorities who, like the presurrender planners, were not comfortable with the European dichotomy between administrative and regular courts.[34] U.S. policy, however, demanded more fundamental reforms. A committee headed by Col. Charles L. Kades (1906–96), Deputy Chief of Government Section, was formed in February 1946 to draft a model constitution to be presented to the Japanese officials responsible for constitutional revision.[35]

The point of major contention within the SCAP drafting committee was the transfer of administrative authority to administrative organs of the proposed Supreme Court. The views of the majority coincided with concerns of postwar Japanese progressives who urged the removal of jurisdiction over judicial administration from the Ministry of Justice.[36] Kades repeatedly questioned the powers the committee on the judiciary had proposed for the courts, arguing with perceptive foresight that the "kind of Supreme Court established in this draft might develop into a judicial oligarchy." The solution, which did not fully satisfy Kades, was to provide for cabinet appointment of all judges and electoral review with potential dismissal of Supreme Court justices.[37] By these means some assurance of political accountability would balance the implicit powers of judicial review.

No record was kept of the discussions during the marathon thirty-two-hour conference held on March 4–5, 1946, among the Americans who submitted the model draft and the Japanese who translated its provisions.[38] The result, however, was acceptance of nearly all of the American proposals on the judiciary. Japan's postwar constitution, as revised by a joint American and Japanese effort and later during deliberations in the Diet, includes nearly all of the provisions and much of the language related to the judiciary of the original SCAP model.[39] The provisions for judicial independence were almost identical. The Constitution of Japan provides:

> Article 76. . . . . All judges shall be independent in the exercise of their conscience and shall be bound only by this constitution and the laws.[40]

> Article 80. The judges of the inferior courts shall be appointed by the Cabinet from a list of persons nominated by the Supreme Court. All such judges shall hold office for a term of ten (10) years with privilege of reappointment, provided that they shall be retired upon the attainment of the age as fixed by law.
> The judges of inferior courts shall receive, at regular fixed intervals, adequate compensation, which shall not be decreased during their terms of office.

Several themes emerge from the events and concerns that led to the particular institutional structure of Japan's independent judiciary. A judiciary free from direct political direction and control was institutionalized from the beginning. The postwar reforms from both American and Japanese perspectives were intended to preserve this independence but also to end administrative—particularly procuratorial—influence and to elevate the status of judges over the procuracy. Balancing judicial autonomy with political accountability was more of an American concern. Less apparent but still evident was the underlying emphasis on the need for public trust in a professional judiciary. In combination with events in the early 1970s these themes reinforced the tendency toward even greater judicial autonomy.

Despite the attempt to assure a degree of political accountability, Japan's new constitutional structure has operated in fact to ensure greater, not less, judicial autonomy and political insulation. The first and only attempt by one of the political branches of the Japanese government to openly influence the courts came in 1948. On May 6, the House of Councilors Judiciary Committee announced that it was opening an investigation into district court decisions in a half-dozen criminal cases in which the courts had denied detention or otherwise had been too lenient, in the view of the committee, in not applying the full rigor of the law. The Supreme Court protested, charging that the inquiry infringed on the constitutionally protected independence of the judiciary. The Legal Affairs Committee responded by formally deciding on October 17 to widen the investigation to include the operations of the procuracy as well as the courts. The *Urawa* case, described previously, became the focal point. The Supreme Court responded with a strongly worded formal denunciation of the Committee's actions:

> The investigatory authority set out in article 62 of the Constitution is merely a supplementary authority for collecting information required for the exercise of the legislative powers, consideration of the budget, and other powers vested in the Diet and each house by the Constitution. . . .
>
> The judicial power, however, belongs exclusively under the Constitution to the courts; other state organs are absolutely unauthorized under the Constitution to interfere in any way with its exercise. In this sense . . . actions of the Committee in reviewing and criticizing findings of fact or sentencing can only be viewed as violating judicial independence and exceeding the scope of investigatory authority for national administration entrusted the Diet by the Constitution.[41]

The protest was effective. The affair ended and there was no subsequent repetition. The Supreme Court thereby established its autonomy from any legislative oversight or even formal critique of pending cases with an implied assertion of the Court's ultimate authority to define the limits of legislative authority to supervise the judiciary.

At least to this extent, Kades' fears of a judicial oligarchy have been realized albeit without the powers that would have given such concerns cause. Yet political checks remain and do influence indirectly judicial administration. Those who administer the career judiciary are mindful that their autonomy depends on the trust of the public generally and more immediately those who exercise political leadership. The cabinet's constitutional authority to appoint judges enables the ruling party to ensure that the judiciary itself maintains a corps of effective and competent judges whose decisions are within predictable and generally accepted parameters. Individual judges also function within the shadow of potential political intrusion. There is no known instance of a judge being directed by others, including judges, how to decide a case. Only a few incidents involving suggested outcomes have occurred. The best known and most controversial took place in the early 1970s when Kenta Hiraga, the Chief Judge of the Sapporo District Court, offered "friendly advice" to the three judges adjudicating the constitutionality of the Self-Defense Forces in the *Naganuma* case that they be circumspect.[42] It would be a gross exaggeration to characterize such incidents as evidence of a denial of judicial independence. Nevertheless, individual judges cannot help but be aware that in adjudicating highly publicized, politically sensitive cases, they can be held professionally accountable for their decisions. Such oversight is exercised by judges themselves, however, not by political leaders. The response of the judiciary, particularly senior judges in charge of its administration, to the potential politicization of the courts in the 1970s can be argued as having secured the necessary political and public confidence for them to continue to claim immunity from politics.

JUDICIAL AUTONOMY REAFFIRMED

In 1971 the name of Yasuaki Miyamoto was omitted from the annual list of assistant judges who, having served for ten years, were recommended to the cabinet for reappointment and promotion to full judge by the administrative arm of the Supreme Court. The cabinet, as usual, duly affirmed the recommendations and all assistant judges on the list were promoted. From April 1972, however, Assistant Judge Miyamoto was no longer a judge. No reason was given, nor was one required. Past and present practice gave the judiciary the determinative voice in deciding who would be promoted. Judicial autonomy,

thus secure, had little ostensibly to do with the decision. All those involved—except until later perhaps members of the cabinet—knew
the cause. Assistant Judge Miyamoto was a member of the progressive Young Lawyers League (Seihyōkyō), formed in the early 1950s
with reputed Communist Party influence.[43] By 1971 an estimated 230
younger judges had joined, many in the late 1960s at the peak of radical student activity in Japan. Senior judges feared their influence and
had decided to act. Miyamoto's name was purposefully left off the list
of judges for reappointment sent by the secretariat to the cabinet.
Others associated with the League were dealt with less directly but
perhaps no less harshly. Their careers simply came to an abrupt halt.
As they faced out-of-the-way, insignificant assignments, often replac-
ing advancing younger judges, most quietly resigned. The purge was
thus completed.

The Miyamoto incident confirms for some the influence of politicians on the judiciary.[44] Others more accurately assess the incident
in terms of the administrative control of senior judges in the Supreme
Court's secretariat and personnel bureau.[45] Missing in almost all
accounts are the consequences. The incident represented a strong
public statement that the Japanese judiciary would not tolerate any
significant departure from an essentially moderate-to-conservative
approach to legal change and judge-driven social reform. The fear of a
strong cadre of what were perceived to be radical progressive judges
was considered profoundly threatening to Japan's judicial establishment. The Japanese conservative political establishment—and electorate—placed its confidence and trust in an autonomous judiciary.
Those who sought a more active and socially responsive judiciary
were naturally dismayed. Those who feared a subversive, radical element in the judiciary were relieved. One consequence was to ensure
at least for a generation that, unlike career judiciaries in other industrial democracies in the wake of the worldwide rebellions of the 1960s,
the Japanese judiciary would remain obdurately apolitical.[46] The autonomy and the primacy of "the legal mind" had been ensured. At
least as important, Japan's judges secured their tenure.

The protests from Japan's judges were immediate and widespread.
More than a third openly protested in one form or another, and many

others quietly made their objections known. The judiciary became the center of a political storm. Miyamoto received nationwide media attention. Articles and books condemning the action poured forth. Since the Miyamoto incident, no judge has been denied reappointment. Denial of tenure was no longer a viable sanction. Instead, the career judges who persisted in continuing their membership in radical organizations became subject to discriminatory treatment in court assignments and promotions. Control in this form, however, has not provoked public outcry. Indeed, in the view of the public, the Japanese judiciary has remained one of the most trusted institutions of postwar Japanese governance.[47]

Japanese judges thus form a remarkably autonomous bureaucracy for which there are few parallels outside of Japan. In a perceptive essay written as the Miyamoto affair unfolded, Kazuhiko Tokoro analyzed the Japanese judiciary as an amalgam of three separate models—political, professional, and bureaucratic—from each of which separate elements could be detected. Characteristic of the Japanese judiciary, however, was the minimal level of popular participation or control. The Japanese judiciary relies less, Tokoro concluded, on legal rules made within administrative bureaucracies with some popular participation as in "bureaucratic" models; on outside experts, such as lawyers and other legal specialists, as in "professional" systems; or upon the personal values of individual judges, who, if not acceptable to their political principals, can be replaced. Rather the Japanese judiciary is more insulated from popular control in any of these forms than the courts of almost all other industrial democracies.[48]

In the end the judiciary itself, not the political branches of the Japanese government, determines the parameters of responsible judicial behavior. This conclusion is best understood through close examination of the process for the appointment and promotion of career judges as well as Supreme Court justices, the career judiciary's influence on the Court, and the mechanisms for judicial socialization. These are among the principal factors that help to explain the cohesion of the judiciary, its autonomy, its avoidance of ideological extremes, and its honesty and trustworthiness.

THE SUPREME COURT

Despite the potential for at least indirect political or electorate influence on the Supreme Court, it is in fact one of the most autonomous highest courts in the industrial world. Appointments to the court are formally among Japan's most politically significant. The Chief Justice is ostensibly nominated by the cabinet with ceremonial appointment by the emperor and is accorded the same rank and salary as the prime minister. The other fourteen justices have equal rank and salary as ministers of state and are appointed by the cabinet. The statutory requirements for Supreme Court justices are broadly worded. Article 41 of the 1947 Court Organization Law provides:

Justices of the Supreme Court shall be appointed from among persons of broad vision and extensive knowledge of law, who are not less than forty years of age. At least ten of them shall be persons who have held one or two of the positions mentioned in item (i) or (ii) for not less than ten years, or one or more positions mentioned in the following items for a total period of twenty years or more:
(i) Chief judge (*chōkan*) of a high court
(ii) Judge
(iii) Summary court judge
(iv) Public prosecutor
(v) Lawyer
(vi) Professor or assistant professor (*jokyōju*) in law in universities as determined separately by statute.[49]

The pool of qualified persons is very large. Hence the potential for political appointments is rather great. Not since the first justices were selected, however, have party or cabinet-level political considerations influenced even the appointment of the Chief Justice. Rather, who becomes a Supreme Court justice or the Chief Justice has been largely determined by the judges who administer the judiciary.

Illustrative is the *Mainichi Shinbun* Social Affairs Bureau account of the appointment of Ryōhachi Kusaba as Japan's twelfth Chief Justice in February 1990. Two months before the appointment, soon-to-retire Chief Justice Kyōichi Yaguchi visited the official residence of then Prime Minister Kaifu. The purpose was to inform the prime minister of the judiciary's choice for his replacement, a choice made with the participation of the principal administrators of the judicial branch—all career judges themselves. Kaifu did not object. As one official is quoted to have said (translated into idiomatic English): "We wouldn't have the vaguest idea who anyone they might suggest was, and we wouldn't have any way of finding out whether they would be suitable. The Supreme Court people have researched this. We trust their judgment."[50] A similar procedure has been followed in the appointment of every Chief Justice since 1962.

All but four of Japan's thirteen chief justices were themselves career judges. Only one lawyer (Fujibayashi), appointed in 1976, and one procurator (Okahara), appointed in 1977, have held the office. Two University of Tokyo law professors (Kotarō Tanaka and Kisaburō Yokota) were appointed back-to-back as the second and third Chief Justices in 1950 and 1960. The remaining nine were all career judges. Two of the past four previously held the position of General Secretary (Saikōsai jimu sōchō), the judiciary's highest administrative post.[51]

Similarly, by convention a third of all Supreme Court justices are appointed from the career judiciary, with another third from the practicing bar and the remaining five justices being other persons of "attainment in their profession with a knowledge of law." Of the thirty-five lawyers who served on the Court, fifteen were former bar association presidents or vice presidents. All of the eleven procurators appointed to the Court served as the chief procurator for a high court (eight) or the deputy chief procurator for the Supreme Court (three). With the exception of Hisako Takahashi, a career Ministry of Labor official and the first woman to serve on the Court, half of the ten career government officials appointed were former diplomats. The remaining five held the post of chief of the registration bureau attached to the cabinet or one of the houses of the Diet at the time of their appointment. In the cases of those who were not career judges, the recommendations to the prime minister have been based on consultations with the leaders of the major bar associations and senior levels of the procuracy and other government bureaucracies. Partisan party considerations are negligible in comparison to the internal politics of each of these separate organizations. The only real exceptions to this rule are arguably recommendations of scholars, for whom the leaders of the ruling party can more easily be directly lobbied.

The careers of the scholars on the Court have been almost as predictable as the other justices. They have included a number of Japan's academic elite—Shigeto Hozumi (1883–1951), Kōtarō Tanaka (1890–1974), Kisaburō Yokota (1896–1993), Ken'ichirō Ōsumi, Shigemitsu Dandō, and Masami Itō. All except Kyoto University Professor Ōsumi were members of the University of Tokyo Law Faculty. Itsuo Sonobe can also be included in the list. Sonobe was a member of the Kyoto University Law Faculty for fourteen years. In 1970 he resigned his teaching post to become a judge. He was appointed to the Tokyo District Court. Two years later he was transferred to the Tokyo High Court. In 1975 he was assigned to the Maebashi Family Court where he became a division head in 1978. In 1981, he was appointed research judge (*chōsakan*) at the Supreme Court, after which he was transferred back to the Tokyo District Court as head of a division. In 1985 he returned to teaching at Tsukuba University. He was a Professor of Law at Seikei University at the time of his appointment to the Court in 1989.

At any point in time at least a third of the Court—five of the fifteen justices—have spent their entire professional lives, usually from their mid-twenties, as judges. Between 1947 and 1992, for example, 107 persons had served as justices. Excluding the first appointments in 1947, which included three former Great Court of Cassation justices and one former Councillor of the Administrative Court, of these justices, thirty-five held a high judicial post at the time of their appointment, all but one of whom were in fact career judges. Four others had begun their professional lives as judges.

Equally significant are the career paths of the justices selected from the judiciary. Between 1947 and 1997, of the forty-two judges who were appointed to the Supreme Court, thirty-seven were serving as chief judge of a high court at the time of the appointment, seventeen from the Tokyo High Court, thirteen from the Osaka High Court, four from the Nagoya High Court, and three from the Fukuoka High Court. Except for the first justices appointed to the Supreme Court in 1947, who included two judges and the chief judge of the Great Court of Cessation and the president of the Administrative Court, only three career judges have ever been appointed to the Court who were not serving at the time of appointment as the chief judge of one of the four principal high courts. Several were transferred from a chief judgeship in one of the other high courts—Hiroshima, Sapporo, Sendai, and Takamatsu—to the Tokyo or Osaka High Court shortly before appointment to the Supreme Court. For example, retiring (1997) Chief Justice Tōru Miyoshi was appointed the Chief Judge of the Sapporo High Court in May 1991. He was briefly made *chōkan* of the Tokyo High Court just before his appointment to the Supreme Court in 1992. A justiceship is thus the highest rung of a career ladder that is determined first by the judge's seniors and at the finish by his or her judicial peers, not agencies, political or otherwise, outside of the courts.

The relative lack of ruling party or other political influence on Supreme Court appointments is also indicated by the non-career judge appointees. As mentioned previously, the appointments of lawyers, prosecutors, diplomats and even scholars and the handful of career administrative officials have followed predictable patterns. Nearly all have achieved elite status within their respective career or professional organizations. Only a couple have had any career mobility. Itsuo Sonobe, as noted, was one example. Another exception was Shunzō Kobayashi (1888–1982), who, although serving as Chief Judge of the Tokyo High Court at the time of his appointment, had spent most of his professional life as a practicing attorney. He also served as president of the Second Tokyo Bar Association. The predominance of former bar officials exemplifies the influence of the bar itself rather than political leaders on which attorneys are selected to become a justice. One of the legal scholars and two of the former administrative officials were also former judges, and one of the legal scholars was a former attorney. Moreover, all of the former administrative officials were serving one of Japan's most politically neutral administrative posts as head of the Cabinet Legislation Bureau or its Diet equivalent at the time of appointment. Even in the case of the four diplomats appointed to the Supreme Court, all of whom were former ambassadors who rose through the ranks of the Foreign Affairs Ministry, political considerations appear to have been secondary to a purely bureaucratic concern to award members who have served well.

Nor has political change significantly affected the Court. A majority of eight justices of the current court were appointed since the 1993 political upheaval that ended the four-decade-long era of single party rule in Japan. Since 1993 political coalitions have formed the cabinets. Of longest duration has been the LDP-Social Democratic Party (former Socialist Party) coalition. The only apparent change in the composition of the court was the appointment, as noted, of Japan's first woman justice—Hisako Takahashi. Socialist prime ministers too appoint the justices recommended by senior judges and the legal establishment.

As of May 1997, Japan's fifteen Supreme Court justices included one appointed under the first Kaifu Cabinet (Itsuo Sonobe, 1989), one under the second Kaifu Cabinet (Katsuya Ōnishi, 1991), three under the Miyazawa Cabinet (Motoo Ono, 1992; Tōru Miyoshi 1992; Masao Ōno, 1993), four under the Hosokawa Cabinet (Hideo Chikusa, 1993; Shigeharu Negishi, 1994; Hisako Takahashi, 1994; Yukinobu Ozaki, 1994), five under the Murayama Cabinet (Shin'ichi Kawai, 1994; Mitsuo Endō, 1995; Kazutomo Ijima, 1995; Hiroshi Fukuda, 1995; Masao Fujii, 1995), and one under the current Hashimoto Cabinet (Shigeru Yamaguchi, 1997). Thus two-thirds of the members of the current Court were appointed since the end of the era of single-party, LDP rule. Yet, with the exception, as noted, of the appointment of Justice Takahashi, the first woman on the Court and one of the few persons ever to serve without a degree in law, no change in the basic pattern of judicial appointments is apparent.

The youngest justice, Hiroshi Fukuda, was born in 1935, the oldest, Masao Ōno, in 1927. Eight are graduates of the University of Tokyo, seven in law and one (Takahashi) in economics. Five (Sonobe, Kawai, Ijima, Fujii, and Yamaguchi) are Kyoto University law graduates, one (Ono) a Chuo law graduate and one (Endō) a Hōsei University law graduate. Of the six career judges on the Court, all but two (Sonobe and Chikusa) were serving as chief judges of high courts at the time of their appointments: on the Tokyo High Court (Miyoshi and Ōnishi), the Osaka High Court (Ono and Fujii), or the Fukuoka High Court

(Yamaguchi). Three had previously headed the Court's general secretariat (Ōnishi, Chikusa, and Yamaguchi). One of the two former prosecutors on the Court was deputy Prosecutor-General at the time of his appointment (Ijima); the other (Negishi) headed the Tokyo High Court's prosecutor's office. All four of the attorneys on the Court had held elite bar association or governmental posts. Two (Ozaki and Kawai) were former presidents of their respective bar associations. One (Endō) had held important posts in the Japanese Federation of Bar Associations. One (Ōno) had been a member for many years of the Ministry of Construction Central Construction Project Dispute Investigation Committee. Two spent at least a year at the Harvard Law School (Ozaki and Kawai). The one career diplomat (Fukuda) had held a series of posts in the Ministry of Foreign Affairs secretariat. One (Takahashi) served a career in the Ministry of Labor—she is one of the few persons ever to serve with a career in an economic ministry. The insulation of the appointment process from any partisan political influence is evidenced by the fact that no member of the current Court had participated in any partisan political activity. In fact the current Chief Justice Tōru Miyoshi, initially appointed to the Court under an LDP Cabinet, was nominated for the office three and a half years later by Japan's first Socialist prime minister in a half century.

Another striking feature of the composition of Japan's Supreme Court is the age of the justices. Since 1952 only two persons under sixty years of age have ever been appointed to the court, Jirō Tanaka and Ken'ichi Okuno, who each were 58. Only two were sixty. No one born after 1935 has ever served on Japan's highest court, and all but three of the 121 postwar justices have served less than ten years. Not until 1990 was anyone appointed who received his or her legal education in postwar Japan. In 1997 the youngest member of the Court was 62.

DEVELOPING "THE LEGAL MIND"

Japan's career judges staff all of Japan's district and high courts as well as the principal administrative offices necessary for the management of the entire judicial branch. In addition, about thirty *chōsakan* are appointed from the senior ranks of the career judiciary to assist the Supreme Court. As a result, the influence of Japan's career judges extends throughout the judicial system from the Supreme Court through the summary courts.

The Japanese judiciary is structured in ways that ensure the greatest possible cohesion. Certainty and consistency are among the highest aims. Although, in the words of one former Chief Justice, "the Supreme Court is not allowed to order a judge to do or not do something in connection with a case before him upon the pretext of administrative supervision, it may issue general instructions to judges with regard to the disposition of judicial business as a whole." [52] By continual rotation, collegial decision making, seminars, and periodic conferences, particularly among judges of a single district or high court, Japan's judges seek to avoid inconsistency in all aspects of the judicial process from the initial filing of a lawsuit through the final decision on appeal.

The principal means of influence by Japan's senior judges is through their active participation at all levels of Japan's court system. The career paths of Japan's judges spiral from junior positions at the district level, usually beginning with a family court, upward at midcareer to a high court and an educational or research position as *chōsakan* at the Supreme Court, back to the district level as head of a civil or criminal division and then to the position of presiding judge. Thus, nearly all of the class of judges who began their careers in 1967 began as assistant judges with a family court. Twenty years later more than half of the judges who remained active were chief judges of family courts (fifteen) or presided over or headed divisions of district courts (thirteen).

Judicial conferences provide another mechanism for consensus and influence by senior judges. The judicial conferences of each court are responsible for most administrative matters, from management of cases to case assignments. The judicial conference of the Supreme Court in turn exercises administrative control over the entire system from the assignment of judges to selection of the chief judges of the high courts as well as the presiding judges of each court. Conference decisions of the lower court can be significantly influenced by the chief judge and presiding judges, but at the Supreme Court level, except for those justices who were appointed from the career judiciary or on issues of special interest to one or more of the other justices, the secretariat is generally more influential than individual justices, who serve for relatively short periods of time in contrast to the career judges of the secretariat. Rarely if ever does a judicial conference overtly attempt to standardize or unify decisions. Where an issue is being litigated in a number of courts, various judges will express opinions. In the process, some degree of consensus may be reached. Supreme Court justices do not actively participate at this level. Nor would any opinions expressed receive official sanction from either the justices or the secretariat. The turnover on the Supreme Court is also too frequent for any direction from that level to become meaningful.

Moreover, the career judiciary also exerts some influence on the Court through the nearly thirty research judges, who are themselves usually midcareer judges posted to the court to assist the justices. Consistency and whatever degree of uniformity the Japanese judiciary is able to achieve is thus less a result of direction from above than a variety of factors that produce convergence of views among Japan's career judges whatever their particular assignment may be. These factors include conscious socialization as well as an intrinsic homogeneity.

The socialization of young assistant judges is given the highest priority. Again in the words of the late Chief Justice Hattori:

> The most important task of the judiciary is the training of younger, inexperienced assistant judges. In addition to the daily training of junior members of a three-judge bench through hearing and trying cases, the training for assistant judges is roughly divided into five programs. The first is a comparatively short introductory course given to assistant judges immediately after their appointment. Its purpose is to provide them with a general idea of their future work and to aid them in preparing for judicial service. The other four training programs are seminar-type pro-

grams given in the first, third, fourth, and ninth years after their appointment [currently the first, third, sixth and tenth years].[53]

The aim of such training, as explained by the judges in the Legal Training and Research Institute who carry it out, is to ensure the highest degree of competence. The emphasis is technical, to enable soon-to-become full judges who will for the first time be able to decide cases on their own to resolve the cases before them appropriately. In-service training sessions for full judges tend to focus on court administration, such as how to deal with an enormous caseload in the most expeditious manner, and new developments in the law.

In order to give careers wider exposure, included in the judiciary's training program today are a limited number of opportunities for study abroad as well as externships for either a few weeks or a year with participating business enterprises. In these programs judges at an early stage in their careers are exposed to new and different environments. For those selected to go abroad, the programs include externships with foreign courts as well as educational opportunities at leading law schools in the United States and Canada. Some judges are sent to study in law faculties in Europe. Recently, externship programs have been initiated to introduce younger judges to the practical aspects of the media or commercial law. Each year, several judges are assigned to one of the major news media companies for three weeks. Several judges are also selected to spend either ten days or one year with a private company. In the latter case, the judges gain direct experience with a variety of business problems as well as the internal realities of large Japanese enterprises. These programs are organized and administered by the Institute.

Consistency rather than uniformity is the goal. Both, however, are a product of the process and structure for judicial training. Intended or not, consistency and a significant degree of uniformity are fostered by the process of intensive judicial socialization in Japan. The values, expectations, and underlying assumptions of senior judges are inexorably passed down, in the process of three-year rotation to a wide variety of courts nationwide, to assistant judges during their service on three-judge panels in combination with periodic training programs during their first, third, sixth, and tenth years on the bench. However, the same process ensures that the attitudes and values of younger judges also pass up throughout the system. As often divergent opinions merge in the crucible of reasoned debate, what appears to be an unparalleled degree of judicial cohesion, certainty, and consistency becomes the result.

These attributes of Japan's judiciary are strengthened by the educational homogeneity of Japan's career judges. The vast majority are graduates of the law faculties of only two national and two private universities: the University of Tokyo, Kyoto University, Chuo University, and Waseda University. Among all graduates of the Legal Training and Research Institute appointed as assistant judges between December 1947 through April 1955, more than 28 percent were graduates of the University of Tokyo, followed by Kyoto graduates (15 percent), and Chuo graduates (13 percent). In fourth place were graduates of Tohoku University (2 percent), followed closely by Kyushu and Waseda (1.7 percent each).[54] These percentages are remarkably consistent for the entire postwar period with only a slight decrease in the number and percentage of Tokyo graduates and corresponding percentage but not the number of Kyoto and Chuo graduates through the early 1960s.[55]

There was an apparent but brief shift in this pattern between 1961 and 1965. Nineteen sixty one was notable as the only year between 1947 and 1990 in which the graduates of any other law faculty led Tokyo graduates for the largest number and percentage of judicial appointments. In that year of the eighty-eight graduates of the thirteenth class of the Legal Training and Research Institute appointed as assistant judges, at least twenty-one were Kyoto graduates with only eleven listed as Tokyo graduates.[56] Although as a result, a plurality of Kyoto graduates became assistant judges in the period between 1961 and 1965—20 percent as compared to 17 percent Tokyo, 17 percent Chuo, and 5 percent Waseda graduates—in no other half decade did the number or percentage of known Kyoto graduates, or any other law faculty for that matter, exceed that of the University of Tokyo. Although in 1966 the number of known Chuo graduates was greater than for either Tokyo or Kyoto (nineteen to thirteen and six, respectively) and in 1967 Tokyo graduates (at twelve) fell to third place behind both Chuo (sixteen) and Kyoto (fifteen), for the period of 1966 and 1970 as a whole, Tokyo graduates constituted a plurality of 20 percent of all newly appointed assistant judges. Chuo graduates accounted for 17 percent and Kyoto graduates 11.5 percent of the 391 judge total.[57] The only significant change for nearly a half century has been the increase in the number of Waseda graduates to become judges. Although from 1955 the number of Waseda graduates appointed to assistant judgeships was greater than that of any law faculty except for Tokyo, Kyoto, and Chuo, from the mid-1970s, more Waseda graduates were appointed as judges than graduates of all national universities combined. In the 1980s, Waseda replaced both Kyoto and Chuo as the University of Tokyo's major rival. Between 1980 and 1985 more than 13 percent of all newly appointed assistant judges were Waseda graduates, as compared to 32 percent from Tokyo, 8 percent from Kyoto, and 7 percent from Chuo. The percentage of known graduates from all other national universities was about 5 percent with 2 percent from all other private universities. The judicial appointments for 1990 appear to be typical: Of the eighty-one assistant judges appointed, twenty-one (26 percent) were University of Tokyo graduates and fourteen (17 percent) were Waseda graduates. Kyoto and Chuo each had eight graduates (10 percent) with the remaining judges having graduated from the following law faculties: Meiji (five), Hitotsubashi (four), Keio (four), Nagoya (three), Kansai (two), Kobe (two), Kyushu (two), Aoyama Gakuin (one), Chiba (one), Gakushuin (one), Hokkaido (one), Nanzan (one), Osaka (one), Tohoku (one), and the University of the Ryukyus (one).

Several conclusions can be drawn from the educational background of Japan's contemporary judiciary. First, in addition to the common socializing experience in the Legal Training and Research Institute, the majority of Japan's judges also share common undergraduate experiences. Although they lived from childhood in various parts of Japan, more than half spent their formative years as university students in metropolitan Tokyo. They were taught and presumably influenced by a handful of elite legal scholars, who also, as noted below, probably graduated from the same universities. Especially in the case of University of Tokyo graduates, their classmates and closest university friends are most likely to have either become government officials or joined one of Japan's major financial or industrial companies, if not to have also passed the national legal examination and become either a procurator or lawyer. In other words, Japan's judges are members of Japan's small, cohesive economic and political elite.

The relative stability of the judiciary is another predominant characteristic. Of the seventy-seven judges appointed in 1960, for example, forty-five (58.5 percent) were on the bench thirty years later in 1990, including two serving as summary court judges after having retired. One had reached mandatory retirement age and three were deceased. Of the others who had left the bench before mandatory retirement age, three resigned within the first five years, one to join a law faculty, the other two to enter private practice. Eight resigned after serving twenty-five years as a judge, four to become notaries and four to enter practice. All of the remaining seventeen resigned to enter private practice, six having served five to ten years, six serving ten to twenty years, and five, twenty to twenty-five years.

The career paths of Japanese judges follow equally stable patterns. As noted above, Japanese judges do not simply move upwards in a hierarchy of courts. Rather, they spiral upwards in positions in courts at all levels. Thus a favorable career path for an aspiring young judge would include assignment in Tokyo in the administrative arm of the Supreme Court, or as a research judge, or both. A presiding judgeship in a more remote family court, followed by a presiding judgeship with a less remote district court, evidence a normal progression of advancement. Take, for example, the careers of two judges selected at random from those serving on the Tokyo High Court in 1990. One was born in Tokushima Prefecture, on Shikoku, in September 1937. A graduate of Chuo University, she passed the national legal examination in September 1962, entered the Legal Training and Research Institute in April 1963, and graduated with the seventeenth class. In April 1965 she was appointed assistant judge and posted to the Osaka District Court. Three years later she was transferred to the Kanazawa Family Court. And three years later she was assigned to the Ministry of Justice, where she served for seven years (1971–78). In April 1978 she was transferred to the Urawa Family Court and in 1980 to the Tokyo District Court. A year later she was appointed a *chōsakan*. In 1984 she returned to the bench as a judge of the Tokyo District Court in 1986. In April 1990 she was posted to the Tokyo High Court to head a division.

Also appointed in April 1990 to serve on the Tokyo High Court was the second judge. Born in Aichi Prefecture in March 1941, he also graduated in the seventeenth class of the Legal Training and Research Institute and was initially posted to the Tokyo District Court as an assistant judge. Three years later in 1968, he was assigned to the Hachinohe branch of the Aomori District Court. In 1971 he became an instructor at the Institute and three years after that was appointed to the Naha District Court on Okinawa, becoming a full judge in 1975. He too was appointed *chōsakan* in 1976 and was transferred to an administrative post with the Tokyo High Court in 1977. In 1980 he was transferred to the Tokyo District Court and a year later to the Osaka District Court. In April 1984 he returned to the Tokyo District Court, from 1986 as head of a division until his appointment to the Tokyo High Court.

Emphasis on the features of Japanese judicial organization that produce consistency and a degree of uniformity can be misleading. All said, Japanese judges do not walk lock-step together. They do not all think, act, or feel alike. Wide disparities in belief, political preference, social outlook, and basic values exist within the Japanese judiciary as in Japanese society as a whole. Indeed, were all Japanese judges as conforming as some might erroneously conclude, efforts to ensure consistency would be unnecessary.

What is important and what is carefully inculcated is, in the words of one young Japanese judge, the development of "the legal mind." In a conversation with the author, she said, "Assistant judges . . . learn much from senior judges. What we learn is, however, not specific opinions concerning legal issues or perspectives of the Supreme Court. Instead, senior judges teach us how to read case files, make research, evaluate evidence, write memoranda, and how to develop what is called 'the legal mind.'" She continued: "Although the concept of 'the legal mind' has various aspects . . . one of the most important . . . is that when you find, through discussion, your opponent's legal theory superior and more persuading than your own, you must accept it. This is true even though . . . it contradicts your own personal principle or political viewpoint."

The combination of the judiciary's concern to maintain its institutional autonomy with the emphasis on consistency and the analytical demands of "the legal mind" contribute to the courts' cautious conservatism. These forces are also buttressed by an ever-present concern to keep the public trust. Although Japan's courts play an instrumental role in shaping public opinion and building consensus on issues of major social and political significance, they tend to remain at the edge of the wave. Seldom do they lead. Like the procuracy, were Japan's judiciary to lose the public and political trust, judges would also lose their independence from political intervention. The judiciary itself is the watchdog ensuring that the public and the politicians have no cause to intervene.

6 Community Confirmed

The Miyamoto affair reveals a basic pattern of judicial—and public—response: the law will be used to protect the individual from expulsion by the community but not prevent the community's routine control over the individual. The values that prompted the angry reaction of Japan's judges to Yasuaki Miyamoto's expulsion were not merely self-serving. Expulsion is an extreme sanction for any community. To break the bonds of belonging and to deny the material and psychological benefits of membership is the harshest action short of physical violence a community can take. Even temporary expulsion by ostracism and the rupture of the benefits of cooperation can be a severe and effective penalty.

Expulsion also costs the community. To cast out any member is itself a self-threatening measure. The loss of a member reduces the number of those who contribute to the community's sustaining activities and its collective strength. The more closely knit, cohesive, and interdependent the community, the more severe expulsion becomes for both those expelled and the community itself. As a sanction expulsion is seldom used and only then as a last resort.

Hardly any pattern of law in contemporary Japan has been more pervasive than the judicial use of legal rules to maintain stable relationships, to borrow Dan Foote's phrase, and to restore the balance in negotiating consensual termination.[1] From divorce to employee relations, the courts have consistently refused to apply or to enforce explicit legal rules or principles in ways that would allow unilateral expulsion and skew a balanced, bargained-for, and mutually agreed end to ongoing relationships. In these cases the courts in effect protect individuals with less bargaining leverage against the community or those with social, political, or economic advantage. Judicial responses and judge-made rules do not, however, eliminate the consensual nature of the relationship and the capacity of the parties to agree to terminate their relationship. Community remains a consensual matter. The effect is less, moreover, to protect the weak against the strong than to prevent unilateral rupture and, in so doing, to confirm community.

VILLAGES AND VILLAGERS

Murahachibu was the traditional village sanction. An extreme form of ostracism, its imposition by the village deprived the deviant members and their households of the benefits of cooperative village life. The penalized households were denied all forms of mutual aid and social communication except for community aid in the case of fire and, according to some, funerals.[2] All agree that the penalty was extreme and in many instances meant economic and social ruin. Even under Tokugawa rule, in extreme cases judicial relief was available. Herman Ooms describes such a case that occurred in the late 1820s in a village located on what is today the northernmost outskirts of Tokyo. A suit was filed with the office of the official (*daikan*) with supervisory responsibility in the village in Edo (now Tokyo). The petition was couched in terms to demonstrate that, unless resolved, official interests were at stake—tax and corvée labor. The suit was settled by mediation with both sides acknowledging wrongs.[3] At least superficially, the relationship and community were restored.

Similar petitions for state protection persisted at least into the late 1950s. Procurators and judges responded. Criminal actions were brought, and in at least a half-dozen decisions between 1911 and 1939, Japan's highest court repeatedly held that, without just cause, *murahachibu* constituted the crime of intimidation (*kyōhaku*) under article 222 of the Criminal Code.[4] As stated in more than a half-dozen decisions of Japan's highest court, with only slight variation in the 1920 case of *Fukuda v. Japan*, which Takuzo Hanai, representing the defendant, lost on appeal: "When a group of people in a certain locality, on a trivial pretext and without a reason that appears just and proper according to social conceptions [*shakai-teki kanjō*] jointly decide entirely to break off relations with a certain person of such group and his family, cutting off supplies of the necessities of life and giving notice thereof to such person, they threaten to ignore the personal character of the person and to treat him as an inferior who is unfit to lead the communal life. It is an intimidation of harm that may have the result of impairing the reputation which he as an individual enjoys, and is enough to cause fear. . . . [Such] act . . . constitutes the crime of intimidation."[5]

Although there have apparently been no postwar Supreme Court cases, at least two high courts reaffirmed these early decisions.[6] The Nagoya High Court applied similar reasoning to a youth club for hazing.[7] We know very little about the background to these cases or, indeed, what the consequences may have been. Even the identification of the principal defendants and the actual sanctions applied are not evident from the reported decisions. They did serve, however, to make the point—at least in extreme cases in which those affected complained to the authorities—the law's most stringent rules condemned unilateral expulsion without good reason from the village.

FATHERS AND SONS

Judicial protection of members of a community from arbitrary or unreasonable expulsion has not been limited to hamlets and neighborhoods. For Japanese the family is the fundamental social unit. Under the Civil Code and Family Registration Law, prior to the 1947 amendments, the *ie* was the legally recognized family unit. Each *ie* had a registered hereditary head (*atoku*) whose legal authority over adoption, marriage, divorce, and legal residence was extensive. Consent of the head of the household, enforced through the family registry by requiring an imprint of his or her registered seal on registry forms, was a prerequisite to effect changes in legal relationships within the extended family. It is generally conceded today that the drafters of the code provisions were less concerned about the realities of family life than they were about ensuring that the legal structure of the family replicated the ideology of the Meiji state, construed in familial terms with the emperor as the head of a nationally extended family. There appears to have been less concern over the actual ability of heads of household to exercise their authority to control the members of the house. The code itself included safeguards against arbitrary refusals to permit changes in the composition of the family desired by those most concerned.

The early cases on the authority of the head of the household under the code, particularly with respect to the right to determine residence, tended to affirm the absolute nature of this authority. It was not difficult, however, for the courts to hold that the right to remove family members from the *ie* was abusive. The first reported case was *Sonoda v. Sonoda.*[8] A long line of subsequent decisions further defined the limits of the authority of the head of the household to manage the *ie* as a whole.[9] Mark Ramseyer provides a catalog of cases in which abuse of right and good-faith principles were used to constrain the head of the household's authority to expel family members, his principal source of leverage for controlling their activities and conduct.[10] The end result was to ensure that heads of households did not exercise arbitrary power. They had to have some degree of consent and offer some degree of reciprocity in exchange for compliance.

HUSBANDS AND WIVES

Since the abolition of the *ie* in 1947, the issue of expulsion and rupture of familial relationships has been most acute in the area of divorce. Japan's Civil Code provisions governing family relations, enacted in 1898, have permitted divorce either by agreement or by judicial decree. The procedure for consensual divorce has long been quite simple. The parties need only send signed (sealed) notification of their decision to the appropriate registry office. Prior to the Occupation reforms, regardless of the respective ages of the couple, the consent (represented by seal) of their parents, grandparents, or guardian was also required. The postwar reforms eliminated this requirement, except for couples under the age of twenty-five. Since these reforms, divorce, like marriage in Japan, requires only mutual consent and for-

mal notice for registration.[11] Divorce by consent in Japan is easier to
obtain than in almost any industrial democracy today.[12] All that is
necessary to terminate a marriage is agreement of the spouses and
compliance with the otherwise neutral and relatively simple registration procedures. No third party assent—ecclesiastic, judicial, or familial—is necessary.

Without mutual consent, however, legal divorce can be effected
only by judicial decree. The grounds for judicial dissolution of a marriage were quite narrow before the war, limited to desertion, imprisonment, profligacy by the husband, adultery of the wife, or acute illness.[13] Drafters of the Civil Code expressly rejected a proposal by
Shigenobu Hozumi to include "discord that makes life together un-
bearable" (kyōdō seikatsu o nasu ni taenai fuwa) as an additional
ground.[14] During the postwar revisions of Japanese family law, along
with relatively minor rewording of the other grounds, a similar but
even more open-ended basis for contested divorce was added: "grave
cause making the continuation of the marriage difficult" (kekkon o
keizoku shigatai jūdai na jiyū).[15] Japan's postwar judges have not,
however, taken advantage of the potential flexibility of this addition
to make contested divorce upon petition by either husband or wife
less difficult. The process itself poses barriers.

The party seeking a contested divorce must first petition the family court. A panel of two lay conciliators and a judge posted to the
family court is assigned the case and meets separately at first with each
spouse. The lay conciliators take charge. The judge is seldom present
until the end. The role of the judge is primarily to review whatever
agreement is reached to make certain that its terms do not transgress
any applicable public policy principles. In most instances, especially
if the conciliators are seasoned veterans, such review and approval is
routine.

The room where they meet is typically sparsely furnished, except
for a few chairs and a conference table at one end of which sits the
panel with the parties at each side facing each other as well as evoca-
tive pictures on opposite walls, typically with children or on the order
of Millet's Angelus depicting the farming couple in a field at evening
prayer. The panel elicits the reasons for the petition, the background

and circumstances of the marriage, the couple's financial situation, and relationships with members of their families. Questions regarding how well the wife gets along with her husband's mother are frequently asked. Concern for minor children, if any, is evident as the conciliators and less frequently the judge (if present) question each spouse. Several meetings may be scheduled, often months apart as in the case of formal trial proceedings. Once convinced that the divorce is inevitable, the panel will mediate a settlement that they and, hopefully the parties, consider to be fair. Today conciliators try to avoid injecting their own views, but they inexorably express values held by the community at large as well as those shared within their particular social status. If either spouse objects and cannot be persuaded to accept a settlement, the petitioner must file a formal petition with the district court.

After the most extensive observation of family court and judicial practice undertaken by any scholar, University of California law professor and anthropologist Taimie Bryant concludes: "[I]nvestigation into how the legal system actually operates with respect to divorce reveals that it is quite difficult to effect a divorce by judicial decision. An individual may seek a judicial divorce in the district court on grounds of adultery, desertion, absence of the spouse for more than three years without any contact or knowledge of his or her whereabouts, incurable mental illness, or grave causes that make continuation of the marriage difficult. However, the requirements of proof of any of these grounds are so rigorous that in fact it is extremely difficult to divorce a spouse against his or her wishes." [16]

Bryant carefully understates the difficulty. Take, for instance, her account of the 1981 decision of the Tokyo High Court quashing a decision by the Tokyo District Court, which had granted a divorce nine years earlier to a husband who had lived apart from his wife for more than twenty years at the time of the district court decision.

Immediately after the marriage in 1946, the man had fallen ill requiring hospitalization and treatment that resulted in separate living arrangements for the first eight years of marriage. Although the couple began living together in 1954, they did not get along, an unhappy situation compounded by co-residence with the husband's mother. About two years later (1956–57) the husband began to shun his wife, and their relationship deteriorated rapidly. In 1958 the husband moved out in order to take a position at a private university. In the years following that move, he met a woman with whom he subsequently developed a serious relationship. By 1959 the marital relationship had ruptured completely, but separation continued to last for at least twelve years before the husband filed for divorce on the ground of "grave cause making marital continuity difficult." A divorce was granted by the court of first instance (Tokyo District Court), but it was denied by the appellate court (Tokyo High Court) in a decision reflecting concern that the courts not permit a party responsible for the marital breakdown to ride roughshod over an innocent spouse.[17]

"Ultimately," Bryant writes, "48.5 percent of the 5054 divorce cases handled by the district court in 1982 were resolved by judicial decision. Forty-six percent of the divorce petitions were granted, 2.5 percent refused, and 19 percent were withdrawn." "It is significant," she continues, "that in 60 percent of divorces granted, one party was absent. This reflects the fact that most divorces are granted for desertion, disappearance for at least three years, or irremediable mental illness—all cases in which mediation is impossible."[18]

Bryant's respondents gave two reasons for the reluctance of judges to grant contested divorces.[19] One was concern over allowing blameless spouses to be forced into a divorce. The second was that without such insistence on fault, women would suffer disproportionately. For many Japanese wives, divorce may not necessarily be a welcome alternative to an unhappy marriage. The reality of family life in Japan, some might argue, has made it considerably easier for many Japanese women to remain married but estranged and separated from their husbands than to be freed from matrimonial ties. As a noted American anthropologist privately remarked on the basis of comments by his Japanese wife on the difficulty of life for women in the United States, in Japan a wife may be socially constrained in her role in terms of her obligations as homemaker and mother, but she is not bound by social expectations that she should necessarily become either the sexual or social partner of her husband. Ronald Dore contrasts the expectations of a traditional Japanese bride: "In the traditional family there were many roles in which a bride could be successful. She could be a good daughter-in-law, a good sister-in-law, a good house-cleaner, a good rice-planter, a good link with another rich and influential family, an efficient performer of ceremonial duties *vis-a-vis* the ancestors or neighbors, as well as being successful as a source of emotional and sexual satisfaction for her husband—if, indeed, the latter counted for much at all. In the new conjugal family she can still prove her worth as housekeeper, as mother and as maintainer of her husband's prestige, but the number of roles is whittled down."[20] Dore notes the likelihood of greater intimacy between wives and their husbands as a result of the changes in traditional patterns of life in Japan. However, anachronistic as such observations have become, studies of contemporary family life in Japan point out the continued emphasis on a "division of labor" between husband and wife, with the wife assuming the paramount roles of mother and homemaker.[21]

Although such a life may be personally unfulfilling, Japanese women have been able to satisfy community requirements as proper wives while living almost completely cut off from their husbands. On the other hand, until recently at least, divorce could have harsh social consequences. The Civil Code provision for mutual obligations of support among siblings applies to divorced but not married sisters. Presumably some Japanese would prefer that their divorced sisters remain in unwanted marriages so they do not have to assume the legally imposed burden for their support. The loss of a married name has also carried social stigma. Remarriage was rare.

Japanese law does not provide the divorced wife the protection of either common law dower rights or, as in many jurisdictions, civil law community property. The Civil Code's separate property regime often leaves the divorced wife with limited economic benefits. The bar of contested divorce thus has the effect of protecting dependent wives. Without the bargained-for consent of the wife, husbands are unable to obtain a divorce. Wives are thus empowered to extract from husbands seeking divorce a larger settlement than the law would otherwise assure them. While such protection many benefit an economically dependent spouse resisting divorce, it leaves unprotected the equally dependent spouse who seeks a divorce. Effect, however, should not be confused with motive.

In a series of decisions beginning in 1987 the Japanese Supreme Court modified the rules against contested divorce. The changes made, however, reveal the tenacity of the concern for preventing any rupture of a marriage without mutual consent. The first and most important case, *Kōno v. Kōno*, was decided *en banc* on September 2, 1987.[22] Again, Taimie Bryant captures the critical facts:

> The petitioner was a company president who left his wife of 12 years in order to live with the mother of two children he and his wife had adopted. During their cohabitation, two children were born to the petitioner and his extramarital partner. Since the petitioner had stopped paying support, the wife had supported herself on proceeds from the sale of a house purchased by her husband and through the sale of dolls she made. However, ultimately she was reduced to living with her brother's family. Despite the lack of emotional or financial support from her husband, the wife consistently rejected his divorce demands because the stigma of divorce would tarnish her and their daughters' family registry. The husband characterized her reasons as greed and spite, which suggests that he failed to meet the price she demanded for a consensual divorce.[23]

From prior cases, the wife had every reason to refuse her husband until he accepted her terms. Prior cases had made clear that, under similar facts, no divorce would be decreed. The husband petitioned nevertheless, and despite denials by both the district and high courts, he continued with an appeal to the Supreme Court. To the surprise, one imagines, of both client and his attorney, he won. The court quashed the lower court decision and granted the divorce, affirming the petitioner's claim in stating: "[W]hen one or both spouses no longer desire to live together in pursuit of a permanent spiritual and physical union, the marriage has lost the reality of communal life, and there is absolutely no prospect of reconciliation, the marriage must be considered to have lost its substantive foundation as a part of social life. To continue such a marriage simply on paper in the family registry is unnatural."[24]

Subsequent petty bench decisions refined the new standards established by the grand bench precedent to include "the totality of circumstances" that could justify granting a contested divorce. The principal factors, however, remained those explicit in the 1987 decision: the length of time the spouses had been separated, the presence of dependent children of the legal marriage, and the financial or psychological hardship the reluctant spouse (nearly always the wife) might experience were the divorce granted. In each case, the petitioner had established an extramarital relationship that could not result in marriage without divorce.

How long the couple had lived separately was considered the threshold question. In the September 1987 Grand Bench case, the parties had been separated for thirty-six years. In subsequent cases, the parties had lived apart for thirty years, twenty-two years, sixteen years, and fifteen and a half years.[25]

In a March 1989 decision, the Third Petty Bench refused to allow a contested divorce on the grounds that a ten-year separation was too short. The official commentary on the case indicated that as society changed, a shorter period of separation might become acceptable.[26] A year and a half later, the First Petty Bench appeared to have thought society had changed sufficiently to reverse and remand a judgment of the Tokyo High Court that had denied to grant a contested divorce in a case in which the couple had lived separately for less than eight years.[27] Although, as most comments on the case point out, other circumstances distinguish the two decisions, the Court apparently rejected the idea that the length of separation could be the sole determinant.[28] Whether the marriage is retrievable appears to be the principal underlying concern.

In a 1993 case in which the husband contested a divorce sought by his wife, the Supreme Court continued to take the more lenient stance. The Third Petty Bench decision in *Kōno v. Kōno* rejected the *jōkoku* appeal of the husband to have a divorce decree reversed.[29] After living with her husband for more than seventeen years, the wife had allegedly fled the home nearly ten years earlier, leaving two children (who were adults by the time of the Court's decision). The wife was thus not only responsible for the separation, she had also allegedly established a relationship with another man. The Supreme Court refused to reverse the decree, concluding that the Tokyo High Court had properly determined that the couple had lived apart for a substantial length of time and that the circumstances demonstrated "grave reason making continuation of the marriage difficult." Although the period of separation remains a critical factor, other evidence of the complete breakdown of the marriage balanced by concern for the social and economic position of the wife—and her responsibility for the separation—made the contested divorce easier to grant.

So long as the protesting wife's financial security can be assured, granting the contested divorce has increasingly become an unwanted but acceptable option. The courts have in effect accepted the view that they should allow divorce when the couple has lived apart for a long period of time, reconciliation is out of the question, and either the wife seeks the divorce or is at least adequately compensated.[30]

In many of these cases the Court faced the dilemma of deciding which family—which community—to maintain. Both husbands and wives had established new *de facto* family units. The idea of somehow preserving both was not an option. In Japan divorce makes strangers. Becoming strangers has been the prevailing metaphor for marital dissolution in Japan. As Bryant notes, it influences all aspects of negotiations for divorce and many of the legal consequences.[31] The idea that after divorce all bonds are broken and all relationships are severed has precluded alimony as well as negotiated financial settlements that involve periodic future payments as well as legally imposed visitation and other rights of noncustodial parents to maintain relationships with their children. To illustrate this point, Bryant quotes a conciliator attempting to persuade a wife to accept a smaller lump sum settlement instead of a larger amount to be paid over time, "After all, you cannot expect a total stranger to behave as though he or she is obligated to you."[32]

Several points deserve repeated emphasis. The law remains passive. The marital partners enjoy extensive freedom to order their lives as they wish, with all of the dysfunctional consequences that may result because of significant differences in dependency between husbands and wives. No attempt is made to redefine the legal rules related to marriage or divorce to ensure that behavior conforms to legal rules or that the legal rules necessarily conform to social practice. The autonomy of the family remains intact. The state does not intervene. No meaningful effort has been made to reform Japan's marital property rules. Indeed, so long as "community" is maintained—that is, the formal marital relationship and the family as a formal, but not necessarily functional, social unit is preserved, there is little if any state or even social intervention. Nor is any effort made to preserve the marital relationship against the wishes of both spouses. As explained, consensual divorce in Japan requires no formality other than registry notice. The confirmation of community in the case of contested divorce cannot be equated with an attempt either to regulate or to enforce community. Bryant believes that the motivating concern in conciliation is primarily to eliminate or at least reduce the social "static" of marital conflict.[33] In effect, the courts merely resist becoming an instrument of dissolution where the marital partners themselves fail to agree. If judges must decide the issue, they choose to confirm the community.

The law also changes. Japan's legal rules may not conform to social practice, but social practice does influence the legal rules. Changing attitudes toward marriage and the family within the community at large as well as by judges themselves have already resulted in a somewhat more flexible approach to contested divorce. These changes will continue, due in part to influences from abroad, including the experiences of Japanese living overseas. Whether these social changes and foreign influences will someday transform the persistent communitarian orientation of Japanese society or law remains to be seen.

EMPLOYERS AND WORKERS

Labor relations is one more area in which judges have responded with legal rules to confirm community. Japan's nineteenth-century Civil Code rule for employment contracts is familiar: unless the parties

have specified the duration of the contract, either party may terminate the agreement with two weeks' notice. The German and French
code rules are nearly identical.[34] Even in European socialist law, the
codified rule was essentially the same.[35] The United Kingdom was
exceptional in its early recognition of a presumption that the employment contract was intended in the absence of stated term to
continue for a year. Similarly during the past century, the right of an
employer to terminate unilaterally with notice has been subjected in
legal systems throughout the industrial world by statute, administrative regulation, and judicial decision to a variety of constraints.[36]
Whatever the means or the wording, in most systems except the
United States, employers must today justify termination either in
terms of the conduct of the employee or business needs.[37] In this respect Japan is unexceptional.

In light of the prevailing American rule allowing "at will" termination without notice and European practice, Japan's postwar labor law reforms predictably did not alter the preexisting rule. The
1947 Labor Standards Law continued to allow unilateral termination
with notice—albeit extended from two weeks to thirty days or with
pay—and to permit immediate termination if the enterprise is dis-
continued for unavoidable causes or for "reasons attributable to the
worker."[38] However, like many of their counterparts in both common and civil law jurisdictions, Japanese judges have created what
Daniel Foote aptly describes as an "edifice" of limitations on the
right of the employer to dismiss workers.[39]

A few early decisions construing article 20 of the Labor Standards
Law, as detailed by Foote, followed accepted scholarly views and the
language of the provision allowing employers to terminate workers
without cause with a month's pay.[40] Troubled by the consequences of
the rule, Japanese judges sought ways to restrict the freedom of employers to dismiss employees without justification, first by imposing
a requirement of cause and then by requiring that "cause" be reasonable while defining quite narrowly the parameters of reasonableness.
In many cases the courts could rely on company employment rules,
mandated by law for employers with ten or more employees. In other
instances the courts cited the right-to-work guarantee of article 27 of

the postwar constitution.[41] For a short period Tokyo District Court judges construed article 20 to include an implied requirement of "just cause" based on "the common sense of society" (*shakai tsūnen*). By 1955, however, the courts had settled on the "abuse of right" (*kenri ran'yō*) doctrine as the rationale to restrict unilateral termination with notice or pay. As discussed more fully in the next chapter, the abuse of rights doctrine gives the courts considerable discretion. It enables judges to be faithful to the language of the code or statute and yet achieve desired results. The doctrine, as it has been developed and used by judges, gives them the flexibility to reach what they consider to be a just outcome in a particular case without having to resort to a generally applicable rule. Foote suggests that one of the possible attractions of the abuse of rights approach in the early 1950s was that judges needed a more flexible rule to avoid invalidating dismissals resulting from the Red Purge or employee discharges by Allied Occupation of U.S. forces in Japan. In most cases, he concludes, the results for Japanese employers were nearly the same.[42] Although the statutory right of the employer to dismiss without cause was affirmed, its exercise has been repeatedly denied as an abuse under sufficiently varied circumstances that the effect has been to impose a general rule that effectively restricts unilateral discharge except in cases of employee misconduct that results in at least a reasonable likelihood of concrete harm to the employer.

The Supreme Court formally affirmed the abuse of right approach in two petty bench decisions in the mid-1970s, long after it had become the prevailing lower court rule. The first decision in 1975 involved a company's discharge pursuant to a union shop agreement of a worker who had been expelled by the union.[43] The Court remanded the case to the Tokyo High Court to determine the validity of the union's action, instructing the court to invalidate the company's action as an abuse of right if it found that the union's action was improper. The second case, decided two years later, also applied the abuse of right doctrine in invalidating the dismissal of a radio announcer who had overslept his early morning news broadcast twice in a two-week period, despite recognition that the employee's misconduct had damaged the company's social standing and demonstrated his "lack of responsibility."[44]

Foote goes on to show how the courts have checked attempts by employers to maneuver around these decisions.[45] Judges have imposed a requirement that dismissal during probationary periods have an "objective and rational" basis.[46] They have not permitted companies to discharge temporary workers unless justified by changes in business conditions.[47] They have even extended a reasonable grounds requirement to cancellation of "tentative" offers to new employees.[48]

In terms of both the reasons judges give to justify their decisions and the results they reach, Japanese judgments on unilateral termination have much in common with American and European cases. The decisions manifest the judges' concern for the economic well-being of the individual employee who, without job security, faces a bleak future, particularly in Japan, where nearly all hiring by medium to large firms is limited to young, entry-level workers and managers. In many instances the effect of the Japanese cases like those elsewhere is to redress an imbalance in bargaining leverage between employer and worker. By denying the employer the right to discharge employees, except in the most egregious instances of misconduct, workers can and presumably often do negotiate for a better package of benefits. Otherwise employers would not persuade them to resign or to agree to termination. However, in addition to doctrinal differences, the Japanese cases reflect a more distinctive set of shared values.

The attitude of the worker is an important factor. Employers have not been permitted to discharge employees for bad attitude, poor performance, and even theft in cases where the employee shows remorse, offers to make reparation, accepts the company's authority, and, in the view of the judges, is likely to avoid such behavior in the future.[49] The same factors that judges, procurators, and the police use to evaluate the likelihood of correction and that lead victims of wrongs to pardon are taken into account in denying employers their most extreme sanction—dismissal.

Equally significant, the standards the courts have imposed to prevent unilateral dismissal have not extended to include protection of workers from work-related requirements and personnel decisions. Employers have wide latitude in dismissing workers for failure to accept overtime work, job transfers, and employer-imposed work rules.[50] The Supreme Court has also long allowed employers to make "reasonable" unilateral changes in work rules, which have binding force on all employees regardless of any lack of consent.[51] Thus, in the view of many labor law scholars, the courts have been able to balance the needs of the company for flexibility with the needs of employees for job security.[52]

As in the case of divorce, one consequence of denying employers the right of unilateral termination in Japan as elsewhere is, as noted, to enable the employee to bargain for better terms in order to reach mutual agreement on termination. Unlike the divorce cases, however, the courts at the initiative of the employee can simply award damages, avoiding the problems of any further dealings between the disgruntled employer and disaffected employee. In the United States, for example, employees commonly sue for a monetary award for wrongful discharge based on breach of contract or tort. In Japan, although employees also commonly seek monetary damages, nearly the same number sue for reinstatement, either seeking injunctive relief from the attempted discharge by means of a provisional disposition (*kari shobun*) or judicial confirmation of the continued validity of the employment relationship (*kakunin seikyū*, the civil law equivalent of a declaratory judgment). Between 1991 and 1995, for example, employees filed 3,485 suits seeking confirmation of the employment contract or injunctive relief against employer termination, in contrast to 4,071 suits for wages.[53] In seventeen of the cases cited by Dan Foote, only two involved claims for damages or other monetary awards. In ten the employee-plaintiff sought a provisional disposition to prevent discharge and in five judicial confirmation that the employment relation continued in effect. Although the problems of proof of negligence may make a tort claim for wrongful dismissal problematic, a contract claim would not be subject to similar hurdles and the amount of damages would be the same. Such an argument assumes, of course, that judges faced with tort actions would not ease the rules regarding evidence of negligence, as they have in pollution, drug-related injury, and other toxic tort cases or simply rely on their demonstrated creativity in redefining article 20 of the Labor Standards Law. The likely answer is that workers subject to wrongful discharge seek reemployment followed by voluntary retirement as a condition of settlement rather than monetary awards (other than back pay). Many, it appears, do in fact go back to work. In other words, a significant number of Japanese employees who have been discharged are willing to continue to work for the employer armed with the court order despite, as Foote notes and as explained below, the extensive freedom the employer has to assign workers to difficult or unpleasant tasks.

If one views the firm as a community or—not coincidentally—in familial terms, the choice to return to work makes more sense. The community of workers and managers itself ordinarily provides protections beyond the purview of the state. At least in some companies, the distinction between workers and managers, employers and employees is not distinct except as to office. The dynamics of the Japanese firm as a community restrain managers whose own positions could be put into jeopardy by decisions they make. Where firm loyalty and consensus rule, a significant degree of perceived fairness is inexorably present. Unless considered fair by the vast majority of other employees, arbitrary or retaliatory measures imposed by managers in the upper echelons of the corporate hierarchy are less likely to occur.

Moreover, as in the case of conflicts between the individual obligation to two communities in the context of family law, so too in labor relations, the courts show greater flexibility when the worker is being forced to choose between obligations to the family and to the company. In one of the exceptional departures from the general rule recognizing the right of employers to dismiss workers upon refusal to accept a transfer, a 1968 Tokyo District Court case held that a company had acted unreasonably in transferring an employee who was responsible for the care of an elderly mother, older brother, and younger sister in addition to his spouse and children.[54] As Foote notes, the 1986 Supreme Court decision in *Yoshida v. Toa Paint Co.* is more typical.[55] In that case the employee refused to accept a transfer that would have required him to leave his mother and his wife. The Court found that the inconvenience of transfer was in effect one that the employee could normally be expected to endure.

LANDLORDS AND TENANTS

Sometime presumably near the turn of the century, Ichibei Sano bought a building on land owned by the Reigenji Buddhist temple in metropolitan Tokyo. On June 1, 1903, Sano and the temple entered a ground rent agreement with a three-year term with an additional clause that provided that "whenever use is needed by the landlord even though within the term, the land shall be vacated within six months from the time of notice." Despite the expiration of the three-year term, the temple made no effort to reclaim the land for eight years. However, in September 1911, the temple notified Sano that it was cancelling the land lease. Sano ignored the notice, and six months later the temple sued for vacation. The Tokyo District Court dismissed the action. The reason given was that the clause in question was simply a "model" provision (*reibun*) commonly used in agreements of this kind and was not intended by the parties to have any effect. In the court's words:

> Under the land lease document there is, as [the plaintiff] asserts, an inscription to the effect that [the defendant] is to leave within six months whenever [the plaintiff] is in need of the relevant land. Nevertheless, should a special agreement be made in a case where a person who owns a building on someone else's land rents the site to the effect that at the point the landowner is in need of it the lease is to be extinguished by notice of such and the relevant site is simultaneously to be vacated and the building given up, such lessee will not be able to own the relevant dwelling even for a day in peace. For this reason, only under special circumstances and not in the ordinary situation do the parties have the intention to make such a special agreement. . . . We must find that this was a provision drafted in accordance with a model provision [*reibun*] customarily used at the time [the defendant]

bought the building. Thus the parties did not have the intention to be bound by the prescriptive period in the same. For this reason, we are unable to say that the special agreement above was actually formed. Consequently, we hold the declaration of intention made by [the plaintiff] based on such special agreement is without such effect.[56]

Concern that ground lease tenants would not have "even a day in peace" were agreements enforced to allow landowners to cancel ground leases with six months' notice whenever they needed the land echoed for a decade in the cases that followed. Neither the temple's lawsuit nor the outcome was unusual. Japanese courts consistently rejected landowner efforts to oust tenants from leased land and buildings after the expiration of the lease agreements. Landowners responded with more explicit provisions and even longer fixed terms. But, in case after case, as with the labor contracts, the courts continued to refuse to enforce the contracts according to their explicit terms.

Gaps in statutory law and the consequences of the new Civil Code's property regime were the underlying cause. By the time Sano and the Reigenji temple concluded their deal, Japan had established a new property regime based on continental European law. The Civil Code included three forms of land tenure, defined as property or "real rights" (*bukken*): ownership (*shoyūken*), a right of use for the purpose of owning a building (*chijōken* or superficies), and a right of use for cultivation or grazing (*eikosakuken* or emphyteusis). Except for mortgages (hypothecs) and other security interests, other legal rights related to possession and use of land were recognized simply as leases (*chintaishaku*), which were classified as one form of contract or obligation (*saiken*). The dichotomy between property and contract was significant in that property rights could be enforced against subsequent purchasers, foreclosing creditors, and other third-party claimants. In contrast, contract rights were enforceable only against the consenting parties.

Enactment in 1899 of the Immovable Registration Law ensured greater certainty and security of transactions in land under the code system by providing for nationwide identification of property in land

and a mechanism for determining the validity and priority of rival claims.[57] The registry system thus reduced not only transaction costs but also the risks associated with the creation and transfer of interests in land. However, land registration also provided an effective substitute for the code for both limiting and creating enforceable rights against third parties. Lack of registration in effect transformed the effective rights of the property holder to the equivalent of a contractual claim. Conversely, through registration, contractual arrangements acquired the attributes of property as enforceable claims against third parties.

The new land registration requirements produced immediate tensions. Existing land use arrangements had to satisfy the defined requirements and registration procedures of the code and the new registration law in order to receive legal protection as property rights. The separate statutory provisions for the enforcement of the new code did allow a year's interval for registration from July 16, 1898, the date the code became effective. But the Immovable Registration Law did not become effective until June 16, 1899, leaving only a month for registration. Some tenants were able to have their interests registered personally, but others became embroiled in disputes with their landlords over whether their arrangements constituted a superficies or a lease. Unable to persuade their landlords to agree, some tenants sued for provisional registration. In most of these lawsuits, apparently, the courts rejected the tenant's claim that the ground rent agreement constituted a superficies. In response, in 1900 legislation was introduced in the Diet to provide that arrangements for the use of land owned by another person for the purpose of owning a building or bamboo trees, if registered within a year, would constitute a superficies and be valid even against bona fide third parties. The bill was enacted with minor change as the Law concerning Superficies.[58]

The Superficies Law proved to be insufficient. Many landlords remained unwilling to cooperate. They simply refused to agree to registration, insisting that they had not intended to establish a superficies on their land but merely to enter a contractual lease. Their intransigence as well as tenant concerns were presumably motivated in part by the drastic increases in the cost of land, particularly in urban areas, as a result of successive land tax increases in 1897, 1904, and 1910 and the rising demand for housing and commercial space caused by the economic boom between the Sino-Japanese and Russo-Japanese Wars (1894–1905). Landowners were not able to realize the full market value either by sale or renegotiation of the rent for any land encumbered by a registered superficies. Unless their tenants' rights were registered, landlord-owners were able to sell the land free of any tenancy claims or threaten sale as leverage in bargaining for increases in rent. By 1908 the problem had again become sufficiently serious to provoke additional legislative efforts to protect tenants. The result was the enactment in 1909 of the Law concerning the Protection of Buildings.[59] This statute quite simply provided that, whether or not registered, either a superficies or lease for the purpose of owning a building would have the effect of a property right.

Very little is known about these urban landlords and tenants. They have been largely ignored by those who study Japanese social history. Unwarranted, however, is any assumption that these disputes pitted greedy landlords against weaker or more vulnerable tenants who would lose their livelihood or shelter were the law not to recognize their rights to possess and use land they did not own. These urban tenants should not be confused with their sharecropping counterparts in rural Japan. The success of their legislative proposals in a predominantly landlord Diet suggests that these urban tenants represented politically powerful interests. It seems likely that these disputes reflected the tensions between established landowners and commercial entrepreneurs, especially the owners of small factories, shops, and other establishments that were profiting mightily by the general industrial growth of Japan's cities but were not inclined to share their gains through increased rents with the owners of the land they were using. The political influence of these urban tenants is evident in any event in their legislative success.

The Building Protection Law did not, however, fully resolve the conflict. The issue of termination still loomed. True to nineteenth-century freedom of contract and party autonomy principles, under the Civil Code the duration of ground rent arrangements, whether construed as property or contract, was left to the agreement between the parties. In the case of a superficies, in the absence of mutual agreement, the code authorized judicial determination of duration upon petition by the party concerned but only within the limits of a minimum term of twenty years and maximum term of fifty years. The code provisions on leases were considerably less protective of tenant interests. Article 617 provided for tenancy at will in the event the parties have not fixed the term by mutual agreement. However, prior notice of termination must be given a year beforehand for leases of land, three months beforehand for building leases, and only a day beforehand for conference rooms or movable property. Furthermore, article 604 imposed a maximum term of twenty years on any lease. The lease could be renewed for another term not to exceed twenty years, but each renewal required new agreement, and thus either party could refuse any new agreement. The term limitation was especially advantageous to landlords in that theoretically it gave them the necessary leverage—in inflationary environments—to demand increases in rent.

Within a few years after the enactment of the Building Protection Law, landlords in increasing numbers began to seek judicial relief to evict tenants upon the alleged termination of their leases. In 1919 the number had reached 282, and by 1922 Japan's district courts were adjudicating nearly 500 cases a year for vacation of land. Presumably most cases were brought by landlords against tenants.[60] The Tokyo District Court's decision in the action brought by Reigenji against Sano was typical of the judicial response in the series of reported landowner suits brought against tenants between 1905 and 1933, analyzed by Tadao Hozumi in his 1961 study of judicial interpretation of contracts in Japan.[61]

Hozumi found only twenty-nine reported decisions, but because only a fraction of all cases were reported, particularly lower court decisions, these cases were probably typical of the vast number of other unpublished decisions. As noted, about two hundred to five hundred landowner lawsuits for vacation of land were brought each year between 1912 and 1922. The courts dismissed more than half. Hozumi's findings included two notable increases in the number of actions brought after 1911, which he attributed to the enactment of the Building Protection Law. "Since landlords could no longer petition for the lessee's vacation of land solely on the grounds of a change of the lessor-landowner," Hozumi concluded, "they began to advance the expiration of the term fixed in the contract or an agreement on the right to give notice as grounds [for termination]."[62]

The judicial responses were remarkably consistent. In nearly every instance, the courts refused to enforce the language of the lease, finding in all but seven of the twenty-nine cases that the term as stated constituted boiler plate, merely a "model" provision (*reibun*), not intended by the parties to be effective. As explained by the Tokyo Court of Appeals in a 1909 decision: "Taking into account the opinion of expert witness A, we are able to find that in the City of Tokyo the custom is observed for such inscriptions in land lease instruments not to bind the parties as they are considered model provisions [*reibun*]. Accordingly, we find that the parties here too relied on such custom and that they were not bound by the purport of the stipulation inscribed in the above."[63]

In one line of cases represented by the Tokyo Court of Appeals, the courts held that custom controlled, not the language of the agreement. In other cases, the courts reached a similar conclusion but justified their holding on the grounds of an implied intent that the term of the lease provided in the contract was only included to mark the point in time at which the parties intended to renegotiate the rent, not terminate the lease. In a 1920 case, Japan's highest prewar court, the Great Court of Cassation, even held that such implicit intention overrode the otherwise mandatory maximum term of twenty years prescribed by article 604 of the Civil Code.[64]

Consequently, by 1920 Japan's judiciary had effectively transformed the basic legal rules of both contract and code governing leaseholds. By "interpretation" they imposed a legal regime in which neither the parties' stated intentions nor the provisions of the code prevailed. To enter a lease, particularly a ground rent agreement, thus placed landowners in the unenviable position of almost total loss of control over its duration without the tenant's consent and voluntary surrender of the leased premises. There was no certainty that a leasehold could ever be effectively terminated by the landlord, at least under the aegis of the law.

With the mounting number of landowner lawsuits to force eviction during the period between 1905 and 1920, the number of legislative proposals for the protection of tenants introduced in the Diet also increased. Although several were approved by the lower house, most died in the House of Peers until, finally, in 1921, a Land Lease Law and a House Lease Law were enacted.[65] The two statutes tended to confirm what the courts had held. Leaseholds were now by statute converted in effect into property rights, and landlords could not effectively limit their duration. Without proof of "just cause," a lease was all but automatically renewed.

Prior to 1991, the Land Lease Law had been amended only four times and the House Lease Law only twice. On March 19, 1991, the Kaifu Cabinet introduced a bill in the Diet for a new Land Lease and House Lease Law as a major component of the Japanese government's effort to constrain spiraling land and dwelling costs. Enacted on September 30 that year, the Land Lease and House Lease Law substituted a single statute regulating land and building leases for the Law Concerning the Protection of Buildings, the Land Lease Law, and the House Lease Law.[66] The statute established a new legal framework over all ground rents and residential leasing arrangements. The 1991 statute retains the features of the 1921 statutes except for leases defined as "fixed-term land leases," a category that covers only ground rent agreements with stated terms of at least fifty years that include specific provision denying their renewability and that are established by notarial deed (kōsei shōsho). Otherwise the statute continues to require "just cause" for termination despite expiration of the stated term. The statute also includes provision for mandatory conciliation of disputes involving increases in rent in the case of residential leases.[67]

Judicial treatment of unilateral landlord termination of land and house leases parallels the approaches judges have adopted in dealing with contested divorce and unilateral employee discharge. The courts remain passive. They do not intervene to ensure protection of tenants any more than they do for workers. The terms of the lease and the conduct of the landlord may seem outrageously unfair. Still the courts tend to avoid intervening to impose or to enforce external standards—even those of the community at large—to reform the terms of the contract. To the dismay of many reformist Japanese critics, they respond reluctantly if at all to enforce even those terms explicit in the law. As in the case of contested divorce, the courts simply refuse to allow termination. It is as if the courts were unwilling to provide the instrument for rupturing the relationship even where the parties have arguably bargained for its termination.

Without question for all relationships noted here, the courts have responded in this manner out of concern for the ostensibly weaker side and the hardships that wives, workers, and tenants may face outside of the community of family and firm or the protection of shelter. The outcomes are not, however, examples of particularized justice. No effort is made to determine whether in any of these cases the particular wife or worker or tenant in fact faced such hardship. Only in recent divorce decisions have the courts confronted the consequences in individual cases of a general rule against allowing contested divorce on husbands, their extramarital partners, and children.

RELATIONAL CONTRACTING

Business transactions commonly occur in the context of ongoing, long-term business relationships. Single-spot transactions are the exception, not the rule. In this sense, the vast majority of business transactions everywhere are "relational." Nearly all existing studies of contract practices in both Japan and the United States note the prevalence of relational contracting in both countries.[68] At least a superficial similarity thus appears to pertain in contracting practices on either side of the Pacific. Nevertheless, Japan is usually considered distinctive at least in the pervasive pattern of relational contracting and related practices. The distinction between "repeated dealing" and long-term contractual commitments also often appears to be blurred. In addition, ongoing business arrangements seem to persist despite economic factors that would appear to make them significantly more costly. Finally, relational contracting in Japan is often thought to make legal rules irrelevant.[69] Each of these features relates to a common issue—the extent to which either party is able to terminate the relationship unilaterally as a matter of practice, community expectation, or law.

Some ongoing business relationships take the form of formal, legally binding, long-term contractual commitments. Most, however, are the product of repeated dealing. Negotiated and documented agreements are relatively rare in any society. As a matter of cost, convenience, habit, or security, repeated deals rather than prearranged commitments are the most common form of continuous business relationships. In the United States, for example, the most stable "repeated deals" in business and commerce appear to be between businesses and their insurance agents, accountants, and law firms.[70] The advantages of institutional memory as well as personal relationships explain their persistence. Similar considerations would also apply in Japan. But for Japan the list has to be expanded. Enduring relationships without contractual commitments have characterized all sectors of postwar Japanese commerce and industry.

What distinguishes repeated dealing from long-term contracts is the freedom of either party to stop. However persistent a pattern of repeated deals may be, each party is free to seek a better deal elsewhere. Indeed the purpose of contract in this context is to restrict each party's freedom to withdraw from the relationship. Contractual commitments are unlikely as long as either or both wish to retain the flexibility to end the relationship at will. The legal rules governing contract formation, it should be noted, do allow one-sided constraint in Japan. Lacking the requirement of consideration or the "mutuality" of obligation, it is theoretically possible in Japan (as in other civil law systems) to lock one party into a transaction without obligating the other.[71] Only in instances of extreme and unreciprocated dependency by one side of the transaction, however, would such contracts make much sense. Yet, even under these circumstances, such contracts would generally be unnecessary and rare. One-sided dependency would itself ensure the repetition of deals and reduce the need for a fixed contractual commitment. Indeed, contractual commitments usually occur only when each side perceives that it will gain by binding the other to the relationship. Thus a degree of mutual dependency and benefit is generally a prerequisite for contracted long-term arrangements.

In Japan these distinctions are not so clearly drawn. To be sure, repeated dealing is the norm, but contracts are used and long-term commitments made. Yet, repeated dealing alone seems to create expectations that such relationships will continue. And they do persist. Despite costs and conflicts, long-term business arrangements endure. Japanese businesses appear to be able to avoid termination and to deal with bad bargains in ways that differ from other countries and seem to make legal rules less relevant.

Ronald Dore refers to the "dense web" of long-term relationships that give Japanese markets a "natural immunity" to imports and penetration from overseas sellers, eliminating any need for formal trade barriers.[72] Mark Tilton expands on the theme in a detailed study of how four raw materials industries—aluminum, cement, petrochemicals, and steel—coped with decline.[73] Tilton describes a *system* of long-term business dealing and cartels, operating with the aid of trade associations and the active encouragement and support of government officials, and enforced through refusals to deal. Dore and others also emphasize the bonds of interdependency and mutual trust that bind the parties and allow them to cooperate with mutual flexibility and the capacity to make ongoing adjustments in response to changing market conditions and competitive demands.[74]

The mutual expectation of repeated dealing does have benefits. Neither party may perceive that each is completely free to cease doing business with the other at any time. Both may view the relationship as binding and be willing to provide the other an opportunity to make adjustments. In each instance, they are likely to tolerate the degree of vulnerability that dependence on future dealing produces. Thus they are more apt to devote resources and invest in the relationship. In the absence of binding commitments, the parties themselves can be expected to work to create conditions of mutual dependence. Hostage-taking is one example, but more positive incentives can also be created. Michael Smitka, with the automobile industry as the example, puts it very well:

> Firms strive to make their mutual commitment to the transaction tangible, to provide assurance to each other that they have a vested interest in continuing the relationship. In Japan, the auto assemblers have avoided vertical integration into parts manufacture, and do not maintain production facilities for items such as small metal stampings. Unlike GM in the United States, which often invested in parts production in competition with outside suppliers, Japanese firms made a clear commitment to purchase from someone. . . . In turn suppliers have often specialized in the automotive market and in many cases built dedicated production facilities near their prime customers' plants. Both sides are thus visibly interdependent, with a clear separation of roles. Furthermore, a supplier typically has overlapping contracts for different types of parts with different time horizons. This makes it virtually certain that both sides will be interacting into the foreseeable future. In the short term it is simply impossible for either side to walk away from the other.[75]

Moreover, the expression of willingness to continue to do business in the future implicit in repetition and a pattern of continued dealing can create tacit understandings and expectations. To the extent that these are recognized within the community, the parties can incur moral if not legal obligations either to continue dealing or to justify termination.

Nearly all observers also agree that in Japan business and commercial transactions take place within a system of private ordering in which norms are created and enforced often with little apparent reference to the law and the legal system. Such patterns of extralegal norm-creation and enforcement are not limited to Japan.[76] Studies also show that the parties to ongoing, long-term relationships do avoid both courts and the law, irrespective of their particular business culture.[77] In both Japan and the United States—and presumably everywhere else—businesses tend to deal with grievances through compromise and flexible adjustments. Strict adherence to legal rules and "rights" is as uncommon in the United States as in Japan. More complete empirical data may be necessary to determine in what contexts and to what extent they negotiate conflicts and disputes "within the shadow of the law." Nevertheless, unless the parties consider that termination or rupture of the relationship could result in a lawsuit, lawyers are unlikely to become involved and legal rules are less relevant than business considerations to the resolution of business disputes.

In Japan, as elsewhere, business relationships do break down. The price of continued dealing may become too great or other benefits of doing business may expire. In such cases even weak law can be quite relevant. To the extent that the legal rules allow one party to end the relationship, either side can justify walking away, despite objections from the other, with little concern over becoming entangled in a lawsuit. However, even without strong sanctions enforcing rules that preclude or restrict unilateral termination of ongoing business relationships, resort to the courts has social repercussions. For the courts to hold that the party has violated a legal rule in treating the other unjustly can activate community condemnation and allow the imposition of refusals to deal and other community sanctions. If the unilateral termination of repeated deals and other ongoing commercial relationships is prohibited without the consent of the other party, a negotiated end to the relationship becomes as necessary in business as it is for divorce, employment, and leases.

The courts have not articulated a general rule for ongoing business arrangements. They have instead applied the good-faith doctrine of article 1 of the Civil Code consistently in holding that unilateral termination of a business relationship without notice or any attempt at negotiation, irrespective of the terms of an explicit agreement, can result in liability for expenses incurred in reliance on its continuation.

Among the earliest decisions is a 1942 Great Court of Cassation case in which the Court held that, in response to a buyer's request for a price reduction, the seller could legally terminate an ongoing sales relationship after the parties failed to reach agreement.[78] In 1961 the Tokyo District Court awarded damages to a golf shoe distributor on counterclaim in a lawsuit brought to enforce a promissory note brought by a golf shoe manufacturer who had been selling about 90 percent if its output to the defendant for three years.[79] The defendant also manufactured golf shoes and had been selling them through a separate distributor. When the defendant reduced the prices of its products, the plaintiff was forced to do likewise. The court held that the arrangement could be terminated only when one of the parties has committed an "unfaithful" act that made it difficult for the relationship to continue. Apparently, however, the plaintiff had not given the defendant any notice that it intended to terminate the relationship. Nor did it attempt to settle the matter through negotiation. An Osaka District Court decision the same year held that an exclusive distributorship without a fixed term could be unilaterally terminated in the absence of "special circumstances" that as a matter of fairness would require its continuation.[80] Termination, the court concluded, had to be made in good faith, which meant adequate notice for and negotiations with the other party, in order to minimize any damages. Even in the case of good-faith termination, the court continued, the terminating party would be responsible to compensate for any damages sustained as a result.

A 1971 decision by the Supreme Court reiterated the good-faith requirement for negotiation and duty to compensate for expenditures made in reliance on the continuation of a contract despite its expiration or termination.[81] The case involved a contract to purchase on a continuous basis the entire output of a sulfur mine. The agreement had a term of less than a year but included provision for automatic renewal. Shipments were made and accepted for more than a year. The price of sulfur had fallen below the contract price several months before the first shipment. After the second shipment, as the deterioration of prices continued, the defendant requested that the plaintiff cease any further shipments and refused to accept any more ore. The seller sued for damages for breach of contract. The district court rejected the claim. The Sapporo High Court reversed, holding that the contract had been automatically extended and the original contract price continued to be in effect. The Supreme Court affirmed the decision but emphasized that the good-faith principle obligated the defendant to accept the ore. Both courts also noted that the investment by the seller to have the sulfur mined also imposed an obligation on the buyer.

In these cases the courts did not make clear whether non-contractual arrangements could incur similar liability. Nevertheless, even in the absence of a long-term commitment, repeated dealing may give rise to similar good-faith duties to give notice, to negotiate over termination, and to compensate for reasonable expenses resulting from expectation of continued dealing. More recent cases suggest a more restrictive trend. In a 1987 Sapporo High Court decision in the *Hokkaido Ford Tractor Company case*, for example, the court held that a manufacturer could not terminate without cause an exclusive dealership pursuant to the terms of the contract. The contract provided for a one-year term subject to automatic renewal unless either party gave the other three months prior notice. In response to the manufacturer's notice of intent not to renew the exclusive dealership, the dealer sought a court order prohibiting the manufacturer from selling the product to anyone within the contract territory. The Sapporo District Court upheld the manufacturer's rights under the contract and dismissed the petition. On appeal from the ruling, the Sapporo High Court refused to construe the language of the contract to allow the contract to expire at the end of the stated term. The court considered the clause to be unreasonable in light of the long-term relationship between the parties (more than fifteen years) and the consequent injury the dealer would suffer were the dealership to be terminated.[82]

In a superbly reasoned and researched study of corporate governance and relational contracting, Curtis Milhaupt presents an exhaustive review of Japanese cases and commentary on precontractual obligations by banks to loan applicants. "Prior dealings," he concludes, "heighten the probability that negotiations will give rise to justifiable expectations of contract formation, imposing on both parties the obligation to continue negotiations with due care and in good faith." He goes on to quote from an Osaka District Court case in which the court awarded damages to a bank customer for unjustified delay in carrying out a promissory note discounting agreement: "[Once the parties] have begun negotiating with a view to entering into a contract, and negotiations have progressed to a stage where the parties have begun to place a degree of confidence in each other, . . . a legal relationship which is governed by the principle of good faith and fair dealing . . . is deemed to have come into existence."[83]

The application of the good-faith doctrine does not require a contract, but rather simply that a "legal relationship" between the parties has come into existence. The determinative factor for the courts in finding this legal relationship appears to be the degree of trust that dealings between the parties has created. Extended to repeated deals, this approach suggests that courts at least implicitly stress the degree of dependency that the conduct of the terminating party has fostered as evidenced by the other party's reliance on the continuation of the relationship in the form of investment in the enterprise or opportunities foregone.

Unlike divorce, employment, and leases, however, not all precontractual negotiations or repeated deals should or will be viewed as creating binding obligations to continue without mutually agreed upon withdrawal. The problem faced by Japanese judges is that, by blurring the line between contracts and repeated deals, they may make business relationships too rigid and impair the healthy dynamics of competitive markets. To some extent at least until recently, the dearth of cases mitigated this problem. The general reliance on substitute mechanisms for settling disputes also meant that judges could assume that only the most egregious cases of this sort of "market failure" would result in litigation and that the cases they adjudicate, almost by definition, reflect a serious breach of trust or other hidden conflict. Concern over imposing a rigid rule that would seriously impair business flexibility and economic change also explains the legal rule that has developed in these cases. The courts do not hold that unilateral termination in business dealings must be justified by a strict requirement of reasonable cause. Rather the courts stress notice and negotiation—in other words, time—time to allow the other party to make necessary adjustments and to recoup at least a portion of any losses that may be sustained as a consequence of the termination.

The state—as represented by the judiciary—also intervenes in a remarkably passive way. With few exceptions, these are private law rules. No official or functionary, police or prosecutor, is charged with their enforcement. Rather they require the initiative and will of those affected—those who have "rights" or legal claims—to activate the mechanisms of judicial adjudication available for their enforcement. The autonomy of the parties to determine their relationship and its governing norms remains, but the courts act in ways that, intentionally or not, prevent unilateral expulsion and thereby balance the leverage the dominant players bring to the game. Yet, for the most part, judges have not been willing to intervene in ongoing relationships to help redress similar imbalance to protect weaker members of the community or allow them to assert greater independence or to resist controls.

In conclusion, the legal rules in these cases were significant. Neither the formal mechanism for law enforcement nor legal rules were irrelevant simply because of the relative strength of community controls and the corollary weakness of coercive means of law enforcement. Legal rules establish standards of conduct in a communitarian society. To the extent that the judges themselves retain the public's trust and accurately express the sense of the community, their views carry weight, and the rules they articulate do not require coercion to be effective. In this way judges foster consensus and thus establish the legal parameters of social behavior.

7 The Sense of Society

Unazuki is a hot springs resort located on the Kurobe river at the entrance to one of Japan's most spectacular gorges about ten miles inland from the Toyama Bay on the west coast of Honshu, Japan's main island. Unazuki's thermal water is pumped from the Kuronagi spa about five miles up the river. The first pipeline for the water was built in 1917. Permission to maintain the duct was obtained from the original and subsequent owners of the land it crossed. Sometime in the late 1920s or early 1930s, Yajirō Shinagawa purchased a tract traversed by the duct. He thereupon demanded that the railway company that owned and operated the duct either remove it or purchase the land for double the amount it would cost to build a new pipeline around the tract. The company refused. Shinagawa then sued for a court order to have the duct removed and to forbid entry. Shinagawa had the law on his side. Civil Code principles of ownership required owner consent for such entry. Under article 209 of the code, for example, even neighbors had to obtain permission for temporary entry necessary for construction on their own land. Shinagawa lost. In 1935 on his second appeal, the Great Court of Cassation affirmed lower court decisions in favor of the railway company. "Needless to say," the Court stated, "an owner of land can ask for protection through the judicial process to undo or prevent invasion or threat of invasion to the right of ownership." "But, it is another matter," the Court continued, "where the damage caused by such invasion is negligible and its removal is extremely difficult and would require a tremendous amount of money even if possible."[1] If, in addition, the landowner seeking judicial protection has purchased the land aware of the invasion and seeks to profit from the situation by demanding that the other party either buy the land or remove the obstruction, "refusing to consider any other alternative means of solving the dispute," the Court concluded, "[t]he claim here cannot be considered anything but an abuse of right. If we look at the matter from the perspective of the common sense of society [*shakai kannen*], it is repugnant to the purpose of [the law's protection of] the rights of ownership and goes beyond the scope of the permissible exercise of these rights."

Shakai kannen and similar expressions for "the sense of society" are among the most frequently used phrases in Japanese judicial opinions.[2] In judgment after judgment, Japanese judges invoke the "sense of society" as a controlling source of value and standard for their decisions. Some may dismiss the phrase as an irrelevant appendage or hortatory device. Others may view it as a transparent veil for judicial value judgments. Both may be right. Nevertheless, like the phrase in the Meiji Constitution that judges exercise their authority "in the name of the emperor," these words too may have a significance to those who use them that others may miss. Dan Foote is surely correct. "Ultimately," he concludes, " 'the common sense of society' is what the courts determine it to be."[3] Yet, judges themselves still feel bound by what they themselves discern as the community norm. The postwar constitution mandates that judges shall adjudicate according to their "conscience."[4] This conflation of conscience and community seems best to explain many of conclusions that judges reach.

Previous chapters have described how judges respond to expulsion from community and the rupture of relationships in adjudicating criminal cases, family relationships, employment, landlord tenant contracts, and ongoing business transactions. As illustrated by the *Unazuki Hot Springs* case, this chapter examines the complex variety of community values and norms that appear to motivate judges in adjudicating cases in which legislated legal rules logically lead to unwanted conclusions. By resort to two general principles of civil law—the prohibition against any "abuse of rights" and the mandate of "good faith"—both initially introduced by judicial decision but now codified, Japan's judges have been able to establish standards of conduct for both individual and collective actors that affirm their perception of community values in the face of contradictory legal rules.

As detailed below, the abuse of rights and good faith principles has spawned decisions that the courts have by consistent and repeated holdings developed into relatively predictable rules and doctrines. Nevertheless, both principles continue to function akin to captured pieces in a game of Japanese chess (*shōgi*). Either principle can be dropped into the game and come into play at any time. In effect both represent an appeal to communitarian equity over law.

ABUSE OF RIGHTS

The abuse of rights doctrine was informally introduced into Japanese law during the process of drafting Japan's first Civil Code. The code project, which began in the mid-1870s with translation of the French Code Civil, was undertaken with the assistance of the French jurist Emile Gustav Boissonaide (1829–1910). Finally completed and enacted in 1890, although never enforced, Japan's first Civil Code reflected its French origins. Boissonaide's commentary drew heavily on French legal theory, including the still-developing limitations on the exercise of conceptually absolute property rights. Echoing mid-nineteenth-century French legal doctrine, Boissonaide presented ownership as a natural law but not an absolute right. The exercise of ownership and other property rights was circumscribed by equally paramount moral standards, the rights of others, and the general welfare. Any exercise beyond these boundaries would be an abuse.[5]

The new Civil Code of 1896 (Books I, II, and III) and 1898 (Books IV and V) did not include any mention of "abuse of rights." No express limitation on the exercise of legal rights was included other than the requirement of article 90 invalidating contracts and other "juristic acts" (*hōritsu kōi*) contrary to "public policy and good morals" (*kōjō ryōzoku*). Japan's first generation of civil law scholars continued, however, to draw on French law and to refer to limitations on the exercise of property and other rights. Ei'ichi Makino is credited with the first systematic study of the doctrine as developed by French scholarship. As explained by Michio Aoyama, Makino argued that the abuse of rights doctrine developed in Europe to prevent the use of legal rights as an instrument of oppression by the strong against the weak.[6]

For Makino, writing in 1905, the doctrine reflected changing attitudes within Europe toward libertarian values as countervailing concerns for collective social needs and community had begun to take
hold. He viewed the trend as a reflection of the "socialization"
(shakaika) of law.[7] Makino thus subtly reformulated the French debate, emphasizing in the process limitations in the interests of the
community over the protection of the individual and individual rights
on which the codes were premised. The French concern with the motivating malevolence of individual actions and more abstract moral or
social restrictions on individual autonomy represents a similar but
still quite separate equation.

Early Japanese cases affirmed the nineteenth-century liberal premises of the code. Ownership was deemed an absolute right. In *Kiyono
v. Takuchi*, for example, the Great Court of Cassation allowed the
owner of land to restrict the flow of thermal water being used for a hot
springs spa.[8] Without explicit statutory or regulatory provision or a
recognized customary rule to the contrary, the Court reasoned, a landowner has the right to excavate the land and use whatever water he
found regardless of the effect on neighbors. The Court did recognize
some limits, however, in cases involving the traditional riparian rights
of downstream owners.[9]

The courts retreated from this stance in subsequent decisions. As
in the *Unazuki Hot Springs* case, property owners had to take into account community interests. Landowners and other holders of property would not receive judicial protection in exercising their rights in
ways that caused significant community harm. In 1917, for example,
the Great Court of Cassation reversed a Tokyo Court of Appeals
(kōsoin) judgment absolving a landowner from liability to his ground
tenant's mortgagee for wilful destruction of the mortgaged house.
The landowner had the structure demolished after the tenant failed
to remove it pursuant to a court judgment. In the words of the Court,
the landowner had "overstepped" the limits of his rights and violated
the rights of others.[10] As detailed previously, the notion was also used
extensively to protect tenants from termination of their leases.

The courts did not restrict the doctrine to property rights. The earliest cases also included decisions denying an absolutist construction

of the powers of the head of the family "house" or *ie*. As in the case of ownership, the first lawsuits challenging the authority of the head of the household under the code, as noted, generally recognized its absolute nature. It was not difficult, however, for the courts to hold that the right to expel family members or to withhold consent to their choice of residence or even to reject their choice for a marital partner could be abusive and thereby craft a constraint that precluded its arbitrary exercise.

In 1919 the Great Court of Cassation further extended the doctrine to establish a basis for an action for damages in tort.[11] The case—and its popular title, the "Hat Rack Pine case"—concerned an ancient pine, locally venerated because of its legendary use by a sixteenth-century warlord. The tree died as a result of damage caused by the emissions of smoke from the steam engines of a state-owned railway. Citing precedents that recognized that the intentional or negligent exercise of legal rights beyond legally recognized limits would constitute a delict (tort), the Court proceeded to articulate a standard for setting the bounds: "Among persons living as a community in any society, though the acts of one person may extend some detriment to another, such acts do not always constitute an infringement of rights. The other person must tolerate some such infringement as an unavoidable aspect of community life. However, when these acts overstep the limits of what is generally recognized in our society as what the injured party should tolerate, it is properly held that such exercises of rights are delicts."[12] The Court went on to say that those living along a railroad line must tolerate some injury because of the need of the community for transportation. Yet, it found that, had proper precautions been taken, the particular injury in the case could have been avoided. Thus, the railway had overstepped the limits of "what our society considers tolerable." The Court thus held the state as owner of the railway liable for the injury to the "hat rack pine."

Had the operators of the railway taken reasonable precautions to prevent harm, the community interest would have presumably prevailed. In an equally well-known decision in 1916, the Court quashed the decisions of the Osaka District Court and Court of Appeals, both of which had held the Osaka Alkali Company liable in tort under the abuse of rights theory for the damage to farmers caused by sulfur emissions whether or not the company had been aware of the potential for injury.[13] The lower court decisions in this case are today commonly regarded as precursors to the application of abuse of rights in postwar pollution cases. As Sono and Fujioka point out, Japanese judges have defined permissible conduct—whether as an exercise of rights or a matter of tortious conduct—in terms of what the community can reasonably be expected to tolerate or endure.[14] Although judges make this determination in each case, they do so as interpreters of community values.

Few Japanese abuse of rights cases are exceptional with respect to either the application of the doctrine or their outcomes. Surveys of European and even American cases reveal factual counterparts to nearly all of the Japanese decisions.[15] The Belgian judges of Ghent who decided in 1950 that the village of Courtrai should not be compelled to renovate the land they had misappropriated to build public roads would have had little difficulty, for example, in deciding the *Unazuki Hot Springs* case.[16] Nor would the judges of the Court of Lyon, who held that a landowner of Saint Galmier had abused his right of ownership by pumping so much of the fabled mineral waters from his well that his neighbor could no longer obtain sufficient volume from his own, have balked at the Great Court of Cassation's 1938 decision in *Samejima v. Honda*.[17]

In that case, the plaintiff, Kiku Honda, owned a restaurant famous for its garden, which featured a pond filled daily from wells. When a neighbor dug his own wells for a pond of his own and, despite Ms. Honda's warning pleas, deepened them, Ms. Honda's wells went dry. The garden misfigured, her restaurant went out of business. Affirming a judgment in favor of Ms. Honda, the Court held that the right of the landowner to use subterranean water is limited by the rights of others. "If his exercise of his right exceeds the extent permissible in light of the common understanding of society [*shakai kannen*], his conduct is to be considered tortious, being an abuse of right."[18]

The adaptation of the "abuse of rights" doctrine by Japanese judges illustrates prevailing patterns of Japanese judicial development. First, a European legal doctrine was introduced into the Japanese legal structure by Japanese scholars. It was then recognized and applied by judges in cases where the application of existing legal rules would, to the judges, have resulted in a decision contrary to the judges' perceptions of justice as defined by their "sense of society." The introduction and application of the good faith doctrine followed similar lines. Indeed, the conformity of the Japanese decisions to prevailing European cases and doctrinal developments is striking. As in the employment discharge cases, Japanese judges have responded during the course of the century in like manner to their European and American counterparts in accommodating nineteenth-century legal rules to the social problems of an industrial society. They have dealt with similar demands in similar ways. Only the odd case here and there and the ubiquitous invocation of the "sense of the community" appear on the surface to distinguish the Japanese approach.

GOOD FAITH

The first judicial affirmation that an exercise of private law rights is subject to an overriding principle of "good faith and fidelity" is said to have occurred in a judicial decision in 1920.[19] The case involved a commonly used arrangement to secure a loan. Instead of creating a formal hypothec (mortgage), the borrower would simply sell land to the creditor subject to a repurchase agreement. The creditor would then register as the new owner with a repurchase agreement registered as a contingent interest in the property with priority over subsequent purchasers and creditors. Apparently such an arrangement was intended when Otokichi Mukaiyama sold a tract of land to Masajirō Yoshikawa subject to a repurchase agreement under which Mukaiyama would reacquire ownership upon payment of 517 yen plus the registration tax of twelve yen eight sen, for a total amount of 529 yen eight sen. Accordingly, Mukaiyama tendered 518 yen prior to the due date. Yoshikawa refused, however, to reconvey the land. Thereupon Mukaiyama sued. He lost in the Nara District Court as well as the Osaka Court of Appeals. On the *jōkoku* appeal, however, the Great Court of Cassation decided in his favor. The repurchase contract became effective, the Court held, despite the minor discrepancy between the contract price and the amount tendered. "The principle of good faith," the Court declared, "governs contractual relationships."[20]

The earliest scholarly discussion of the good faith doctrine by a Japanese scholar appears to be by Otoshirō Ishizaka (1877–1917), who devoted several pages to the principle in his treatise on Japanese civil law.[21] Ishizaka's influence appears to have been rather limited. Joseph E. de Becker's unparalleled works in English on the Japanese Civil Code of the early 1920s do not contain any references to either the good faith or abuse of rights principles.[22] Nor apparently do other Japanese treatises before the mid-1920s.[23] Ei'ichi Makino was again a commanding influence. In his essay on the relevance of laws published in 1922 and reprinted in 1925 in a book of collected writings under the same title, Makino pointed to a number of decisions in which the courts, he argued, were at least implicitly enforcing a requirement of good faith in the exercise of contract and other rights.[24] The first comprehensive treatment of the good faith principle by a Japanese scholar, however, was the five-part series of essays published in 1924 on the "Good Faith Principle in the Law of Obligations" by Hideo Hatoyama (1884–1946), published in 1924. Hatoyama cites Makino's contemporaneous work, but Hatoyama himself deserves full credit for the first detailed study of the good faith principle in Japanese.[25]

As Makino had observed, the courts were already deciding cases in ways that could be understood as imposing a good faith requirement. In effect Hatoyama and subsequent scholars, drawing heavily from German law, provided a rationale that not only explained but also justified the decisions judges would continue to hand down. The scholars incorporated the principle into the main body of Japanese jurisprudence and thereby in effect fully legitimated what the courts had been doing. Later, under the continued influence of German law, both scholars and the courts extended the application of the good faith principle beyond the law of contracts and other obligations, transforming it into a governing principle of Japanese private law.

CONSISTENCY WITHOUT COHERENCE

In 1947 both the abuse of rights and good faith principles were added as express provisions of the Civil Code.[26] Article 1 of the code as amended now reads:

1. All private rights must conform to the public welfare.
2. Rights shall be exercised and duties shall be performed in accordance with the principles of good faith and fidelity.
3. No abuse of rights shall be permitted.

During the half century since the amendment, however, the courts have not developed either principle into a doctrinally coherent theory. Instead, the two continue to play a remedial role as discretionary devices that allow judges to avoid the logic of the otherwise applicable legal rules. By the early 1950s, some patterns could be discerned. The principles were most often used in disputes involving leases, usually arising out of landlord efforts to oust their tenants. The abuse of rights principle was identified as a limitation on property rights, while the good faith mandate remained more closely associated with contracts. As in the case of *Mukaiyama v. Yoshikawa*, the good faith principle was applied frequently in disputes over tender and performance as well as collateral contract duties. Nevertheless, no clear line of demarcation separated the two principles. They could be applied almost interchangeably in many cases. The good faith principle has been used generally, however, to define rights and duties. In cases in which the good faith principle would preclude the exercise of a right, any attempt to enforce it will be deemed abusive. Whatever the context, violations of either principle give rise to claims for damages.

There is no dearth of cases. Uchida estimates that the courts have applied the good faith principle in more than five hundred contract cases since 1947.[27] In a detailed review of all published Supreme Court decisions between 1971 and 1984 in which either the abuse of rights or good faith or both principles were raised, Summary Court Judge Toshio Ogamino notes that, in addition to the forty-nine separate Supreme Court cases reviewed, during the same period the principles were also raised in at least 196 high court and 338 district, family, or summary court cases.[28] Except in the most frequently litigated disputes, as in labor relations and leases, in which the courts have repeatedly applied the principles in similar contexts, any meaningful generalization is elusive. For example, of the forty-nine Supreme Court decisions, three involved claims brought by state employees—especially members of the self-defense forces—against the state for failing to take adequate safety precautions;[29] two involved the right to set off (sōsai) a claim against a debt;[30] one, as a defense against extinctive prescription (statute of limitations);[31] eleven, leases;[32] two, sales agreements;[33] one, to effect a change of registration to conform to actual parentage of child in dispute over succession;[34] one, to challenge an employee dismissal;[35] five involved repossession of automobiles;[36] five, corporate management disputes;[37] five, promissory note enforcement;[38] six, litigation-related issues;[39] one, to establish the right to any excess over public auction proceeds under a secured transaction created by registration;[40] and in six, one or both principles were raised in miscellaneous disputes, including the landmark case recognizing a "right" to sunlight and another requiring good faith negotiation.[41] In two-thirds of the cases, the court accepted the argument and applied one or both principles.

Nearly all of these cases reflect a much larger volume of both Supreme Court and lower court decisions in each area. In 1966, for example, in Satō v. Fukui, in an en banc decision, the Supreme Court held that the good faith principle barred debtors from raising the defense of prescriptive extinction in an action to enforce a debt where they had acknowledged the debt unaware that the period had lapsed.[42] Such knowing acknowledgment of a debt would have otherwise revived the debt. Since 1966 the courts have disallowed the defense in an increasing variety of contexts.[43] In 1970 in a case involving the rights of a debtor under a land repurchase agreement to repurchase land sold to secure a loan reminiscent of the 1920 decision in Mukai-yama v. Yoshikawa, the Third Petty Bench of the Court held that, having repeatedly refused partial payments that together amounted to more than the total owed, a secured creditor could not in good faith claim that the repurchase right had been extinguished despite the lapse of the statutory period.[44] A few of the cases involve misconduct by the party asserting the defense, such as the defendant in a damage action resulting from the collision of two trucks, who had made a false statement to the police as a result of which the plaintiff had been prosecuted for criminal negligence.[45] The majority, however, involved breaches of trust in the context of ongoing relationships. Examples include the employer who had misled an injured employee to believe that he would be able to continue with the company once he had completed a rehabilitation program, an elder son who had delayed for more than twenty years transferring registration of ownership of farmland to his mother as required pursuant to a conciliation agreement, as well as the trusted bank customer who deceived the bank into believing that he was the true holder of an innominate (mukimei) deposit account.[46] Like the expulsion cases described previously, the courts in these cases disallowed the use of legal rules to evade both legal and moral duties arising from relationships of trust and ongoing relationships.

Once the Supreme Court has recognized the application of either principle in a specific category of cases or well-defined context, repeated and consistent application in similar cases has enabled the courts to produce an identifiable corpus of legal rules. The previously described development of the "abusive discharge" doctrine is among the best-known examples. Others include the "right to sunlight" and related "rights" to a healthy environment, and, most recently, a precontractual duty to negotiate in good faith. In these cases, significant community, as well as individual, interests are at stake. Accordingly the courts view of the "sense of society" rather easily leads to the application of legal doctrine at variance with the individual rights of the code. Where community interests can be argued to require greater certainty or consistency, the courts have been less willing to depart from the established roles. This tendency is illustrative of the development of the concept of impossibility of performance (rikō funō) and the "changed circumstances doctrine" (jijō henkō).

ENVIRONMENTAL RIGHTS

Mitamura and Suzuki were neighbors. Both had purchased homes in a wealthy suburban Tokyo district in the late 1950s. A few years later

Suzuki built a second story. He did not obtain the required permit, and the new addition violated the required building standards. It also obstructed Mitamura's sunlight and ventilation. Mitamura sold his house and sued for damages. The Tokyo District Court held that the violations of the Building Standards Law did not themselves give rise to a claim for damages as a delict (tort).[47] Nor had, the court found, Mitamura's house declined in value as a result of Suzuki's construction. Mitamura won on appeal, however, as the Tokyo High Court found that the illegal additions evidenced Suzuki's bad faith and that Mitamura's sunlight and ventilation had indeed been impaired. Suzuki appealed to the Supreme Court. The Court affirmed the high court's judgment, holding that "in instances where sunlight and ventilation are impaired by the acts of a party that constitute an abuse of rights, it is proper to recognize a claim for damages in delict."[48]

The Supreme Court's recognition of a claim for damages for obstruction of sunlight as a result of new construction in *Mitamura v. Suzuki* had immediate consequences. Although the court did not define with any precision what the limits of this new "right to sunlight" might be, the possibility of a claim reinforced the bargaining leverage of residents in urban neighborhoods negotiating for compensation from developers as well as local governments in negotiating over construction permits.[49] In effect, as noted by Sono and Fujioka, this case, combined with its prewar antecedents and subsequent decisions filled a missing gap in Japanese tort law by creating a law of nuisance.[50]

PRECONTRACTUAL DUTIES

Since the mid 1960s Japanese courts have in an increasing number of cases imposed liability for damages for failure to continue to negotiate in good faith.[51] As described by Tohoku University Professor Shōji Kawakami, the good faith principle has provided the foundation for liability in cases of failure to satisfy requirements or to provide information essential for the performance of contractual obligations as well as to negotiate to conclusion.[52] Kawakami lists nearly twenty-seven cases, including two Supreme Court decisions, as of 1988.[53] By 1993 the number had grown to more than thirty cases.[54] It is worth noting that the Supreme Court decisions did not initiate this development but represented its culmination. Only after two decades of lower court decisions did Japan's highest court finally in the mid-1980s affirm the application and establish basic parameters for the good faith principle in the context of precontractual negotiations.

Two dominant patterns emerge. First, the courts appear to be quite consistent in the application of both principles. For example, despite a variety of circumstances, all attempts by landlords to cancel leases and evict tenants were held to be in violation of good faith or abusive or both. A similar degree of protection against repossession of automobiles may be emerging. Only two cases involved long-term commercial relationships—one a suretyship—but the principles were applied in both. A second pattern in these and other cases has been to deny resort to legal mechanisms of enforcement to the party with the ostensibly stronger bargaining position. The parties to these transactions are thereby induced either to resort to extralegal means to enforce their claims or, where such extralegal leverage is not available, to reach negotiated compromises.[55]

CHANGED CIRCUMSTANCES

Supervening events will relieve a party from the duty to perform a contractual commitment under two doctrines of Japanese civil law: impossibility of performance (*rikō funō*) as a result of circumstances that are not attributable to the fault of the obligor and the principle of changed circumstances. Both reflect the courts' "sense of society."

Impossibility of performance of a contractual obligation exculpates breaches of contract unless such impossibility arises out of circumstances that are attributable to the fault of the party required to perform. This conclusion results from a generally accepted construction of article 415 of the Japanese Civil Code, which provides: "If an obligor fails to effect performance in accordance with the tenor and purport of the obligation, the obligee may demand compensation for damages; the same shall apply where performance becomes impossible as a result of a cause attributable to the fault of the obligor." The risk of loss provisions for sales under the Civil Code are to similar effect. Article 536 provides:

(i) Except in the cases referred to in the preceding two articles, if the performance of an obligation becomes impossible for any cause not attributable to the fault of either party, the obligor shall not have a right to receive counter-performance.

(ii) If performance becomes impossible for any cause attributable to the fault of the obligee, the obligor shall not lose his right to demand counter-performance; however, if he has received any benefit through being relieved of his own obligation, he shall return such benefit to the obligee.

Article 415, it should be noted, is construed in light of other provisions of the Civil Code and a significant dose of German law theory to pivot both an obligor's discharge and liability for breach on the idea of impossibility. That is, in cases where it is determined that performance of an obligation is impossible, discharge occurs if the cause is not attributable to the fault of the obligor. On the other hand, liability for damages arises if the cause is attributable to the obligor's fault. However, until performance, including court-ordered specific performance, becomes impossible (or the obligee rescinds the contract, for instance, under articles 540–48 of the Civil Code), the obligee has only the right to demand specific performance and delay damages. Thus only one of two functions of "impossibility of performance" is to discharge an obligor. The requirements for such discharging impossibility are (1) that the performance is "impossible" and (2) that this impossibility results from a cause not attributable to the fault of the party seeking discharge.

A rather elastic standard is said to apply in all contexts, but Japanese courts tend in practice to construe the requirements at least for discharging impossibility quite stringently.

The applicable standard for determining impossibility is "the commercial sense of society" (*shakai no torihiki gainen*).[56] A 1917 decision by the Great Court of Cassation in *Ota v. Koji* reflects what was in effect an overruling of an earlier decision in which absolute physical impossibility, not merely hardship, was held to be required.[57]

In a number of cases immediately prior to World War II the extreme hardship, although not the absolute impossibility, of locating vessels for shipment of scrap iron was similarly held to constitute discharging impossibility under the "commercial sense of contemporary society."[58] Although there is little in the way of detailed analysis of the facts in any of these cases, it appears that performance was precluded by more than commercial impracticality. In each case the discharged party was, apparently after some effort, unable to procure the required ships or supplies. Furthermore, there is no indication in any of these cases that the courts equated economic hardship or loss with "extreme hardship." In fact, it is possible that the ships and scrap iron could not have been obtained at any price at that time.

There is, nevertheless, at least one early lower court decision in which impossibility was determined by an express balancing of economic gain and loss. In this case—*Hasegawa v. Hakodate Senkyō K.K.*—a shipowner successfully claimed damages against a salvage company for failure to perform a salvage contract.[59] While being towed by the defendant company, the vessel sank again as a result of high seas. The court found that it was "impossible" to salvage the ship pursuant to the contract because any benefit to be gained by the shipowner was outweighed by the costs involved in a second attempt to refloat the ship. The *Hasegawa* case, however, did not involve discharging impossibility. A finding of impossibility was necessary in that case to support the shipowner's claim for damages.

An early postwar lower court decision in *Fujisawa v. Nakamura* suggests commercial impracticability or economic loss could constitute discharging impossibility.[60] But in this case too the facts cluster closer to the absolute end of the impossibility continuum. The dispute arose during the closing months and presumable chaos of the Japanese occupation of Korea. The case involved a contract made in Korea in 1944 under which the defendant Nakamura was to manufacture and supply fishing net dyes to the plaintiff Fujisawa on a continuing basis and a claim by Fujisawa for return of the deposit with damages. Both parties were Japanese and had returned to Japan following the war. The court held as follows:

> Where the amount of the goods and term of the sale in a sales contract for the continuing supply of goods between merchants are not decided upon beforehand, and where, because of circumstances that could not have been foreseen beforehand by either side at the time of the conclusion of the contract, delivery of the contract goods has become difficult and, as for the buyer as well, accepting delivery of the goods by paying transportation costs has become impossible in terms of profitability within the scope of price controls, we recognize that in the absence of special circumstances to the contrary that to perform the obligations both sides bear in accordance with the tenor of the contract has become actually and economically impossible for reasons that cannot be attributable to the fault of either the seller or the buyer.

Apparently the seller was not able to obtain transportation for the dyes as a result of a freight-car shortage and informed the buyer that he could not make delivery unless the buyer provided an alternative means. The buyer did not respond.

The basic standard for negligence determines whether impossibility is attributable to the fault of the obligor—that is, whether the party claiming exculpation has exercised the care required of a person in his position to avoid impossibility.[61] The burden of proof ordinarily is on the party claiming discharge.

Discharging impossibility is sometimes treated as identical to the concept of force majeure (*fuka kōryoku*).[62] The term *force majeure* is specifically used in several separate provisions of the Japanese Civil and Commercial Codes.[63] *Force majeure* can be understood as a more limited concept encompassed by the notion of "impossibility for a cause that is not attributable to the fault of the obligor." Common to both concepts, however, is the notion that a party is not discharged by impossibility caused by an external supervening event if the event could be foreseen and its consequences could have been avoided by taking proper precautions. What measures must be taken will depend in turn on the standard of care required by the party in the circumstances of the case.

In the *Hasegawa* case the court found that the bad weather conditions were foreseeable and the loss of the salvaged ship could have been prevented if proper care had been taken. It held that high seas and weather conditions did not constitute *force majeure* that would excuse nonperformance by the salvage company. In contrast, in *Vacuum Oil Co. v. Dampfsschiffsrederei Union A.G.*, where a carrier was sued for loss of oil during transport, the court held that the loss was the consequence of bad weather and high seas and could not have been prevented by the exercise of care required of a party in those circumstances.[64] In short, the weather conditions could constitute discharging *force majeure*. The court did not address the issue of whether they were foreseeable.

Should the event causing impossibility occur while a party is in delay, the ultimate impossibility of performance can almost always be attributable to the fault of the party responsible for delay to the effect that he is not excused from nonperformance (breach). For instance, in *Watanabe v. Mizumi*, the Tobacco Monopoly Sales Law, which made private trading in tobacco illegal, was enacted during the defendant's delay in making delivery under a private sale of tobacco.[65] So finding, the court held that performance was impossible for reasons attributable to the fault of the seller and awarded damages under Article 415.

The authors of two excellent studies in English conclude that existing precedents indicate that Japanese courts are relatively *liberal* in allowing discharge and that the Japanese rules are roughly equivalent with the idea of impracticability because of the extreme and unreasonable difficulty, expense, injury, or loss involved under American law.[66] The language and standards used by Japanese courts to some degree bear out this conclusion. Nevertheless, Japanese courts, at least at the level of the Supreme Court, have yet to reach a decision that warrants the label "liberal exculpation" in terms of the factual pattern and situation in the reported cases.

Underlying Japanese courts' restricted application of the Civil Code provisions on discharging impossibility is an implicit emphasis

on the *pacta sunt servanda* principle. Such strict enforcement of contractual duties in turn has led to the development of the doctrine of
changed circumstances. Japanese scholars, primarily Masaakira Katsumoto (1895–1993), favorably impressed by the use of the *Geschäfts
grundlage* theory in Germany and *imprécision* in French law during
the economic chaos that followed World War I, introduced the doctrine of changed circumstances in the mid-1920s. In 1926 Katsumoto
published a one-thousand-page treatise on the changed circumstances
doctrine in civil law. The work constituted a monumental survey of
the doctrine as it had evolved in western law from the time of Ham-
murabi's Code into the medieval maxim *clausula rebus sic stanibus*.
For Katsumoto, and subsequently the courts, the doctrine was
grounded in the good faith principle as a device by which old legal
rules could be reformulated to solve new problems.[67] The doctrine
was not fully acknowledged by Japan's highest court until 1944 in
Okunokōji v. Ichida.[68] The parties in that case had concluded a contract in 1939 for the sale of land on which the plaintiff intended to
build a factory. After the plaintiff had made the down payment but
prior to the subsequently extended date for final payment, July 31,
1941, price control regulations had been enacted that made official
approval of the purchase price mandatory. Although the defendant
made proper application on July 9, 1941, no decision had been reached
by the date for payment, and registration of ownership was not transferred. The plaintiff thereupon notified the defendant of his intention to rescind the contract on August 1, 1941, and to claim return of
the down payment. The court held that under such circumstances the
buyer might be entitled to rescind, for it would be contrary to the
principle of good faith to require the parties to be bound by the contract for so long a period of uncertainty. Thus the court quashed the
judgment and remanded the case to the court below, ordering it to determine whether official approval would have been expected at the
time of the notification of rescission.

  In prior cases, the Court had held that the rule of *pacta sunt servanda* precluded excuse from performance even in cases of drastic
economic change. In a 1920 case, for example, the Great Court of
Cassation reversed a Tokyo Court of Appeals decision rejecting a suit

to enforce a repurchase agreement for a price that was, because of inflation, twenty times less than the actual value of the property.[69]

These prewar beginnings were affirmed early in the postwar period. *Hirai v. Shibata*, for instance, involved a contract concluded in 1945 for the sale of a house and building.[70] Hirai, the seller, refused to transfer registration on the day for performance, and Shibata brought the action to endorse for registration of ownership in his name. Hirai pleaded rescission on the basis of changed circumstances as a result of inflation that had trebled the value of the property. The Supreme Court held for Shibata. As in the case of impossibility of performance resulting from *force majeure*, the court stated the change of circumstances doctrine does not relieve a party of his duty to perform where the changes occur while the party is in delay of performance.

Similarly in *Suzuki v. Kawanoe*, the Supreme Court held that the doctrine did not apply to foreseeable changes in circumstances.[71] In that case, the appellee's predecessor in title had agreed in 1944 to sell a house to the appellant. Before the change in ownership was registered, the seller's own home was destroyed in an air raid. The seller argued that under the changed circumstances doctrine he had the right to rescind the original contract because the sale had been made on the assumption that the second house was not needed and the sale would not have been concluded if it had been known that the seller's own home would be destroyed. The Supreme Court, however, reversed a Nagoya High Court decision recognizing the defendant's argument and denied application of the changed circumstances doctrine holding that the destruction of the house (located in Fukui, an industrial city of moderate size) by fire during a wartime air raid was foreseeable at the time the contract was entered.

A series of cases in the early 1950s culminated in a 1954 decision in *Iguchi v. Ikegami*.[72] The case involved the enforcement of an agreement to terminate a lease and vacate a house located in Osaka concluded in the fall of 1943. The lessee did not vacate as promised and, after some delay, the lessor brought an action for eviction. The lessee defended on the grounds that the severe housing shortage in Osaka that occurred after the conclusion of the agreement, caused by air raids and a postwar increase in population, constituted a change in circumstances that permitted the lessee to rescind his agreement to vacate. The Supreme Court rejected this argument, refused to apply the doctrine, and ordered the eviction on the grounds the circumstances did not reveal a requisite "conspicuous unfairness" in enforcing the contract. The plaintiff had failed to satisfy each of the criteria the majority set out in the case:

1. A substantial change of circumstances must have occurred after the contract was formed.
2. The changes must have been unforeseeable.
3. The changes have occurred by events for which neither party is responsible.
4. Demand for performance under the term of the contract must be "conspicuously" unfair.[73]

Although the doctrine of changed circumstances has continued to be recognized ostensibly as applicable law in Japan, in these and subsequent cases *Okunokōji v. Ichida* remains the sole reported decision by the highest Japanese court in which relief under the doctrine has been afforded. *Taiyō Tochi K.K. v. Okoda* is typical.[74] This case involved a lot requisitioned during the Occupation for a parking lot next to a hotel in downtown Tokyo used by U.S. military forces. Prior to the requisition, the land was subject to a lease between Okoda and the Taiyo Company. Okoda brought the suit in 1954 for judicial affirmation of the validity of the lease. Taiyo argued that, given the uncertainty of the parties' legal relations, the lease should be terminated on the grounds of impossibility of performance and changed circumstances. The court held the lease to be valid. It reasoned that, although performance was temporarily impossible for reasons that could not be attributable to either party and since neither was greatly inconvenienced, the good faith principle did not require termination of their legal relations.

The Japanese Supreme Court also seems to have consistently refused to relieve contract parties from losses due to inflation even where the value of the contract has been reduced to almost nothing.[75] In a case in which payment for the sale of mining rights concluded in 1936 did not become due until 1952, the court denied that any existing law enabled automatic adjustment in the amount of contract price. Lower court decisions under similar circumstances have required price adjustments or have allowed rescission.[76]

The themes articulated by Makino echo throughout the Japanese decisions. Japanese judges are less concerned with the moral behavior of the parties than with the harms their actions inflict on the community and its members. They seldom if ever respond as guardians of universal standards of conduct but rather as interpreters of the community's conscience and sense of fairness. They note the inability of the parties to negotiate settlements between them and see the resort to the judicial process as a failure of both personal and community mechanisms for maintaining relationships. The wrongs they perceive to have been committed are harms to the family, the neighborhood, fellow workers—the immediate communities—rather than the society at large or the state. The wrongfulness of the behavior is less an infraction of any abstract standard of fair play or honest dealing than the selfish pursuit of individual interests at the expense of others or a misuse of authority and the law against those in a position of subordination to whom benevolence is owed. Nevertheless, the obligations of business contracts and other consensual relationships are not easily avoided. The courts do not readily accept excuses. The courts implicitly agree that certainty and consistency are community values. Particularized justice is not an overriding concern. However subtle, the communitarian bias of Japanese judges' "sense of society" provides the Japanese decisions their distinctive cast.

8 Between the Individual and the State

Japan's postwar constitution was intended by its makers to allocate governmental powers to ensure political accountability to the electorate. Equally important were the individual rights against the state guaranteed to the Japanese people. Although the Meiji constitution had also included a long list of rights guaranteed the emperor's subjects, none were absolute. All were subject to legislative—but not administrative—curtailment. The postwar Constitutional Problem Investigation Committee—usually referred to as the Matsumoto Committee in deference to the prestige of its chair, Jōji Matsumoto—was appointed by the Shidehara Cabinet in October 1945 to study revision of the Meiji constitution. The committee's original proposal attempted to address the problem by expanding these rights and making them more absolute, without, however, altering the basic constitutional framework of the Japanese state. The Matsumoto draft, as noted, was rejected outright by General MacArthur. A subsequent document was drafted by a small group of lawyers under SCAP headed by Charles Kades. Intended as a model for the Japanese, this document was then revised over two days and a night by a joint American and Japanese working committee. Only after further amendment in the Japanese Diet was it finally enacted as the Constitution of Japan.[1]

The postwar constitution went well beyond even American constitutional freedoms. In addition to a general clause guaranteeing the exercise of "fundamental human rights" (article 11) and most if not all of the guarantees of the American Bill of Rights, the Constitution of Japan, as promulgated, also comprised the right of equality and concomitant freedom from discrimination in political and social relations on the basis of "race, creed, sex, social status or family origin" (article 14); the right to compensation from the state for tortious acts of public officials, including judges and prosecutors (article 17); freedom of occupation (article 22); academic freedom (article 23); the right to minimum standards of life (article 25); the right to equal education (article 26); the right to work, with an affirmative duty to work (article 27); as well as the right of workers to organize and bargain collectively (article 28).

The Japanese Supreme Court has not construed these rights to impose affirmative duties on the state for their realization. Nor has the Court acted otherwise to ensure their implementation as fully as some might conceive them.[2] If the Supreme Court has not taken the opportunity to use these provisions to expand the welfare state, it has also only rarely construed more narrowly than other industrial states the responsibilities of the state toward its citizens in the absence of implementing legislation. In other words, the justices have tended to defer to the political branches of government and the political process rather than craft constitutional mandates themselves. A substantial measure of self-restraint is evident. As discussed in chapter 5, despite the potential for direct inference through the judicial appointment process, there is in fact no evidence of any interest on the part of the cabinet to select judges on any basis, much less to pick them for ideological views or partisan concerns. The strongest argument to support any degree of political intervention that can be made is that the judiciary itself screens career judges to ensure that whatever the personal political leanings of individual judges, their decisions do not manifest ideological views at any extreme, in order to preserve judicial autonomy from such political inference. Whatever the merit of such arguments, all available evidence supports the view that Japan's senior judges share the views of Japan's political elite and, more significantly, the general public. This conservative tendency has not, however, meant stagnation. Just as the Court has in effect perceived changes in the "sense of community" so, equally gradually and with remarkable deference to prior decisions, the justices have adapted constitutional mandates. Moreover, the Japanese judiciary—especially the Supreme Court—has tended to act in ways similar to courts within the civil law tradition, particularly as a judiciary comprising a bureaucracy of career judges.

Despite such self-restraint, whatever its causes, the Japanese judiciary—especially the lower courts—has readily enforced proscriptive constitutional and statutory mandates to protect the individual against the state. The most distinctive aspect of Japanese constitutional jurisprudence, at least from an American perspective, is the relatively greater emphasis on economic freedoms and property rights over the freedoms of expression and "spirit," in the outcome of postwar constitutional litigation. While articulating the outer limits of state regulation over individual property rights and competitive economic activity, the Supreme Court has been less willing, nevertheless, to reform legal standards considered to be widely supported by the community. Japan's justices have consistently construed the constitution in ways that reinforce community preferences and practice against claims for protection of individual beliefs. This tendency is explained in part by the state action requirement of the constitution. Without state action, community practices are immune from constitutional constraints. Nevertheless, the Court has also tended to ignore state involvement in community activities in cases where a finding of state action would have allowed the court to intervene.

INDIVIDUAL FREEDOMS AND THE STATE

Asked in a conversation with the author to name the most important constitutional decisions by the Japanese Supreme Court, a prominent young Japanese constitutional law scholar listed five sets of decisions in which the Court has held legislative measures unconstitutional. Today he would surely add a sixth—the April 1997 constitutional decision on the separation of the state from religion.

The most significant decision related to legislative acts, he remarked, was *Kurokawa v. Chiba Prefecture Election Commission*, in which the Court declared that the allocation of seats in the Diet for the 1972 lower-house election under the Public Office Election Law was unconstitutional.[3] In 1985 the Court reaffirmed this decision, again holding that the allocation for the House of Representatives under the Public Office Election Law as amended and applied to the 1983 lower-house election was similarly unconstitutional.[4] Taken chronologically, the first case was the Court's 1962 decision in *Nakamura v. Japan*.[5] At issue was a provision in a customs statute permitting confiscation of contraband cargo owned by a third party without knowledge of the crime or notice of the customs action.[6] The Court held that the lack of notice under the provision violated the constitutional guarantee of procedural due process of article 31 and the protection of property of article 29. The third set of cases came a decade later in *Aizawa v. Japan* and two companion cases. The challenged measure was article 200 of the Criminal Code, which mandated a significantly harsher penalty for patricide than ordinary homicide (article 199).[7] The Court ruled that article 200 constituted a denial of equality under the law. Three years later in 1975, the Court decided the *Pharmacy Location* case.[8] In that decision the Court invalidated a provision in a business licensing statute that restricted the location of new pharmacies under the freedom of occupation guarantee of article 22 of the constitution. The most recent case mentioned was *Hiraguchi v. Hiraguchi* in 1987.[9] Citing the *Pharmacy Location* case, the Court held that a provision of Japan's Forest Law restricting the right of a co-owner of forest land from petitioning for partition as provided in the Civil Code violated the protection of property rights of article 29.[10]

In all but one of these cases—*Nakamura v. Japan*—the Court departed from earlier decisions. In 1964, for example, the Court upheld the constitutionality of the allocation of seats per district for the upper house of the Diet in a broadly worded opinion that appeared to leave the issue of apportionment entirely to the legislative branch.[11] A majority of the fifteen justices had in 1950 similarly affirmed the constitutionality of article 205 of the Criminal Code, which imposed a more severe penalty for those guilty of inflicting a bodily injury resulting in death against a lineal ascendant than against other victims, noting a "universal moral principle" that "attributes special importance to the moral duties of the child toward his parents."[12] The provision of article 200 had also been deemed constitutional in a series of decisions commencing with a companion decision in *Otōki v.*

Japan.[13] The *Pharmacy Location* case was preceded by two major decisions, both upholding the constitutionality of statutory business licensing restraints, including location restrictions. The first was the 1955 *Bathhouse* case, in which the Court unanimously upheld the criminal conviction of a public bathhouse operator for operating without a license.[14] The defendant argued unsuccessfully that a site restriction requiring that new bathhouses be located at least 250 to 300 meters away from any existing establishment violated the freedom of occupation guarantee of article 22 of the constitution. Such a restriction, the Court stated, served the public welfare by ensuring more even distribution of public bathhouses and preventing the risk to hygiene that could be caused by excessive competition. In 1972, the Court in effect affirmed this decision in *Marushin Sangyō K.K. v. Japan.*[15] In that case the Court upheld a 700-meter site restriction that applied to shopping malls.

In only one case—*Aizawa*—did the Court in effect overrule an earlier decision. Even in that instance, the Court carefully distinguished its leading precedent, acknowledging that a crime against a lineal ascendant could be punished more severely as in the case of article 205 of the Penal Code. As in the malapportionment cases, the Court emphasized the degree of imbalance rather than requiring equal treatment. However cautious, the Court nevertheless redefined the legal principles of the earlier cases and made an abrupt change in direction as a new generation of justices, notably in the mid-1970s, revisited constitutional decisions of the 1950s and early 1960s.

In each instance where the Court has declared a legislative measure unconstitutional, further judicial action has been unnecessary in order to effectuate the rulings. As Nobuyoshi Ashibe points out, each was followed by either an administrative or legislative or combined response to eliminate the violation.[16] The 1976 decision in *Kurokawa v. Chiba Prefecture Election Commission* and the 1985 decision holding Japan's distribution of lower house seats under the prior electoral system unconstitutional have had the most dramatic effect. Despite the acute sense of frustration the justices may have felt in their inability to fashion a remedy to cure the system themselves, the influence of these decisions was considerable. They helped to undermine the legitimacy of the existing electoral system and thereby contributed significantly to the political reforms of 1994. For those accustomed to a judiciary that actively exercises remedial or corrective powers, the Japanese judiciary may seem in these cases weak and impotent. A more sanguine view of the Japanese judiciary and its constitutional role would emphasize in response its legitimizing and consensus-building function.

The malapportionment cases are not isolated examples. The Court's consistent refusal to adjudicate the constitutionality of Japan's Self-Defense Forces under the prohibition of war and armaments clauses of article 9 also exemplifies the legitimizing role of the courts.[17] So long as the Supreme Court has refused to decide the issue one way or another, neither side has had much comfort. The issue has remained a contentious political question, ultimately, it appears, to be determined with minimum judicial influence. The result seems to be, in the words of one Japanese scholar, a process of "transformational interpretation," in which public acceptance is in effect the determining factor.[18]

The judiciary's response to these two highly contentious issues illustrates the interrelationship of Japanese institutions and culture in constitutional adjudication. The judiciary's legitimizing function has been a critical factor in the democratic realization of constitutional ideals. The Court has protected its institutional autonomy and has been able to signal those issues on which national consensus has been reached—at least in the minds of the justices. This caution and the unwillingness (or perhaps more accurately inability) to exercise more coercive powers has helped, it can be argued, to buttress broader support for the courts and the constitution itself. Perhaps because it is the least coercive branch of government, it can be trusted.

The decisions of the 1970s and 1980s also collectively define the most important parameters of Japan's constitutional jurisprudence and illustrate again the Court's sense of Japanese society. They demonstrate first that Japan's constitutional system is not static. Although the Court's approach has been cautious and perhaps passive, as noted by some of Japan's leading constitutional law scholars, neither passivity nor consistency has prevented change.[19] As noted, in all but one of the cited decisions since the 1960s, the Court significantly modified without reversing its prior decisions. The Court has in effect remained very close to the national consensus. Its decisions reflect directions in which the majority of Japanese appear to wish to move. As presaged in the *Nakamura* case, concomitant with the enactment of the Administrative Procedure Act, the courts have begun to display considerable concern over administrative procedural protection.[20] The *Aizawa* case is similarly indicative of the Court's concern with substantive justice in criminal law, evidenced by a spate of recent cases.[21] The Court contributes to this consensus but does not venture too far ahead. Rather it remains just at the crest of public consensus, adding to the momentum of change and allowing it to continue but not leading the way.

The role of the Supreme Court should be distinguished from that of the lower courts, particularly at the district level. Illustrated in the development of legal rules discussed in previous chapters, Japanese district courts and, albeit less frequently, high courts have played a more active role. The Supreme Court, after long delay in adjudicating cases on appeal, in effect has allowed lower courts to develop both judicial and public consensus. Critics might counter that the Court only acts to allow change once the pressure from the lower courts becomes irresistible. Both views are probably accurate, depending upon the issue involved.

A further reminder is in order. As explained previously, the judges in Japan's lower courts also include the most senior. They occupy the positions of greater influence as the presiding judges of each panel on which they sit. Thus any dichotomy between the pattern of decisions emanating from Japan's lower courts from those by the Supreme Court does not reflect purely generational differences. Although the views of younger judges are more pronounced at the district court level, many of their peers at mid-career staff the administrative and research posts of the Supreme Court itself where their influence is also felt.

The Court has also demonstrated a commitment to a pivotal principle of the postwar constitution—the protection of the individual from the state. Although careful not to step ahead of public consensus and unwilling to transform constitutional norms into imperatives requiring positive state action for their fulfillment, the Court has ensured that the constitution's guarantees of individual freedoms place meaningful limits on the state's authority and powers. As a result, with respect to the state, the Japanese people are among the world's most free.

COMMUNITY VALUES

The change in direction of the 1970s and 1980s was not uniform. In other cases the Court has also had the opportunity to reexamine earlier constitutional decisions. Although a few have been modified, none have been significantly altered. The Court's views on freedom of expression exemplify this consistency. In the 1957 *Lady Chatterly's Lover's case,* the Court upheld the convictions of a prominent publisher for selling and a well-known novelist for translating copies of D. H. Lawrence's controversial novel.[22] The Court rejected the argument that obscenity was protected under the freedom of expression guarantee of article 21 of the constitution and reaffirmed both prewar and postwar precedents on the definition of obscene writing. Once again the Court's understanding of the "sense of society" controlled. As the Court stated in making the determination of what writings are prohibited as obscene:

> The standard for the court when it makes such a decision is the good sense operating generally through the society, that is, the prevailing ideas of society [*shakai tsūnen*]. These, as the original decision puts it, "are not the sum of the understanding of separate individuals . . . they are a collective understanding that transcends both. They cannot be rejected by separate individuals who hold to an understanding opposed to them." The judgment of what the prevailing ideas of society are is, under our present system, entrusted to judges. . . . it cannot be denied that courts have the authority to determine what constitutes the prevailing ideas of society.[23]

In 1969 the Court expressly affirmed this decision as controlling precedent in a case that upheld the convictions of the translator and the publisher of a Japanese version of a portion of the Marquis de Sade's *In Praise of Vice*.[24] The two cases continue to be followed.[25]

Care must be taken in comparing the community values at stake in the Japanese obscenity cases with those at issue in similar cases in the United States or Europe. They are not the same. Community concerns over sexually explicit literature—the "good sense" of society—in Japan lack the religious dimensions that pervade the conflict between pornography and free expression in the United States and elsewhere. Whether or not encompassed within a very broad definition of morality, pornography in Japan does not trigger deeply rooted conflicts between religious beliefs and secular values. In Japan, Western concepts of religion require redefinition.

LAW AND RELIGION

Few societies are perceived from the outside as secular as Japan. "Religion," Edwin Reischauer notes, "occupies a more peripheral position in Japan" than in any society in the West or, perhaps, any other nation.[26] Japan lacks any indigenous belief system incorporating coherent doctrine, universally applicable standards and rules, or a transcendental vision. In the words of Karel van Wolferen: "Concepts of independent universal truths or immutable religious beliefs, transcending the worldly reality of social dictates and the decrees of powerholders, have of course found their way into Japan, but they have never taken root in any surviving world-view."[27] Yet religion by most definitions prospers in Japan. Shinto folk beliefs, Buddhist sects, Christian congregations all thrive, side-by-side, frequently in mixed rituals attracting the same participants. Where else but Japan would a bride and groom don traditional garb for a Shinto ceremony in the morning, then change into Western wedding clothes for a Christian church service in the afternoon? The environment seems to spawn all manner of new "religions," groups, and cults. One must therefore approach the topic of religion in Japan with care. The problem of definition is acute. While religious organizations, ritual practices, and folk belief abound, only within narrow, social confines can one identify religious subcultures as communities with shared values and mutual acceptance of a coherent system of belief and universalist claims.

The problem of defining Japanese religion poses a significant barrier to any comparison of the Japanese experience with those societies whose political cultures have been influenced fundamentally by the religious and legal traditions of the Mediterranean world. In such societies the claims of "reason" after the Enlightenment set into motion profound and continuing conflict. The separation of church and state in these societies has common historical parameters. Whether in England or Egypt, similar concerns produce the tensions in construing the state as "secular" and defining its relationship to established ecclesiastical authority as well as deeply rooted values. In such societies shared understandings connect ideological conflicts over validity and expression in law of any values originating in or buttressed by religious belief. Whether the issue is the legal prohibition of abortion in Kansas or of bank loans with interest in Kuwait, the foundations of political controversy are the same. Contemporary cultures and institutions have evolved out of a theocratic tradition defined by the fusion of moral norms and legal rules. Religion may thus seem peripheral in Japan to those who see through lenses colored by such tradition. Japan may actually be different, however, only in contrast to those societies shaped by Mediterranean law and religion. Hence, what seems to us peculiar to Japan may be better understood as a mirror image of our own peculiarity.

The separation of law and morality is not, as noted previously, a uniquely Japanese phenomenon. The earliest notions of law and religion introduced into Japan from T'ang dynasty China also reflected such separation. In Imperial China, from at least the third century B.C., law was understood as an instrument of state regulatory control, with administrative rules backed by explicit penalties. The extent to which the imperial state's legal rules should reflect moral (familial and Confucianist) norms had been debated and generally settled under Han imperial rule (206 B.C. to A.D. 220), several centuries before the first T'ang emperor. No claim was made, however, that either

Confucianist norms—and certainly not Buddhist "law"—could be construed as was natural law in the Western tradition as a legal order within which man-made law was to conform.

Natural law concepts were thus first pervasively introduced into Japan along with other Western concepts and understandings about law as well as religion in the mid-nineteenth century. Within the context of traditional views of law as regulatory rules and customary principles, positivist conceptions of law as rules and principles recognized or made by state institutions were readily understood and adopted. In contrast, natural law theories remained a rather rarified topic of academic study more akin to Japanese discourse on Western literary styles than a viable element of the organic legal order that was in the process of being created.

One consequence has been the continued separation of law from morals as distinctly different, albeit interrelated, sources for proper conduct. Furthermore, as explained in greater detail below, both law and morals were and continue to be relatively weak in comparison to custom and community practice as the wellspring of social norms. This separation has also enabled Japan to avoid what Judith Sklar so aptly describes as an American tendency to legalize moral issues.[28] Although the United States is not alone in transforming moral controversy into legal disputes, in few other societies do moral and ethical questions seem as readily litigated. Japanese courts thus seldom confront controversies that arouse as deep public passion as lawsuits in the United States involving the constitutionality of laws against abortion, sodomy, or the death penalty.

The dearth of deeply divisive moral disputes, particularly in the interpretation of constitutional questions and legislative activity, is another factor that helps to explain the seemingly greater cohesion of Japanese society. Unless related to political ideology, legal rules regulating social conduct are not as potentially contentious for Japan as for other societies.

The closest the Japanese Supreme Court has come to dealing directly with the constitutionality of a legal rule grounded on traditional moral values was the series of cases involving articles 200 and 205 of the Criminal Code that treat the killing of a lineal ascendant as a more serious offense and thereby subject to a more severe penalty than ordinary homicide. None of these decisions caused any significant public outcry. Indeed, the Japanese public appeared to be almost indifferent.

What we mean by morality and religion differs so fundamentally that any comparison is profoundly difficult. The consequences are illustrated by the official reconstruction during the nineteenth century of traditional Japanese animism, ancestor worship, and ritual practices into a Western conception of religion. From the outset, the modern Japanese state confronted the dilemma of defining Shinto in order to use its association with imperial ritual and ancestor worship for purposes of statecraft and national unification. In the end, Shinto was established as a state "religion." In so doing, elements of myth and ritual that had long defined the legitimacy of the state and governance were absorbed along with local community practices into the category of religion. This transformation of traditional practices and symbolic ritual necessarily, as Carol Gluck observes, forced the intrusion of civic responsibility and state loyalty into the sphere of individual conscience and belief.[29] The result was not only conflict with Japan's initial guarantee of freedom of religion under the Meiji constitution. As State Shinto along with the imperial institution became more closely affiliated with ultranationalist and militarist aims in the 1920s and 1930s, Shinto itself acquired an indelible cast.

For the American victors of the Pacific War, the redefinition of the imperial institution in purely temporal terms along with the disestablishment of Shinto was high on the agenda of intended reforms to demilitarize and democratize Japan. One of the earliest directives of the Supreme Commander for the Allied Powers (December 15, 1945) prohibited any "sponsorship, support, perpetuation, control and dissemination of Shinto by the Japanese national, prefectural, and local governments, or by public officials, subordinates and employees acting in their official capacity."[30] Japanese officials also appreciated the problem of Shinto, and at least one suggested early on the elimination of the "religious character" of the shrines and treatment of imperial Shinto ritual as the "private religion of the imperial family."[31] This proposal had the merit of rupturing the relationship between Shinto and nationalism and by the same stroke, enabling the postwar state to control the symbols of Japanese nationalism. Had Shinto reverted back to community rituals and practices, it could then have lost its prewar association with militarist ultranationalism while the state could have found ways to honor those who sacrificed their lives during the war free from the influence of State Shinto and ultranationalism. This approach did not prevail. The provision on religious freedom in Japan's postwar constitution that ultimately emerged from the drafting process and Diet deliberations dealt with the central issue of the Meiji regime along American lines. Article 20 provides:

1. Freedom of religion is guaranteed to all. No religious organization shall receive any privileges from the State nor exercise any political authority.
2. No person shall be compelled to take part in any religious act, celebration, rite, or practice.
3. The State and its organs shall refrain from religious education or any other religious activity.

The former policies regarding shrines were thus dramatically reversed. What had been public now became private. The rituals and symbols for honoring Japan's war dead passed beyond the control of the state. Absent state control, the fundamental question remained of how to define the state's relationship to shrine worship (jinja shinkō), especially the role of community involvement in tutelary shrines.

Remarkably not until the late 1960s did the courts face the issue of state involvement in Shinto ritual under the postwar constitution. Until 1967 there was hardly any litigation involving article 20; apparently none that dealt with the separation of church and state under paragraph 3. The landmark case remains the 1977 *en banc* decision of the Supreme Court in *Kakunaga v. Sekiguchi,* otherwise known as the *Tsu Groundbreaking Ceremony* Case.[32]

The *Tsu Groundbreaking Ceremony* Case involved a legal challenge to the inclusion of a Shinto ceremony at public expense in the commencement of construction of a public gymnasium. The city had invited a local shrine to conduct a customary purification rite on the building site. The participating priest and four other shrine employees received a 4000 yen (approximately U.S.$30) honorarium in addition to reimbursement of 3663 yen for expenses. Afterwards, a resident of the city brought suit to require the mayor to reimburse the city personally for the total amount expended, alleging that the city had violated the separation of church and state provision of article 20(3) of the constitution as well as article 89 of the constitution prohibiting any expenditure of public funds for "the use, benefit or maintenance of any religious institution or association" and a provision of article 242-2 of the Local Autonomy Law, which allows a "citizen's suit."[33] The Tsu District Court dismissed the action.[34] The court agreed that the ceremony constituted a religious activity but concluded that it was a customary event without substantive religious purpose. The funds expended, concluded the court, were simply compensation for services performed. Thus the city's actions did not violate either the constitution or the Local Autonomy Law. On first appeal, the Nagoya High Court held that the ceremony was a religious ritual peculiar to Shinto worship, a recognized national religion, and not merely a customary event.[35] Municipal sponsorship and payment of public funds for the ceremony thus contravened articles 20(3) and 89 of the constitution as well as provisions of the Local Autonomy Law. On appeal to the Supreme Court, a ten-justice majority agreed with the district court and reversed the high court judgment.

The majority opinion construed the purpose of article 20 as a corrective measure to expand the Meiji constitution's protection of freedom of religious belief. The 1946 constitution, the Court noted, provided for unconditional freedom of religious belief and the separation of religion from politics as a response to various abuses that had resulted from the close relationship between Shinto and the state following the Meiji Restoration. Article 20, the majority concluded, requires the state to maintain neutrality among religions but does not require an unreasonably or impossibly absolute separation from religion in every educational, cultural, or routine endeavor supported by governmental authorities.

The *Tsu Groundbreaking Ceremony* Case can be read as establishing a de minimus standard for construing the separation of church and state requirement of article 20(3). So long as the challenged activity or expenditure is not intended or does not have the effect of aiding, supporting, or suppressing any particular religion, it does not violate article 20. The questioned religious activity can also be viewed as one that had become more of a civic ceremony without significant religious content for the participants. The Court was implicitly concerned with the problem that to hold otherwise would have embroiled the Japanese judiciary in a swarm of controversial cases and the charge that it was attempting to root out historic community practices. The case did not directly involve the nexus between Shinto and the military, but the issue was so closely related that the implications of the lawsuit were apparent to all concerned. The state's constitutional relationship to Shinto could not be disentangled from the state's separation from its military past. Community as well as national rituals to honor those who died in military service would remain the central issue.

COMMUNITY AND THE STATE

In February 1993 the Third Petty Bench applied the *Tsu* "intention or effect" test to dismiss two related challenges to municipal government involvement in the restoration and support of local stone memorials to Japan's war dead (*chūkonhi*).[36] In the late 1970s residents of Minoo City, a municipality in the northern suburbs of Osaka, brought three separate damage actions against the mayor and public school officials. In the first suit, filed in 1976, the plaintiffs sought repayment of municipal expenditures to repair and relocate a memorial as well as the lease of public land for its site. Brought a year later, the second action similarly challenged official participation and the use of public funds for annual Shinto and, in alternate years, Buddhist memorial services held at the memorial. A third suit, also filed in 1977, questioned the legality of payments the city made to the Minoo Branch of the Japan Bereaved Families of Soldiers Killed in Action Association (*Nihon Izokukai*), which maintained the memorial.

Chūkonhi memorials to local soldiers were first constructed following the Russo-Japanese War (1904–1905) along with the establishment of local army reservist organizations throughout the country. As a reservist group was formed, a *chūkonhi* memorial would be erected, usually in an open area adjacent to a school. The monuments facilitated close identification between the local community and the military by honoring those who had lost their lives serving the emperor and the nation. Their identification with local spirits (*kami*) through enshrinement reinforced the notion that their "spirits" would also protect their families and the community.[37]

The Minoo *chūkonhi* was similarly erected in 1917 by the Minoo Branch of the Imperial Army Reservists Association. Like many other *chūkonhi*, the Minoo monument was removed and buried during the Occupation. In 1952 the monument was recovered and restored to its original foundation by the Minoo Branch of the Japan Bereaved Families of Soldiers Killed in Action Association. Because of the need for the site as a result of the expansion of the adjacent school, in 1972 the monument was again removed and relocated nearby on land purchased for this purpose by a municipal land development corporation and leased to the association at a cost to the city of about eighty-five million yen (U.S.$850,000). Except for the brief period during which the monument was buried, Shinto and Buddhist services had been held in alternative years at the memorial since 1940. School offices and other facilities as well as chairs and desks were used for these services. City employees also helped to plan the services and used city stationery and other property for the invitations. The mayor and other city and school officials actively participated, and the mayor, the school principal, and members of the school board all received honoraria for attending the ceremonies.

The suits were first adjudicated by the Osaka District Court. In the first two cases, decided respectively in 1982 and 1983, the Osaka District Court ruled in favor of only some of the plaintiffs' claims.[38] Both sides thus appealed both judgments. The Osaka High Court consolidated the two cases, and, on July 16, 1987, dismissed all claims against the defendants. The plaintiffs then appealed to the Supreme Court. In 1993 the Third Petty Bench affirmed. The Court agreed that the high court had properly dismissed both suits. The third suit was not decided by the Osaka District Court until 1988.[39] Following the lead of the High Court and perhaps anticipating the Supreme Court's 1993 response, the Osaka District Court dismissed the suit on the grounds that the subsidy was provided to promote the welfare of the bereaved families and not to aid any particular religious belief.

In effect the Supreme Court treated the memorial and the services as if the aims of the Occupation had been fully achieved. The justices disassociated the commemoration of Japan's war dead from its association with Shinto and Buddhist ritual and belief. The *chūkonhi* and the services, the five justices all agreed, were intended to honor fallen soldiers, not to promote religion. The assistance of Minoo City and the school did not in either intent or effect "aid, foster, promote, or suppress" any particular religion.[40] Nor did the organization of bereaved families to which assistance was extended constitute a religious group. Support for the group's activities too did not violate article 20.

Those opposed to the actions by the city and school officials in these and similar cases criticize the Court's argument. The identification of prewar Japanese ultranationalism, the military, and the imperial institution with Shinto, they argue, continues. As a result, any official support for Shinto shrines and memorials—especially those related to Japan's war dead—represents an unconstitutional involvement of the state with religion. Any participation of Japanese public officials in ceremonies at the Yasukuni shrine in Tokyo, for example, causes political controversy. As the national shrine dedicated to the spirits of Japanese soldiers, Yasukuni, like the prefectural defense-of-the-nation shrines (*gokoku jinja*) and the *chūkonhi*, was used to identify the military and the state with Shinto. It remains closely associated with the military establishment. Ironically, without this nexus, the principal target—commemoration of militarist nationalism—could not be challenged under article 20. Thus any official involvement with Yasukuni or the prefectural shrines to honor Japanese war dead continues to produce lawsuits similar to those in the *Minoo Chūkonhi* cases.[41] Official use, particularly in schools, of the putative national anthem *kimi-ga-yō* is also challenged under article 20.[42]

In April 1997 the Supreme Court for the first time upheld such a challenge.[43] In a landmark *en banc* decision, reversing a judgment by the Takamatsu High Court, a majority of thirteen justices agreed that donations of public funds to the Yasukuni Shrine as well as the Ehime prefectural Defense-of-the-Nation Shrine violated the constitutional principle of separation between the state and religion.[44] The Court ruled that the Governor of Ehime Prefecture had exceeded "socially and culturally acceptable limits" under article 20 in donating prefectural funds to the shrines. The donations, the majority argued, could not be regarded as a matter of customary social courtesy. Rather, the intention and effect was to aid, encourage, and promote a particular religious organization.

Only two justices dissented. Chief Justice Miyoshi, joined by Justice Kabe, argued that as the central national memorial for Japan's war dead, the Yasukuni shrine had a special role that could be distinguished from its religious function. Ceremonial mourning also was supported by the public, and both the central and prefectural governments could be obligated to participate. Thus they concluded that the Ehime prefectural donations did not exceed the limits of permissible state involvement with a religious organization. In a concurring opinion Justices Takahashi and Ozaki maintained that the separation between politics and religion should be complete. They still supported the *Tsu* test but sought clearer guidelines for assessing the intent and effect of donations to shrines. Justice Sonobe also concurred with the result, but he argued that any donation of public funds to shrines should be viewed as unconstitutional. No guidelines were necessary. Justice Sonobe was the only member of the Court to have participated in the Third Petty Bench decision in the *Minoo Chūkonhi* case, which was unanimous.

The *Ehime Shrine Donation* decision appears to be less significant as the first case in which the Court has held government support of Shinto shrine ceremonies to be unconstitutional than as an affirmation of the *Tsu* formula and implicit recognition that the "sense of society" today may favor support for local community memorials and ceremonies for Japan's fallen soldiers but not the more politically sensitive national Yasukuni Shrine or even the prefectural Defense-of-the-Nation shrines, at least in the form of direct donations. Taken together, the decisions reflect a deference to the local community and local practices insulated from national politics.

THE INDIVIDUAL AND THE COMMUNITY

In her book *In the Realm of a Dying Emperor*, Norma Fields writes movingly of the grievance of Yasuko Nakaya that was transformed in a process culminating in the most significant decision by the Japanese Supreme Court on the application of article 20 with respect to individual religious belief.[45] For Fields as an outsider, the facts are simply stated:

> Nakaya Takafumi was killed in 1968 in a traffic accident while on the job as a member of the Self-Defense Force in Morioka in northern Japan. Three years later, the Self-Defense Force branch in Takafumi's native Yamaguchi Prefecture, together with the prefectural Veterans' Association (a private organization established to "bridge the gap" between the public and the SDF) initiated proceedings to enshrine his spirit in the local (prefectural) Defense-of-the-Nation Shrine. His widow, a Christian, registered her unequivocal objection to these plans. Nevertheless, she eventually received a communication from the shrine in which her husband's name appeared with the title *mikoto*, indicating that he had become a deity. In consultation with her minister, Mrs. Nakaya filed suit in 1973 against the Yamaguchi Prefectural Branch of the Self-Defense Force and the Veterans' Association. She charged them with a violation of the constitutional provision for separation of religion and state as well as violation of her religious rights. Fifteen years later, overturning substantial recognition of these claims at the district-court and high-court levels, the Supreme Court ruled in favor of the defendants.[46]

Reading about the case in the *New York Times* in 1988, Fields writes, the thought that "a widow could not prevent the state from turning her deceased husband into an object of veneration, and this denial would be cynically ratified by the highest judicial body of the land, filled me with rage and despair."[47]

The 1988 *Yamaguchi Shrine* case stands out for the public attention it has received and the criticisms Fields and others level against it. Its prominence is explained less, however, by whatever grievance motivated Yasuko Nakaya or by its addition to legal doctrine on the construction of Japan's postwar constitutional guarantee of freedom of religion than by its ultimate significance in confirming community norms despite the role of Shinto ritual in public affairs and its nexus with Japan's military establishment. Nakaya's motives combined concern for the broader political implications of the enshrinement of her husband as well as its contradiction with her religious beliefs. She was also persuaded in progressive Christian study groups that Japanese Christians bore a special responsibility in view of their failure to protest against Japanese militarism in the 1930s. As she told the Supreme Court: "The relation between Yasukuni Shrine . . . and the responsibility of Christians during the war, which I learned in the study groups, and my husband's joint enshrining in the Gokoku Shrine overlapped with the meaning of my husband's death, which I wanted to know."[48]

The *Yamaguchi Shrine* case, along with the landmark 1977, 1983, and 1997 Supreme Court decisions, together reflect judicial deference to community values. The *Yamaguchi Shrine* case, however, indicates a concomitant denial of state protection of the individual against the community. Yet in the end and at great personal cost, Yasuko Nakaya scored a victory of sorts. Her act of protest itself had immediate political influence and is likely to have effected a change in community behavior, ensuring greater sensitivity and accommodation to the beliefs of its members.

The *Yamaguchi Shrine* case was the first article 20 case after the *Tsu* decision to reach the Court. It presented a considerably more complex set of issues. The relevant facts were uncontested. Employees of the local Self-Defense Force (SDF) branch and Yamaguchi Prefecture Veterans Association had petitioned the Yamaguchi Shrine to have a deceased SDF member memorialized or "enshrined" over the protests of his widow. His father and other relatives apparently welcomed the effort and, after the lawsuit was filed, wrote the association urging it to continue the efforts for the rite. The shrine itself was not a party to the suit. Inasmuch as the shrine was acknowledged to be a private religious corporation, the lawsuit was directed solely against the local SDF branch and the association as a claim for damages and revocation of the petition to the shrine for infringement of the personal religious rights of the plaintiff and her deceased husband.

The Yamaguchi District Court ruled in favor of the plaintiff. Concluding that the efforts by the SDF branch and association constituted a concerted act, the court held that the SDF branch had violated the principle of separation of church and state under article 20(3) and thereby infringed the plaintiff's personal religious rights. The court entered a damage award against the state of one million yen plus interest.[49]

The district court carefully distinguished the petition by the association from the enshrinement rites. The association was also said to enjoy legal protection for its religious beliefs, and their exercise even in contravention of the plaintiff's beliefs was not, according to the court, unlawful. However, the petition to seek Shinto enshrinement did itself constitute a religious activity in which the state and its agencies are prohibited from engaging. Hence the efforts by the local SDF branch employees in combination with the association violated the mandate of article 20(3).

The Hiroshima High Court affirmed the district court judgment on all points except those portions that dealt with the association, which the high court deemed not to have the legal capacity to be a party to the suit.[50] The case was appealed to the Supreme Court, and six years later the Grand Bench decision was handed down with a 14-to-1 majority, reversing both lower courts and denying Mrs. Nakaya any relief. No current justice was a member of the Court at that time.

Reviewing the facts, the majority concluded that the state had not acted in this case. The fact that the veterans association was a private party like the shrine not subject to constitutional prescription was not disputed. The only state agency involved was the local branch of the SDF, whose employees, the majority emphasized, had merely cooperated with the association in supporting the petition to the shrine. The majority thus rejected the lower courts' determination that the petition was a concerted or joint action by both the association and the SDF employees. Hence the lower courts were reversed and the case dismissed for lack of the requisite state action.

Although the challengers formally lost in the *Tsu, Minoo Chū-*

konhi, and *Yamaguchi Shrine* cases in terms of the judicial construction of article 20 of the postwar constitution, paradoxically they may have actually achieved much of what they sought. The cases themselves conveyed a mixed message. Customary rituals within the local community may constitutionally receive support. So too may officials provide financial aid and participate in local commemorations for soldiers from the community who have died despite the historical relationship of such commemorations to Shinto beliefs. Any significant state or official involvement without community acceptance, however, is by implication constitutionally suspect. Nor is it likely that public officials will risk official sponsorship of Shinto rituals in support of national aims, especially those in aid of the military establishment. Indeed many mayors may react with caution in supporting even relatively minor ceremonial celebrations, at least in communities where opposition is a likely response. The outcome of Yasuko Nakaya's lawsuit, for example, had direct bearing on the constitutional legitimacy of official connection with Yasukuni rites. Within a year after the decision, nearly a decade before the 1997 *Ehime Shrine Donation* decision, Prime Minister Nakasone announced that all official visits to the Yasukuni shrine would cease, and an increasing number of prefectural and local governments ended the practice of donating funds to Yasukuni and prefectural Defense-of-the-Nation shrines. Ehime Prefecture was one of the last. Equally significant and on a more personal level, few shrines are apt to ignore the express wishes of widows or other close relatives of those they are asked to memorialize. For all concerned, the loss of face and reputation as a result of the public accusation of having committed a wrong remains a substantial deterrent in Japan.[51]

Nonetheless, such victories are won at great personal cost. Acts of defiance toward community solidarity in seeking the aid and intervention of the state usually produce community hostility and denunciation. Norma Fields's descriptions of the travails of Yasuko Nakaya ring true.

Whether or not the majority can be faulted for an excessively fine distinction between private and state action in the *Yamaguchi Shrine* case, the justices' conclusion was accurate at a more fundamental

level. Fields and other critics of the decision miss the point in condemning the Court for denying Yasuko Nakaya protection against the
state. Except in the narrowest legal terms, action by the state was not
at issue in the *Yamaguchi Shrine* case. The real conflict was between
the local community, whatever its formal attire as public agency or
private association, and an individual member. The real representatives of the state were the judges who decided these cases, not the employees of the Yamaguchi SDF branch and members of the veterans
association. Stripped of legal garb and the underlying political concerns, the case involved a challenge to community practice and an
established pattern of life. The plaintiff petitioned for the state to intervene to protect her individual interest and beliefs against the actions taken by and on behalf of the community of which she was a
part. The judicial response was refusal. Acting through the courts, the
state denied her the protection she sought. This, I submit, is the crux
of the case and much of Japanese law.

The pattern is familiar. The community and its consensus governs.
Legal rules, even those of constitution or code, yield to the informal
rules and norms evolved through time and accepted by tacit assent and
community adherence. Rare is the incident of the state overturning
the informal regulations of community life or coercively imposing a
new set of standards without community consent. In cases involving various formal organizations, from religious groups to political
parties, the courts have been reluctant to intervene in internal conflicts or to protect the claimed rights of individual members against
the group. The courts perceive a segmented social order (*bubun shakai*) in which various organizations and communities vie with the
state in their authority over the individual. In effect these communities are viewed by the courts as outside of the law's domain. To be
sure, the legislative, administrative, and judicial institutions of the
state produce new legal rules daily. Their legitimacy and efficacy remain in doubt, however, so long as the informal processes of consensus and assent have not been fully employed.

For the individual in Japan, these patterns of state deference and
community control have obvious costs. Without state protection, the
individual often has little option but to submit and conform to the

community—whether hamlet or firm—that can coerce compliance to its norms and needs. Japanese can and do maintain their own individuality, but within the bounds of what is acceptable to the community. One of the best examples of this is Japan's judiciary itself. To the extent the community tolerates deviance from conventional behavior, the individual may have wide latitude for uncommon personal beliefs and expression. Japanese society's historical religious syncretism and notable acceptance of extraordinarily disparate religious beliefs thus has generally tended to ensure community tolerance of most nonconforming individual religious faiths. Nothing in the *Tsu, Minoo Chūkonhi* or *Yamaguchi Shrine* decisions contradicts in any way the proposition that the individual in Japan enjoys the broadest freedom of personal religious belief.

Often at issue in such cases is less community intolerance of individual religious belief than the individual believer's own intolerance—mandated at least in the case of Mrs. Nakaya by her Christian faith—of community practices, as argued by the Ministry of Justice procurators representing the state.[52] Mrs. Nakaya's claim reflected the inexorable conflict between community norms and universalist religious or secular beliefs. Whether grounded in the exclusivity of a religious mandate or a belief in the universal claims of human rights, the rejection of traditional community practices pits the individual against the community. In each case, the community, not the individual, is being challenged. The Supreme Court's responses are therefore hardly surprising. As in the *Yamaguchi Shrine* case, a majority of justices (concurring and dissenting opinions) may condemn the Self Defense Forces for their insensitivity, but the majority also rejects the individual's claim for state protection. In the *Yamaguchi Shrine* case itself, the Court expressly noted that whereas private infringement of protected religious belief could constitute a delict under the Civil Code, in this case no delict had been committed. The actions of the parties against whom the plaintiff sought legal relief related to their own religious beliefs, which deserve equal legal protection. Between the individual and the state stands the community. The individual must thus submit; legal rules will not be used to effect a major change in community practice.

CONCLUSION

In the 1901–2 Storrs lectures, Kazuo Hatoyama told his Yale Law School audience that two concerns had led to the enactment of the Japanese Civil Code. One catalyst was the desire to end the system of extraterritoriality imposed by treaty with the European powers and the United States. More compelling, in Hatoyama's words, were "the immediate wants of society arising out of social, economic, and political revolutions" and "the need of a systematic and complete code." Judges played an instrumental role in the process of this responsive reception of Western law even prior to the adoption of the code. Hatoyama noted: "The Japanese judges, in seeking just principles to be applied to cases which were entirely novel, examined the jurisprudence of Europe and America, and, in thus appealing to the various occidental systems, they endeavored to eliminate those features of law which were accidental or merely historically important in particular countries, and selected the legal principles which might be said to be absolute and common to all."[1]

Nearly a full century later, Hatoyama's words may sound quaint and a bit hollow. Few today in the West or in Japan would agree that the rules and principles of nineteenth-century European law are either absolute or common to all. Nonetheless, there is truth in Hatoyama's assertion.

By the end of the nineteenth century, transforming nation-states throughout the world had reconstituted the categories, concepts, and principles of Roman law into new codes and statutes. Others would follow, many, particularly in Asia, citing Japan's success. What in hindsight may seem shockingly overbearing as Eurocentric arrogance was in fact accepted as valid by many in Japan and elsewhere. Translated into various languages across the globe, except where English and the Common Law held sway, the words of modern Roman law became the universal language of law. Wherever independent states emerged, unified legal systems were part and parcel of an edifice for centralized national rule. As in Japan, their architects designed them both to reverse the centrifugal forces that threatened these newly defined nation-states and to conform to what appeared to those moved by the vision of the Enlightenment as universal ideals of progress and civilization.

For Japan the creation of a unified national legal system in conformity with what was perceived as the most advanced civilization of the time had a historical parallel. Like the reception of imperial Chinese law a millennium before, Japan's new codes were appreciated both as a symbol of status and an instrument of statecraft. Japan's nineteenth-century nationalist reformers, no less than their seventh-century forbears, borrowed to build a new state and society.

Private law formed the central arch. The Civil Code enshrined the tenets of property and contract in an envisioned order of rules to be enforced, in the language of the law, as rights, by request of the holder with certainty and consistency in result. Behind the blueprints, the promise was grand. Property and contract articulated and secured, the individual was to be enabled thereby to pursue and achieve fullest potential. Wealth would be created and moral imperatives fulfilled. The spirit of this law was profit and progress.

Japan pursued the venture with determination. How deeply accepted or even well understood the moral underpinnings of the codes were we will perhaps never know for sure. It seems unlikely, though, that many Japanese gave much thought to the notion of property as a natural law right or freedom of contract as an ethical imperative—articles of faith for many like the French jurist Boissonade. Individualism and self-regarding conduct were certainly not praised as moral virtues. Even the language of "rights" was new. Nevertheless, by the end of the century, from codes to courts, at least the structure was complete.

The system also worked. Japanese had not been reticent to take advantage of their freedom from ancient restrictions imposed by their warrior rulers. Nor did they shy away from using new rules and rights to advantage. They pushed the limits of all new laws and the opportunities they afforded to enhance their gains. They formed banks and limited liability companies, registered property, and began in increasing numbers to seek judicial enforcement for law-created protections against kin and kind.

Japan's nineteenth-century statutes and codes in this context did not as much unleash Japan's creative forces as they channelled and fixed them. With contract and property legally affirmed and enforced, those with new economic, political, and social leverage could not only drive hard bargains but also now secure their benefits after the initial balance had shifted. As political institutions similarly empower those in control not only to garner favors and largesse, but to protect positions of privilege and influence against future challenge and change, so the rules of contract and property protected past and present gains from future change. The truly powerful, the patrons who never lose their initial leverage over their clients, do not need such protection. The permanently weak, who live out their lives in a state of client-like subjugation, seldom have the means or claims to seek such aid. Only those betwixt and between, who once strong may become weak as their influence and leverage dissipate or change in ways that make self-help a risky substitute, need such law.

The enthymemes, or unstated premises, of assertive individualism and state protection on which Japan's new codes—and the adjudicatory processes for their enforcement, the essence of the new system of rights—were grounded were from their inception in conflict with the communitarian values and patterns of Japanese society. Inevitably confrontation ensued. The rules and principles, the processes and procedures—in other words the intrinsic system of rights of Japan's new codes—could not be reconciled easily with the embedded values of a society in which law meant self-restraint and reciprocal duties without rights and in which autonomy as well as economic well-being had been the paradoxical product of community.

Japan's communitarian bias had never been a matter of free individual or even collective choice. Accurately perceived perhaps as a response to an ingrained sense of mutual need reinforced by habits of mind, community in Japan was also induced from above. It was first and foremost the consequence of both the village structure established for the mobilization of rural resources by Japan's warrior rulers and the economic interdependency intrinsic in intensive cultivation of rice. In Japan as elsewhere, community rested on an overriding perceived need for security from the risks of life as well as for the benefits of collective action. Reinforced in the ceremonies of popular religion and official ideology, community also meant self-sacrifice for the community good. However, self-interest and self-regarding conduct still played a major part in village life.

Behind the veil of harmony and order as moral and official ideals, competition and rivalry for individual, household, lineage, and village gain had long functioned as catalysts of social and economic change. Administrative edicts, regulations, and rules had long been used as weapons in these village rivalries for position and influence. All sides used petitions to distant warrior rulers—litigation, some would call it, in the interstices of administrative governance—in order to achieve through official intervention what could not be otherwise gained. This situation was a far cry, however, from a legal order in which such rivalries could now be waged without constraint. Nor did the new code rules acknowledge any moral claim or community interest superior to the individual assertion of enforceable rights and duties.

In all countries around the globe throughout this century, a familiar sequence of events and forces has challenged classically liberal codes and legal doctrines of nineteenth-century private law. War, economic instability, and social inequities have led to demand for more corrective, direct governmental intervention. Japan's experience is therefore neither unique nor exceptional with respect to the confrontation between the liberal, individualistic premises of nineteenth-century western law and more egalitarian social concerns. What is exceptional, however, is the nature of the Japanese response. Two characteristics stand out.

The first has been Japan's conforming consistency. Japanese law has continued to adhere faithfully to the doctrinal constructs and language of the civil law tradition. Japan has not transformed a borrowed law. Rather it has made the transplant its own. Japanese law has remained conforming and consistent. No new uniquely Japanese rights have been created or doctrines introduced. Only sparingly have the rules or doctrine been reformed. The formal procedures have remained in place. Only adaptations and adjustments have been made. Yet, the law has not been static. Through an ongoing process of learning and teaching from abroad, scholars and judges continue with conforming consistency to adapt old rules and to introduce and apply new principles to continue to deal with constantly changing social, economic, and political wants.

Despite the continued conformity of Japanese law within a now global legal tradition, Japanese judges have fashioned the rules and adapted the doctrines in distinctive ways. Instead of expanding the rights of wives, tenants, and workers for their protection, the courts have rather restrained the rights of fathers and husbands, landlords, and employers to prevent their exercise in ways that seem abusive or overreaching. The result has been less to particularize justice—for, after all, repetition of particularized decisions inevitably leads to conduct-altering generalized predictions. In case after case throughout the century, Japanese judges have denied "rights" in order to ameliorate what they have perceived to be the injustice of property and contract enabling those with greater economic and social leverage to enlist the aid of the state against those with whom they dealt. Rather than developing new rights for the weak, Japanese courts constrained the old rights of the strong.

The second consequence of the twentieth-century confrontation between new law and old norms in Japan has been, as detailed above, to reinforce the community rather than the state. Japanese prosecutors have found in the community effective mechanisms to avoid the counterproductive consequences of the West's excessively punitive and individualistic criminal law and means to reinforce their own discretion and autonomy. Japanese scholars have introduced new theory and doctrines that in case after case enabled Japanese judges to shape the rules and principles of the codes to confirm community. Japanese judges have discovered in their own community ways to ensure consistency in the law and, through self-policing, to maintain public trust and independence.

In the resulting affirmation of community over the state, law has not been transformed into a mechanism for judicial policing to redress bargains or to redefine property. Rather the state remains more passive. The individual thus remains more dependent upon the community than the state. Nor has the Japanese Civil Code lost as completely its primacy. To be sure, as detailed above, Japanese courts have redressed imbalances of bargaining leverage and restricted absolutist claims in the exercise of property rights. They have done so, however, in particularized fashion. Left undisturbed are the code's original principles. *Pact sunt servanda* remains a paramount principle of law in Japan. Nor has legislative or administrative regulation replaced private law as extensively as in other industrial states. As exemplified even by the use of criminal law, the most coercive instrument of state power has been used as a mechanism for officially controlled communal participation and correction. In private law, by refusing to allow unilateral rupture of relationships but leaving undisturbed the legal effectiveness of mutual consent, whether for dissolution of a marriage or termination of employment, Japanese courts have largely left undisturbed party autonomy from the viewpoint of state intervention and enforcement but not the community. Even in constitutional law, the state has been restrained while the community has been affirmed.

Private law rules enable the parties to seek state intervention. But with state intervention, the parties no longer control their relationship. The parameters of their autonomy are subjected to state definition. This is not to say that extralegal rules established by agreement—that is, legally unenforceable contracts and promises—ensure greater party autonomy. To the extent that the parties are able to enforce rules through some alternative, extralegal mechanism, the parameters of their autonomy are similarly determined by those who exercise the powers of enforcement. In either case the enforcer controls. To the extent, for example, that business communities in Japan provide an effective alternative or substitute for judicial enforcement of contracts, these communities define the limits of party autonomy and the applicable rules of the transactions within their ambit.

Community enforcement enables a system of private ordering as an alternative to the state—a system of private ordering that in the abstract is as much beyond the control of the parties as the system of legal ordering by the state. However, insofar as the efficacy of community enforcement depends upon collective undertakings by the members of the community themselves, each participant has a voice in the process that cannot be duplicated in the legal process. By the same token, those outside the community have little or no say.

Community ordering rarely if ever operates in isolation from state ordering through the legal system. The two systems function concurrently and in competition. The modern state always, of course, has the capacity to intervene. Because the state defines its own competence, it retains the ultimate authority to control the limits of community autonomy. By policing transactions through "public law," the state can intervene directly. Enforcing rules through criminal law or administrative processes empowers prosecutors, regulatory officials, and always judges by enabling them to determine which rules govern. Although the extent of such empowerment of each office depends upon the scope of its "prosecutorial" or enforcement discretion, the state, acting through the legislature or the judiciary, has the last word.

In the enforcement of contracts, as in the application of constitutional constraints, the state in effect chooses to restrict its own competence and discretion. By allowing the parties the freedom to determine whether or not to seek to enforce the rules by taking the issues to court, the state permits competition from other systems of ordering. In theory, therefore, the parties have the choice and presumably select the enforcement system that best serves their interests.

Potential litigants can be expected, it is argued, to forecast the outcome of state enforcement and to settle any dispute in conformity with such prediction. As a result legal rules govern without the need (or costs) of actual litigation. Arguments along these lines regarding negotiated settlements with predicted outcomes in conformity to legal rules rest on the pivotal but seldom stated premise that the parties have an unhindered choice to litigate. Moreover, rarely taken into account are the effects of alternative systems of enforcement. If access to court is either precluded or not the preferred system of enforcement, the parties will not bargain in the "shadow of the law" as presupposed. Instead they will negotiate within the shadow of community norms and the predicted outcomes of community enforcement.

In part this results from the nature of such arrangements as reflections of varying degrees of mutual dependency. Judicially created rules that prevent unilateral termination of commercial relationships notwithstanding, the lack of contractual commitments to continue dealing both reflect and reinforce this orientation. In this respect neither the law nor the courts become irrelevant. Rather, both play a positive role in fostering such relational dealing.

Why this is so deserves closer attention. We can speculate that the "social density" of Japanese society, especially within its various communities, contributes substantially to the capacity of the community to enforce effectively accepted community norms. Repeated transactions over long periods of time among the same persons not only facilitate communication and enhance the flow of information, they also foster trust, cooperation, and interdependence, which combine to strengthen even further the bonds and cohesion among the participants. The literature on business transactions and contracting in Japan suggests a predominant emphasis on repeated deals based on relationships established over time and avoidance of spot transactions with strangers. Similar patterns apply in the context of other transactions in other communities.

Putting aside the question of causes, the effects of such a prevailing pattern of interrelationships seem clear—a community whose members share significant gains by continued cooperation, with significant barriers to withdrawal as well as to new entry. Whatever the drawbacks of such communitarian orientation, the cohesion of the participants tends to endure as the well-being and prosperity of each becomes increasingly dependent upon cooperation and reciprocal dealing with the others.

Many would concede the relative importance of community controls and private ordering in Japan but still question the role of the state. Surely, it can be said, legal rules do apply to contracts in Japan and the state does enforce contracts. Litigation rates may be low in Japan relative to other industrial countries, but Japan does have lawyers and judges, lawsuits and enforcement actions. Except in the presumably rare instances when the parties can be certain that community controls will indeed work, do they not negotiate in the shadow of the legal rules?

Whether through the mechanisms of formal enforcement or private ordering in the "shadow" of legal rules, the operation of law in any society has both intended and unintended consequences. The outcomes of lawsuits, criminal law enforcement, and administrative decisions tend in the aggregate to reflect and to define the role and often the value of law in a society at a point in time. The consequences of judicial decisions in cases involving the most intimate or essential relationships or deeply held beliefs form patterns that, intended or not, both reflect and define the spirit of law in Japan.

To the extent that the state offers more or even the same security and protection with fewer costs, community suffers. When the state fails, community gains. The relative weakness of formal law enforcement is therefore one aspect of Japan's communitarian emphasis. The argument need not be repeated at length here, but a lack of judges and trial lawyers, in addition to filing fees, bond-posting requirements, judicially imposed constraints on proof, and other disincentives combine to increase the costs of litigation and effectively restrict access.[2] While these or similar problems are not unique to Japan, they are relatively more severe in the Japanese legal system. As a result, the aggrieved party receives less state protection and therefore has less to gain from state intervention. Weak law enforcement also reinforces the prevalence of ongoing business relationships. Lack of legal protection—or perception that the law does not provide adequate security—inhibits transactions between strangers. Reputation and trust, introductions and go-betweens, become more important. Substitutes for legal means of redress are necessary.

Potential litigants in well-developed legal systems seldom face "sue or suffer" choices. Other means of redress, from self-help to community support, are usually available options. Nevertheless, extralegal mechanisms for redress of business grievances appear considerably less developed and weaker in these systems than in Japan. The published profiles of typical business disputes in Japan reveal a significantly greater emphasis on community-based measures both to resolve grievances and to enforce promises. Boycotts, refusals to deal, and other variants of commercial and social ostracism not only seem to be more prevalent in Japan than elsewhere, they also appear to be more socially acceptable. In addition to the relative weakness and inaccessibility of the formal mechanisms for law enforcement, self-help and community sanctions tend to be more easily and effectively applied.

Business dealing in Japan, for example, occurs in an environment that encourages relational contracting and provides a system of ordering that effectively substitutes for the formal legal system. Although such substitution may not reduce the rules of contract law to irrelevance, it does restrict their application and thus their role in regulating transactions and determining outcomes. Moreover, to the extent that, as a result of Japan's communitarian orientation, potential litigants are discouraged from pursuing claims, the community may indeed retard if not preclude any expansion of the judicial system and the development of legal rules at variance with community preferences.

Communities also compete with the state as a source of protection and benefit to its citizens. To remain cohesive and thus controlling, communities must remain a better source of well-being than the state. Thus their norms and controls have to serve their members better overall than those of the state. If community norms work against the interests of any member for very long, unless exit is foreclosed, that member can leave and thus cease to be subject to community controls. An isolated defection may not have too significant an effect, but multiplied over time, such defections will destroy the community. Community norms will thereby over time reflect the interests of members in general and not reflect preferential treatment to one group or another. Thus community norms can be expected over time to approximate whatever legal norms tend to maximize the interests of community members.

By the same token, however, each of the state's components also competes. Prosecutors and judges as well as bureaucrats and politicians seek public loyalty and support. They too can thus be expected to create and enforce legal rules that serve the broad interests of the public in general and those groups whose loyalty and support is the most crucial. In the process, legal rules as enforced will similarly over time move toward community norms. Differences will of course remain, but the differences will for the most part reflect differences in the interests of separate communities or constituencies. As this process continues, the state inexorably reinforces rather than erodes community cohesion.

Like Japan's traditional villages, from large-scale business enterprises to government bureaucracies, "communities" in effect have become semiautonomous social units. To the extent the state or the politicians allow them freedom from—or for whatever reason do not impose—direct managerial or regulatory controls, they are able to develop and enforce their own autonomous rules of the game. In other words, except in cases where the state chooses to intervene with coercive commands, these "villages" function effectively.

Japan's contemporary communities also share another feature. Most remain closed and controlling. In the United States, the Forest Service and the military are the only close parallels to Japan's governmental "communities" and large-scale bureaucratic enterprises. Entry occurs almost exclusively at the lowest rank. Lateral entry is a rare exception. Exit is possible but, given the lack of lateral mobility in comparable organizations, usually with financial and social risks. Thus at the beginning of one's career as a judge or as a member of one of Japan's larger organizations, the course and end of a lifetime career can be predicted. The individual trades independence for security, a security that is dependent on compliance with the norms of the community and its collective prosperity. Central personnel authorities determine one's career progress. Dependent upon their evaluation of one's contribution to the community, the individual is again forced to conform. Loyalty, hard work, and honesty are rewarded, but often at the expense of self-fulfillment, family, and any conflicting personal or broader societal interests. The community can indeed become the tyrant.

The defining pattern for Japanese law, during the course of the twentieth century, has been its communitarian orientation. How enduring will be this emphasis can only be guessed at. To what extent it will continue into the next century is open to question. Many Japanese plea for reform.[3] Change through learning from the West, concern for individual autonomy, and the views of scholars are also predominant features of the spirit of Japanese law. During the next century, perhaps their combined influence, along with economic imperatives, will produce another transforming change. However, a balance can be struck. As Tatsuo Inoue has eloquently argued: "Reorientation toward individual rights does not necessitate the sacrifice of all the positive aspects of human communality to individualism. Rather, the Japanese experience shows that individual rights are needed to enjoy a richer form of human communality. The tyranny of intermediary communities impoverishes both the communal and individual dimensions of human existence."[4]

More certain is the proposition that Japanese judges will shoulder a large share of the responsibility for whatever change may come through law. They cannot evade or shift it to others. Within law's domain, they will still have the last word.

NOTES

Introduction

1 For a study of the development of law-enforcing institutions and processes in Japan, see J. Haley, *Authority Without Power: Law and the Japanese Paradox* (New York and London, 1991).

2 J. H. Wigmore, *Panorama of the World's Legal Systems* (St. Paul, 1928), 503–20.

3 See, for example, M. Ōki, *Nihonjin no hō kannen* [Japanese people's concept of law] (Tokyo, 1983).

4 F. K. Upham, *Law and Social Change in Postwar Japan* (Cambridge, Mass., 1987).

Chapter 1: Law's Values

1 See H. Tanaka, *The Japanese Legal System: Cases and Materials* (Tokyo, 1976), 143–61.

2 See E. Fujibayashi, *Hōritsuka no chie* [A jurist's wisdom] (Tokyo, 1984), 101–3, on the importance of the Supreme Court in resolving conflicting decisions by separate high courts. The desire to create a unifying system of national law was a major impetus for Japan's reception of western law. See, for example, R. Ishii, *Meiji bunka shi: 2 Hōsei hen* [History of Meiji culture: volume 2, The legal system] (Tokyo, 1954), 18; translated into English by W. Chambliss as *Japanese Culture in the Meiji Era, Volume 18: Legislation* (Tokyo, 1958), 28.

3 I. Suehiro, *Hanrei minpō* [Civil law precedents] (Tokyo, 1923), ii–viii. The quote is translated in Tanaka, *Japanese Legal System*, 147.

4 *Saibansho kōsei hō* [Court Organization Law] (Law no. 6, 1890), art. 49.

5 *Saibansho hō* [Court Law] (Law no. 59, 1947), art. 10 (iii).

6 *Keiji soshō hō* [Code of Criminal Procedure] (Law no. 131, 1948), art. 405 (ii and iii).

7 T. Kawashima, "The Concept of Judicial Precedent in Japanese Law," in E. von Caemmerer, S. Mentschikoff, and K. Zweigert, eds., *Ius Privatum Gentium: Festschrift für Max Rheinstein zum 70. Geburtstag am 5. Juli 1969* (Tübingen, 1969), 87–99.

8 See, for example, M. Rikō, *Ritsuryō kenkyū zokuchō* [Research on the ritsuryō codes] (Tokyo, 1994), 187–89.

9 For example, D. Henderson, "Chinese Legal Studies in Early 18th Century Japan," *Journal of Asian Studies* 30 (1970): 21–56; and P. Chen, *The Formation of the Early Meiji Legal Order* (London, 1981).

10 See Tanaka, *Japanese Legal System*, 59; J. Haley and D. Henderson, *Law and the Legal Process in Japan*, rev. ed. (Seattle, 1988), 599–603.

11 *Shōhō* [Commercial Code] (Law no. 48, 1899). Article 1 provides: "As to a commercial matter, in the event there is no applicable provision of this Code, customary commercial law shall apply; and if there is no applicable commercial customary law, the Civil Code shall apply."

12 R. Pound, *An Introduction to the Philosophy of Law* (New Haven, 1922), 47.

13 For example, S. N. Eisenstadt, *Power, Trust, and Meaning* (Chicago, 1995), 27–30. See also S. N. Eisenstadt, *Japanese Civilization* (Chicago, 1997).

14 M. Damaska, "A Continental Lawyer in an American Law School: Trials and Tribulations of Adjustment," *University of Pennsylvania Law Review* 116 (1968): 1363.

15 *Japan Almanac 1993* (Tokyo, 1992), 253.

16 T. S. Lebra, *Japanese Patterns of Behavior* (Honolulu, 1976), 1–21.

17 V. L. Hamilton and J. Sanders, *Everyday Justice: Responsibility and the Individual in Japan and the United States* (New Haven, 1992).

18 Lebra, *Patterns of Behavior*, 4.

19 Y. Higuchi, "When Society is the Tyrant," *Japan Quarterly* 35 (1988): 350–56.

Chapter 2: Law's Domain

1 See, for example, J. Migdal, *Strong Societies and Weak States* (Princeton, 1988).

2 J. Braithwaite, *Crime, Shame and Reintegration* (Cambridge, 1989).

3 J. Haley, "Japan's Postwar Civil Service: The Legal Framework," in H. K. Kim et al., eds., *The Japanese Civil Service and Economic Development: Catalysts of Change* (Oxford, 1995), 93 n. 16.

4 R. Rabinowitz, "Law and the Social Process in Japan," *Transactions of the Asiatic Society of Japan*, 3d ser., 10 (1968): 42–43.

5 *Nenkan sakuingō* [Annual cumulative index], *Hōritsu hanrei bunken jōhō* [Information on literature on statutes and court decisions] (Tokyo, 1981).

6 E. Tipton, *Japanese Police State: Tokyo in Interwar Japan* (Honolulu, 1990), 69.

7 H. Wada, "The Administrative Court Under the Meiji Constitution," *Law in Japan: An Annual* 10 (1977): 1–64.

8 The immovable registration statute, for instance, provides for the registration of contingent rights in real property. Registration enables the holder of contingent rights to establish priority in a claim for registered ownership once the contingency occurs and the conditions to the claim of ownership are satisfied. As a result, various devices have been used to secure loans either through transfers of title to the creditor with registration of a contingent interest to protect the debtor in possession, as in the case of a sale to the creditor of the real property to be used as collateral with a registered lease and buy-back contract effective upon full payment of principal and interest, or simply the registration of the right to ownership by the creditor as substituted performance for the debtor's repayment of the loan that becomes automatically effective upon default.

9 *Karitōki tanpo keiyaku ni kansuru hōritsu* [Law concerning provisional registration security contracts] (Law no. 78, 1978). See J. Haley, "The Preliminary Contract for Substitute Performance: A Reflection of Japanese Judicial Approach," *Law in Japan: An Annual* 7 (1974): 133–48.

10 See T. Bryant, "For the Sake of the Country, For the Sake of the Family: The Oppressive Impact of Family Registration on Women and Minorities in Japan," *UCLA Law Review* 39 (1991): 109–68.

11 See, for example, A. Tiedemann, "Big Business and Politics in Prewar Japan," in J. Morley, ed., *Dilemmas of Growth in Prewar Japan* (Princeton, 1971), 267–316.

12 J. Haley, "The Politics of Informal Justice: The Japanese Experience, 1922–1942," in R. Abel, ed., *The Politics of Informal Justice* (New York, 1982), 2:125–47.

13 *Chian iji hō* [Peace Preservation Law] (Law no. 46, 1925).

14 Y. Noguchi, *1940 nen taisei* [1940 system] (Tokyo, 1996).

15 See F. K. Upham, *Law and Social Change in Postwar Japan* (Cambridge, Mass., 1987).

16 See, for example, M. Tilton, *Restrained Trade: Cartels in Japan's Basic Materials Industries* (Ithaca, 1996).

17 *Gaishi ni kansuru hōritsu* [Foreign Investment Law](Law no. 163, 1950); *Gaikoku kawase oyobi gaikoku bōeki kanri hō* [Foreign Exchange and Trade Control Law] (Law no. 228, 1949).

18 H. First, "Antitrust Enforcement in Japan," *Antitrust Law Journal* 64 (1995): 137–82; quote, 143.

19 See, for example, J. Haley, "Mission to Manage: The U.S. Forest Service as a 'Japanese' Bureaucracy," in K. Hayashi, ed., *The U.S.-Japanese Economic Relationship: Can It Be Improved?* (New York, 1989), 196–225.

20 *Shiteki dokusen no kinshi oyobi kōsei torihiki no kakuho ni kansuru hōritsu* [Law concerning the prohibition of private monopoly and protection of fair trade] (Law no. 54, 1947).

21 *Gesetz gegen Wettbewerbsbeschränkungen* [Law against Restraints of Competition] (Law of July 27, 1957, BGB1. I 1081).

22 *Yushutsu torihiki hō* [Export Transactions Law] (Law no. 299, 1952); *Yushutsunyū torihiki hō* [Export and Import Transactions Law] (Law no. 188, 1953).

23 *Seizōbutsu sekinin hō* [Products Liability Law] (Law no. 85, 1994). The law became effective on July 1, 1995. See T. Madden, "An Explanation of Japan's Product Liability Law," *Pacific Rim Law & Policy Journal* 5 (1996): 299–300; A. Marcuse, "Why Japan's New Products Liability Law Isn't," *Pacific Rim Law & Policy Journal* 5 (1996): 379–82.

24 See, J. Haley, "Japanese Administrative Law: Introduction," *Law in Japan: An Annual* 19 (1986): 1–14.

25 C. Wollschläger, "Long-term Economic Development and Civil Litigation in Japan, the U.S., and Germany," in H. Baum, ed., *Japan: Economic Success and Legal System* (Berlin, 1996), 89–142. See also C. Wollschlager, "Civil Litigation in Japan, Sweden, and the USA Since the 19th Century: Japanese Legal Culture in the Light of Statistical Judicial Statistics" (paper presented at the 1995 Annual Meeting, Research Committee on Sociology of Law, International Sociological Association, Legal Culture, Encounters and Transformations 3, Tokyo, August 1–4, 1995).

26 J. Haley, *Authority Without Power: Law and the Japanese Paradox* (New York and London, 1991), 71–72.

27 See, for example, "Japanese Discover the Lawsuit," *Los Angeles Times*, Nov. 13, 1995, A6.

28 See J. M. Ramseyer and M. Nakazato, "The Rational Litigant: Settlement Amounts and Verdict Rates in Japan," *Journal of Legal Studies* 18 (1989): 263–90.

29 Upham, *Law and Social Change*.

30 T. Tyler, *Why People Obey the Law* (New Haven, 1990).

31 R. Dore, *Taking Japan Seriously: A Confucian Perspective on Leading Economic Issues* (Stanford, 1987), 74.

32 See, for example, T. Fukase, "Nihon no rippō katei no tokushoku," [Distinctive features of the Japanese legislative process], *Jurisuto*, no. 805 (1984): 16–24.

33 *Gyōsei tetsuzuki hō* [Administrative procedure law] (Law no. 88, 1993). For an English-language translation, see M. Levin trans., "Administrative Procedure Act," *Law in Japan: An Annual* 25 (1995): 141–59. The most thorough study of the statute and its background is L. Ködderitsch, "Japan's New Administrative Procedure Law: Reasons for Its Enactment and Likely Implications," *Law in Japan: An Annual* 24 (1991): 105–37.

34 Marcuse, "Japan's New Products Liability Law," 398.

35 *Shakuchi hō* [Land Lease Law] (Law no. 49, 1921); *Shakuya hō* [House Lease Law] (Law no. 50, 1921). See T. Hozumi, "Hōritsu kōi no 'kaishaku' no kōzō to kinō, 2" [Structure and function of the 'interpretation' of juristic acts, pt. 2], *Hōgaku kyōkai zasshi* 78, no. 1 (1961): 27–71; translated by author in *Law in Japan: An Annual* 5 (1972): 154–61.

36 *Shakuchi shakuya hō* [Land Lease and House Lease Law] (Law no. 90, 1991). See J. O. Haley, "Japan's New Land and House Lease Law, " in J. O. Haley and K. Yamamura, eds., *Land Issues in Japan: A Policy Failure* (Seattle, 1992), 149–73.

37 *Ginkō hō* [Banking Law] (Law no. 21, 1927).

38 *Shokuryō kanri hō* [Food Control Law] (Law no. 40, 1942).

39 *Shuyō shokuryō no jukyū oyobi kakaku no antei ni kansuru hōritsu* [Law concerning the supply and demand and stability of prices of primary foods] (Law no. 113, 1994).

40 For elaboration, see Haley, *Authority Without Power*, esp. 169–91.

41 See *Sato v. Japan, Keishū* 16:193 (Gr. Ct. Cass., 3d Crim. Dept., Dec. 3, 1936). See *Japan v. Sekiyu Renmei, Hanrei jihō*, no. 983:22 (Tokyo High Ct., Sept. 26, 1980), translated in J. M. Ramseyer, "The Oil Cartel Criminal Cases: Translations and Postscript," in J. Haley, ed., *Law and Society in Contemporary Japan: American Perspectives* (Dubuque, 1988), 67–84; discussion of criminal intent, 71–72.

Chapter 3: Law's Actors I

1 See N. Toshitani, *Nihon no hō o kangaeru* [Thoughts on Japanese law], 3d ed. (Tokyo, 1991), 96; and W. Ames, *Police and Community in Japan* (Berkeley, 1981).

2 See, for example, H. Tanaka, *Jittei hōgaku nyūmon* [Introduction to positive law jurisprudence], 2d ed. (Tokyo, 1966), 262–310.

3 R. Torrance, *The Fiction of Tokuda Shūsei and the Emergence of Japan's New Middle Class* (Seattle, 1994), 18.

4 Japanese National Commission for UNESCO, *The Role of Education in the Social and Economic Development of Japan* (Tokyo, 1966), table 62(A), p. 124.

5 See S. Miyazawa, "For the Liberal Transformation of Japanese Legal Culture: A Review of Recent Scholarship and Practice" (paper presented at the 1995 Annual Meeting of the Research Committee on Sociology of Law of the International Sociological Association, Tokyo, August 3, 1995).

6 Z. Kitagawa, *Nihon no hōgaku no rekushi to riron* [History and theory of Japanese jurisprudence] (Tokyo, 1968); Z. Kitagawa, *Rezeption und Fortbildung des europäischen Zivilrechts in Japan* [Reception and continuing study of European Civil Law in Japan] (Frankfurt, 1970).

7 See, for example, E. Makino, *Gendai no bunka to hōritsu* [Contemporary culture and law] (Tokyo, 1918); E. Makino, *Hōritsu ni okeru mujun to chōwa* [Contradiction and harmony in laws] (Tokyo, 1919); E. Makino, *Hōritsu ni okeru seigi to kōhei* [Justice and fairness in laws] (Tokyo, 1920).

8 E. Makino, "Hōritsu ni okeru gutai-teki datōsei" [The concrete relevance of laws], *Hōgaku shirin* 24, no. 10 (1922), reprinted in Makino, *Hōritsu ni okeru gutai-teki datōsei* (Tokyo, 1925), 1–101; T. Uchida, "Gendai keiyaku hō no arata na tenkai to ippan jōko" [New directions in contemporary contract law and the general clauses], *NBL*, no. 516 (1993): 29 n. 6.

9 M. Itō, *Saibankan to gakusha no aida* [Between judge and scholar] (Tokyo, 1993), 23.

10 C. Nakane, *Japanese Society* (Berkeley, 1972), 48.

11 *Bengoshi rinri* [Code of Attorney Ethics] (adopted March 19, 1955, as amended March 27, 1987).

12 Information provided by Japan Foundation of Bar Association, International Section, July 23, 1996.

13 F. K. Upham, *Law and Social Change in Postwar Japan* (Cambridge, Mass., 1987).

14 *Bengoshi hō* [Attorney Law], Law no. 205, 1949, Art. 30.

15 Okudaira, Masahiro, *Nihon bengoshi shi* [History of Japanese bar], (Tokyo, 1914), 1352–61.

16 Toshitani, *Nihon no hō* [Japanese law], 96–120.

17 R. Torrance, letter to author, June 28, 1990.

18 *Tōkyō Asahi Shinbun*, March 2, 1928, p. 2; October 24, 1933, p. 2; April 9, 1928, p. 4; April 13, 1931, p. 11; June 23, 1932, p. 1; July 17, 1932, p. 2; February 20, 1934, p. 11.

19 See, for example, *Tōkyō Asahi Shinbun*, April 25, 1929, p. 11 [Excessive competition is cause of corruption among lawyers]; April 28, 1929, p. 1 [Lawyer arrested for cutting pages from court record]; June 19, 1929, p. 9 [Lawyer arrested for attack on money lender]; July 5, 1929, p. 2 [Prosecutors plan another round-up of corrupt lawyers]; April 13, 1930, p. 2 [Another corrupt lawyer arrested]; April 16, 1930, p. 2 [Another corrupt lawyer arrested for extortion, major round-up in making]; April 18, 1930, p. 2 [Another corrupt lawyer picked up]; April 20, 1930, p. 2 [Another lawyer arrested for fraud]; June 1, 1930 [Five lawyers prosecuted for fraud]; March 6, 1931, p. 3 [Client sues lawyer for fraud]; November 6, 1935, p. 2 [Lawyers arrested on charges of embezzlement]; July 8, 1936, p. 2 [Lawyer arrested for extortion].

20 For example, *Tōkyō Asahi Shinbun*, February 21, 1932, p. 2 [Tatsuji Fuse convicted and sentenced to 4 months in prison for having an article published in violation of the Newspaper Law]; August 7, 1932, p. 2 [Lawyers arrested for contributing funds to left-wing causes]; September 29, 1932, p. 2 [Former judge and an attorney arrested for contributing funds to radical groups]; September 14, p. 2 [Fuse arrested again]; December 4, 1935, p. 2 [Fuse refuses to recant views; prosecutor grants that Fuse never member of Communist Party but demands six-year sentence for pernicious influence]; November 26, 1931, p. 7 [Imamura brought before disciplinary court on charge of deliberately stalling proceedings by charging, against his client's wishes, judge with evasion].

21 See, for example, *Tōkyō Asahi Shinbun*, July 11, 1933 [Acid thrown in face of lawyer acting as counsel for landlord seeking to evict tenants from dance hall].

22 *Bengoshi hō* [Attorney Law] (Law no. 7, 1893).

23 See R. Ishii, *Meiji bunka shi* [History of Meiji culture] (Tokyo, 1954), 18:229; translated into English by W. Chambliss as *Japanese Culture in the Meiji Era* (Tokyo, 1958), 18:292.

24 D. Johnson, "The Japanese Way of Justice: Prosecuting Crime in Japan" (Ph.D. diss., University of California, Berkeley, Law and Social Policy, 1996), 193.

25 Ibid., 80–91.

26 See M. Mitsui, "Kensatsukan no kisō yūyō sairyō: sono rekishi-teki

oyobi jisshō-teki kenkyū" [Prosecutors' discretion to suspend prosecution: Studies on its history and actual practice], *Hōgaku kyōkai zasshi,* vol. 87, nos. 9–10 (1970); vol. 91, nos. 7, 9, 12 (1974); vol. 94, no. 6 (1977). In English, see Johnson, "Prosecuting Crime," 286–99; M. Goodman, "The Exercise and Control of Prosecutorial Discretion in Japan," *Pacific Basin Law Review* 5 (1986): 16–95; D. Foote, "Prosecutorial Discretion in Japan: A Response," *Pacific Basin Law Review* 5 (1986): 96–106; B. J. George, "Discretionary Authority of Public Prosecutors in Japan," *Law in Japan: An Annual* 17 (1984): 42–72; S. Itō, *Mata damasareru kenji* [Prosecutor fooled again], 7th ed. (Tokyo, 1993), 186–89.

27 *Keiji hoshō hō* [Criminal case indemnity law] (Law no. 60, 1931). See M. West, "Note: Prosecution Review Commissions: Japan's Answer to the Problem of Prosecutorial Discretion," *Columbia Law Review* 92 (1992): 684–723. Originally referred to in English as an "inquest of prosecution," the institution was literally created by Thomas Blakemore in order to thwart American demands that Japan adopt a grand jury system to control prosecutorial discretion. See J. Haley, *Authority Without Power: Law and the Japanese Paradox* (New York and London, 1991), 126.

28 See Johnson, "Prosecuting Crime," 487–90.

29 See, for example, R. Appleton, "Reforms in Japanese Criminal Procedure Under Allied Occupation," *Washington Law Review* 24 (1949): 401, 402–3. See also R. Mitchell, *Thought Control in Prewar Japan* (Ithaca, 1976), 99–194.

30 Appleton, "Reforms in Japanese Criminal Procedure," 402 n. 6.

31 See *Japan Weekly Chronicle,* September 29, 1927, 336.

32 R. Yasko, "Bribery Cases and the Rise of the Justice Ministry in Late Meiji–Early Taishō Japan," *Law in Japan: An Annual* 12 (1979): 57–68; R. Yasko, "Hiranuma Kiichirō and Conservative Politics in Pre-war Japan" (Ph.D. diss., Department of History, University of Chicago, 1973).

33 *Asahi Shinbun,* September 9, 1992, 13; see also M. Sato, *Kenji chōsho no yohaku* [In the margins of a prosecutor's notebook], (Tokyo, 1993), 283–85.

34 Daniel H. Foote, "The Benevolent Paternalism of Japanese Criminal Justice," *California Law Review* 80 (1992): 317–90.

35 Johnson, "Prosecuting Crime," 265 (table 1), 295.

36 Foote, "Benevolent Paternalism," 348.

37 Johnson, "Prosecuting Crime," 298.

38 Foote, "Benevolent Paternalism," 349, citing a Ministry of Justice study.

Chapter 4: Crime and Community

1 See D. Black, *The Behavior of Law* (New York, 1976).

2 *Keiji hō* [Criminal Code] (Law no. 45, 1907); *Keiji soshō hō* [Code of Criminal Procedure] (Law no. 131, 1948). The English language literature on the history and basic features of the criminal justice system in Japan is voluminous: In addition to previously cited works, see H. Meyers, "Revisions of the Criminal Code of Japan during the Occupation," *Washington Law Review* 25 (1950): 491–530; A. Nagashima, "The Accused and Society: The Administration of Criminal Justice in Japan," in A. von Mehren, ed., *Law in Japan: The Legal Order in A Changing Society* (Cambridge, Mass., 1963); S. Dando, *Japanese Criminal Procedure*, trans. B. J. George (Hackensack, N.J., 1965); G. Koshi, *The Japanese Legal Advisor* (Rutland and Tokyo, 1970); W. Clifford, *Crime Control in Japan* (Lexington, Mass., 1976); A. D. Castberg, *Japanese Criminal Justice* (New York, 1990); J. Westermann and J. Burfeind, *Crime and Justice in Two Societies: Japan and the United States* (Pacific Grove, Calif., 1991); M. Shikita and S. Tsuchiya, *Crime and Criminal Policy in Japan: Analysis and Evaluation of the Showa Era, 1926–1988* (New York, 1992); R. Thornton and K. Endo, *Preventing Crime in America and Japan: A Comparative Study* (Armonk, N.Y., and London, 1992).

3 On the proposals and debates over revision in English, see R. Hirano, "The Draft of the Revised Penal Code," *Law in Japan: An Annual* 6 (1973): 49–64; D. Johnson, "The Japanese Way of Justice: Prosecuting Crime in Japan" (Ph.D. diss., University of California, Berkeley, Law and Social Policy, 1996), 103–6.

4 See N. Nishida, "Das Japanische im japanischen Strafrecht" [The Japanese in Japanese criminal law], in H. Menkhaus, ed., *Das Japanische im japanischen Recht* [The Japanese in Japanese law] (Munich, 1994), 529.

5 A. Oppler, *Legal Reforms in Occupied Japan: A Participant Looks Back* (Princeton, 1976), 121.

6 See *Political Reorientation of Japan* (Report of Government Section, Supreme Commander for the Allied Powers, September 1945–September 1948), 241–42. A "Dear Mr. Prime Minister" letter from General Douglas MacArthur was necessary to persuade the Japanese government to delete the provisions.

7 Johnson, "Prosecuting Crime," 227–34.

8 From the 1764 treatise on criminal law, *Dei Dellitti e delle Pene* (translated into English in 1776 as *An Essay on Crimes and Punishments*) by

the Italian jurist, Caesar Bonesana, Marquis di Beccaria (1735–1794). *Satō v. Japan, Keishū* 16:193 (Gr. Ct. Cass., 3d Crim. Dept., Dec. 3, 1936), holding that a cabinet order establishing a "crime of preparation" (*yobizai*) as a criminal violation of the foreign exchange control statute exceeded the permissible scope of delegated authority. *Kenpō* [Constitution], arts. 31, 39, and 73.

9 Ministry of Justice, Research and Training Institute, *Summary of the White Paper on Crime, 1995* (Tokyo, 1995), 3, 56.

10 B. J. George, "Discretionary Authority of Public Prosecutors in Japan," *Law in Japan: An Annual* 17 (1984): 51 n. 94.

11 M. Shikita, "Integrated Approach to Effective Administration of Criminal and Juvenile Justice," in UNAFEI, *Criminal Justice in Asia: The Quest for an Integrated Approach* (Tokyo, 1982), 37.

12 Johnson, "Prosecuting Crime," 154.

13 Ibid., 83.

14 Code of Criminal Procedure, art. 461–2, 462.

15 Ibid., art. 461, as amended by Law no. 31, 1991.

16 The 570 summary courts in Japan generally lack jurisdiction over any cases involving an offense not subject to a penal fine at least as an optional penalty: *Saibansho hō* [Court organization law] (Law no. 59, 1947), art. 33(2)(i). Summary courts have express jurisdiction over cases involving habitual gambling, larceny, embezzlement, and accepting or selling stolen property. They also have authority to impose a sentence of up to three years imprisonment with forced labor in these and certain other special offenses under special statutes. Court Organization Law, art. 33(2)(ii).

17 *White Paper, 1995,* 57.

18 S. Miyazawa, *Policing in Japan: A Study on Making Crime* (Albany, 1992), 225–26.

19 *White Paper, 1995,* 58.

20 Criminal Code, arts. 26–2, 26–3 (added to the code pursuant to Law no. 195, 1953), 27, 66, 68(1).

21 See J. Haley, "Restorative Justice: The Japanese Model," in B. Galaway and E. Hudson, eds., *Restorative Justice: International Perspectives* (Monsey, N.Y., 1996), 357.

22 Abe, "The Accused and Society," 334; K. Oyama, "Criminal Justice in Japan IV" (paper prepared for UNAFEI program, c. 1978), 9.

23 M. Shikita, "Integrated Approach," 37.

24 H. Wagatsuma and A. Rosett, "The Implications of Apology: Law and

Culture in Japan and the United States," *Law & Society Review* 20 (1986): 461–98.

25 Ames, *Police and Community,* 136; D. Bayley, *Forces of Order: Police Behavior in Japan and the United States* (Berkeley, 1976), 148.

26 A. Yamaguchi, "Victim Restitution and the Japanese Criminal Justice System," in V. Kusuda-Smith, ed., *Crime Prevention and Control in the United States and Japan* (Dobbs Ferry, N.Y., 1990), 167.

27 Thornton and Endo, *Preventing Crime,* 161.

28 See, for example, F. Igarashi, "Crime, Confession and Control in Contemporary Japan," *Law in Context* 2 (1984): 1–30; Miyazawa, *Policing in Japan,* 158–67, 235.

29 See, for example, Johnson, "Prosecuting Crime," 541–42.

30 Dando, *Japanese Criminal Procedure,* 196, 205–6.

31 Miyazawa, *Policing in Japan,* 81.

32 *Sangiin Sōmu I'inkai no kokusei chōsaken ni kansuru shiryō* [Materials concerning the investigatory authority of the House of Councilors Judicial Affairs Committee], *Sangiin Hōmu I'inchō no Urawa Mitsuko jiken ni kansuru chōsa hōkokusho* [House of Councilors Judiciary Committee Chair report concerning the investigation of the Mitsuko Urawa case], *Hōsō jihō* 1, no. 5 (1949): 77, 96.

33 Johnson, "Prosecuting Crime," 455.

34 A prominent example was the March 1996 visit to Japan by Vivien Stern, the secretary-general of the London-based Penal Reform International, and Andrew Coyle, governor of London's Brixton Prison, at the invitation of the British Council and the Japanese Center for Prisoners' Rights, reported in the *Japan Times Weekly* (International Edition), March 25–31, 1996, p. 7. See report titled Human Rights Watch/Asia, Human Rights Watch Prison Project, *Prison Conditions in Japan* (New York, 1995).

35 Comment to author by Professor Masahito Inouye, August 4, 1996.

36 *Japan Times Weekly* (International Edition), March 25–31, 1996, p. 7.

37 Ibid.

38 *Hōmu Sōgō Kenkyūjō Kenkyūbu kiyō* 29 [Ministry of Justice Combined Research Institute Research Division Bulletin no. 29] (Tokyo, 1986), 20.

39 Wagatsuma and Rosett, "Implications of Apology," 472, 473, 474, 478.

40 T. Rohlen, *For Harmony and Strength: Japanese White-Collar Organization in Anthropological Perspective* (Berkeley, 1974), 79.

41 See, for example, M. Misawa, "Daiwa Bank Scandal in New York: Its Causes, Significance, and Lessons in the International Society," *Vanderbilt Journal of Transnational Law* 29 (1996): 1–51; and E. Feldman, *De-*

constructing the Japanese HIV Scandal, Japan Policy Research Institute Working Paper no. 30 (Cardiff, Calif., February 1997).

42 V. L. Hamilton and J. Sanders, "Punishment and the Individual in the United States and Japan, *Law & Society Review* 22 (1988): 323–24. This point is given less emphasis in their subsequently published monograph, *Everyday Justice* (New Haven, 1992).

43 T. Lebra, "Apology and Self: The Japanese Case" (paper presented for panel, "Righting Wrongs: Compensation, Apology and Retribution in Contemporary Pacific Societies," ASAO Meeting, Kona, Hawaii, February 6–12, 1995); N. Tavuchis, *Mea Culpa: A Sociology of Apology and Reconciliation* (Stanford, 1991).

44 *Asahi Shinbun*, 7 November 1984, 22–23.

45 Hamilton and Sanders, *Everyday Justice*, esp. 167–73.

46 See J. Haley, "Comment: The Implications of Apology," *Law & Society Review* 20 (1986): 499–507.

47 Tavuchis, *Mea Culpa*, 34.

48 M. Goodman, "The Exercise and Control of Prosecutorial Discretion in Japan," *Pacific Basin Law Review* 5 (1986): 39.

49 T. Bryant, "*Oya-ko Shinjū:* Death at the Center of the Heart," *UCLA Pacific Basin Law Journal* 8 (1990): 1, 12–13.

50 Ibid.

Chapter 5: Law's Actors II

1 See J. M. Ramseyer and F. Rosenbluth, *Japan's Political Marketplace* (Cambridge, Mass., 1993), 142–81.

2 D. F. Henderson, *Foreign Enterprise in Japan: Laws and Policies* (Chapel Hill, 1973), 173.

3 See J. H. Merryman, *The Civil Law Tradition*, 2d ed. (Stanford, 1985), 34–38.

4 *Kenpō* [Constitution], art. 76(3).

5 See, for example, *Abe v. Chiba, Minshū* 18:954 (Sup. Ct., 2d P.B., June 26, 1964), translated in D. F. Henderson and J. Haley, *Law and the Legal Process in Japan* (Seattle, 1978), 649–50.

6 Merryman, *Civil Law Tradition*, 34–38.

7 For a detailed account of the formal processes for the selection of judges by the late Takaaki Hattori, a former Chief Justice who spent much of his career as judge in the administration of the judiciary, see Takaaki

Hattori, "The Role of the Supreme Court of Japan in the Field of Judicial Administration," *Washington Law Review* 60 (1984): 69–86.

8 Ibid., 77.

9 As of 1996, 115 judges were assigned to the following administrative, instructional, and research offices of the Supreme Court: General Affairs Bureau (45), Legal Training and Research Institute (27), Office of Court Clerks (10), Family Court Research Bureau (3), Supreme Court Library (1), Research Judges (29). Nihon Minshū Hōritsuka Kyōkai & Shihō Seido I'inkai [Japan Democratic Jurists Association and Legal System Committee], eds., *Zensaibankan keireki sokan: Kaitei shinpan* [Judges' almanac: Revised edition] (Tokyo, 1990), 452–57.

10 See L. Beer and H. Itoh, *The Constitutional Case Law of Japan, 1970 through 1990* (Seattle, 1996), 66.

11 Saikō Saibansho Jimu Sōkyoku [Supreme Court General Secretariat], *Heisei 6 nen, Shihō tōkei nenpo* [Annual Report of judicial statistics, 1994] (Tokyo 1995), vol. 1, *Civil Cases*, 12; ibid., vol. 2, *Criminal Cases*, 5.

12 The autonomy of the Japanese judiciary has recently become the subject of debate. Two respected scholars argue that political actors in fact manipulate judges in order to direct the development of Japanese law. One, University of Chicago Law School Professor J. Mark Ramseyer, joined by his colleague Frances McCall Rosenbluth, argues that "Japanese legislators not only *try* to discipline their judicial agents, but they also largely—however imperfectly—succeed" (Ramseyer and Rosenbluth, *Japan's Political Marketplace*, 162).

13 *Saibansho kōsei hō* [Court organization law] (Law no. 6, 1890), arts. 73 and 74.

14 Ibid., art. 74–2 (added by amendment, Law no. 101, 1921).

15 For an eloquent but extreme argument to the contrary, see J. M. Ramseyer and F. Rosenbluth, *The Politics of Oligarchy* (Cambridge, 1996).

16 See, for example, *Tōkyō Asahi Shinbun*, February 10, 1929, p. 11 (Prosecutor seeks ten years imprisonment in Peace Preservation Law trial of "Red Judge" Ozaki; he asks for three year terms for three other judges on trial); February 11, 1931 (Ozaki sentenced to eight years); May 11, 1931, p. 2 (Prosecutor resigns, seen in company of cafe hostess and mistakenly identified as his brother-in-law, a prominent politician under attack for communist sympathies).

17 For an example of the attitude of judges in the late 1930s toward stricter

penalties for violations of the 1925 Peace Preservation Law [*Chian iji hō*], see R. Mitchell, *Janus-Faced Justice: Political Criminals in Imperial Japan* (Honolulu, 1992), 99.

18 See *Tōkyō Asahi Shinbun*, November 2, 1930, p. 1 [Ministry of Justice unable to reduce budget by 2.1 million yen (U.S.$1.5 million) as requested by government]; November 5, 1930, p. 2 [Judges and procurators oppose reductions in salaries]; November 6, 1930, p. 1 [Twenty judges and ten prosecutors will have to be let go to meet budget]; January 1, 1931, p. 2 [Eleven upper-level employees of the Justice Ministry to retire during year]; March 10, 1931, p. 2 [*Seiyūkai* protests government order for "cessation of work" (*jimu teishi*) at sixty-two courts as economizing measure, charging measure amounts to discontinuation of courts in violation of 1890 Court Organization Law]; March 31, 1931, p. 3 [Editorial criticizes Hamaguchi Cabinet action as improper means of economizing]; May 10, 1931, p. 2, [Judges and procurators strongly oppose proposed salary reductions]; May 22, 1931, p. 2, [Ministry of Justice considers reductions of judges' salaries by imperial ordinance illegal under Court Organization Law]; May 28, 1931, p. 1 [Judges' salaries exempt; procurators protest discriminatory treatment; judges unenthusiastic but "voluntarily" accepting cuts]; June 1, 1931, p. 1, [Salary reductions for all government officials except judges go into effect]; June 10, 1931, p. 1 [Justice Ministry cuts 700,000 yen (approximately U.S.$350,000) from budget]; July 4, 1931, p. 1 [Ministry of Finance announces further reductions in government expenditures necessary because of revenue shortfall]; August 8, 1931, p. 1 [Government must reduce expenditures by 30 million yen (U.S.$15 million) for year; Ministry of Justice considers cuts in sum allocated for jury system to save 1.42 million yen (U.S.$710,000)]; October 1, 1931, p. 1 [Ministry of Finance plans to reduce national budget by 2.2 million yen (U.S.$1.1 million)]; October 4, 1931, p. 1 [Ministry of Justice to have difficulty meeting budget]; October 28, 1931, p. 2 [Amendment to be introduced in Diet to permit lay off of judges and procurators]; November 3, p. 2 [Ministry of Justice agrees to lay off employees if other agencies agree to do same; refuses to agree to more lay-offs of judges and prosecutors]; December 9, 1931 [Last hold-out among judges agrees to voluntary reduction in salary; in response government will not introduce legislation or issue imperial ordinance].

19 The Hamaguchi cabinet's closure of ward courts provoked strong public and partisan opposition. From the *Kokumin Shinbun:* March 10, 1931 [*Seiyūkai* opposed to temporary discontinuance of 62 ward courts];

March 11, 1931, p. 1 [Minister of Justice accused of lacking concern for suffering of people in the countryside by reducing number of ward courts]; March 12, 1931, p. 2 [*Seiyūkai* demands prior disclosure of names of ward courts to be closed]; March 14, 1931, p. 2 [Editorial on "age of cheaters" critical of Government's handling closure of ward courts]; March 15, 1931, p. 2 [Protest letters against ward court closures sent to Justice Minister]; March 17, 1931, p. 2 [Opposition within ruling *Minseitō* to ward court closures]; March 20, 1931, p. 7 [Japan's bar associations issue declaration opposed to court closures; One hundred lawyers visit Ministry of Justice and upper chamber of Diet]; March 24, 1931, p. 7 [Delegates meet to plan nationwide strategy against ward court closures].

20 See *Hōritsu shinbun*, no. 3385 (March 23, 1932); no. 3377 (March 3, 1932): 1 [Presiding judge of Tokyo District Court explains reasons for resignation]; no. 3379 (March 8, 1932): 1 [Great Court of Cassation justice resigns].

21 See Ramseyer and Rosenbluth, *Oligarchy*, 86–87.

22 See comments by new Justice Minister Kisaburō Suzuki, *Hōritsu shinbun* no. 3355 (January 8, 1932): 1. See also *Hōritsu shinbun*, no. 3355 (January 8, 1932): 17; no. 3363 (January 28, 1932): 4; no. 3364 (January 30, 1932): 1.

23 In addition to Mitchell's, *Janus-Faced Justice*, see his *Thought Control in Prewar Japan* (Ithaca, 1976) and *Censorship in Imperial Japan* (Princeton, 1983). Mitchell cites repeated examples of "judges refusing to be bullied by procurators," and their "scrupulous regard for the letter of the law" (*Janus-Faced Justice*, 151, 153). See also Hattori, "Judicial Administration," 74.

24 Suzuki lost his seat in the Diet in the 1936 election. Tetsu Katayama, later to become Japan's first Socialist prime minister, placed first in the same district (*Tōkyō Asahi shinbun*, January 22, 1936, p. 1).

25 Both Hiranuma and Suzuki were instrumental in enabling the enactment of the Peace Preservation Law of 1925 and the subsequent suppression of socialist-communist activities.

26 See, for example, *Tōkyō Asahi shinbun*, July 9, 1936, p.2, on the Minseitō's deliberation of proposals for legal reform that initially included placing the Ministry of Justice's administrative authority over judges under the Great Court of Cassation, selecting judges from the bar, and abolition of the Ministry of Justice. Only two proposals were eventually recommended: the unification of the colonial Korean and Taiwanese legal systems with Japan and elimination of the preliminary trial system

because of its domination by procurators (*Tōkyō Asahi shinbun*, August 11, 1936, p. 2).

27 Nihon Bengōshi Rengōkai [Japan Federation of Bar Associations], ed., *Nihon bengōshi enkakushi* [History of development of Japanese bar] (Tokyo, 1959), 183.

28 A. Satō, "Shihō kanryō to hōsei kanryō," [Judicial administration and legal affairs administration], in *Gendai no hōritsuka* [Contemporary jurists], *Gendai hō* [Contemporary law], (Tokyo, 1966), 6:44–60. On activities by bar to seek reform, see Nihon Bengoshi Rengōkai, *Nihon bengoshi enkakushi*, 183–97.

29 See comment by former Chief Justice of the Supreme Court Kisaburō Yokota in K. Yokota, *Saiban no hanashi* [Speaking about the courts] (Tokyo, 1967), 41.

30 In 1935, for example, procurator Raisaburō Hayashi was appointed Chief Justice of the Great Court of Cassation over objections by career judges who favored Judge Torajirō Ikeda (*Tōkyō Asahi Shinbun*, April 22, 1935, p. 2; May 8, 1935, p. 2). A year later however, Hayashi became Justice Minister and was replaced as Chief Justice by Ikeda (*Tōkyō Asahi Shinbun*, March 13, 1936, p. 1). Hayashi, it might be noted, was a relatively liberal, reformist justice minister. On equality of status of the procuracy and judges, see M. Hasegawa, *Shihōken no dokuritsu* [Independence of judicial authority] (Tokyo, 1971), 85.

31 For a general description in English on presurrender planning for a military occupation of Japan, see M. Iokibe, *Beikoku no Nihon seisaku* [America's Japan policy], (Tokyo, 1985), 2 vols; M. Mayo, "American Wartime Planning for Occupied Japan," in R. Wolfe, ed., *Americans as Proconsuls: United States Military Government in Germany and Japan, 1944–1952* (Carbondale and Edwardsville, 1984), 2–51; R. Ward, "Presurrender Planning: Treatment of the Emperor and Constitutional Changes," in R. Ward and Y. Sakamoto, *Democratizing Japan: The Allied Occupation* (Honolulu, 1987), 1–41.

32 National Archives, Diplomatic Section, Notter Files, T-1221 reel 3, CAC 185/185a, May 9, 1944.

33 Notter Files, T-1221 reel 4, CAC 249, July 7, 1944, p. 2.

34 See comments by Commander A. R. Hussy Jr., Meeting of Steering Committee with the Committee on the Judiciary, Memorandum of 7 February 1946, in K. Takayanagi, I. Omoto, and H. Tanaka, *Nihon kempō seitei no katei* [Process of drafting the constitution of Japan], 3d ed. (Tokyo, 1984), 186.

35 Charles L. Kades describes the committee's contribution to the making of the postwar Japanese constitution in "The American Role in Revising Japan's Imperial Constitution," *Political Science Quarterly* 104 (1989): 215–47.

36 See, for example, Memorandum of Robert A. Fearey, Jr., "Comparative Analysis of the Published Constitutional Revision Plans of the Japanese Progressive, Liberal, Socialist and Communist Parties, Two Private Study Groups (including the Federation of Bar Associations), and Dr. Takano Iwasaburo," in *Foreign Relations of the United States* 8 (1946): 170.

37 Takayanagi, Oneto, and Tanaka, *Nihon kempō seitei*, 186 and 256. Constitution, art. 79(2) and (3).

38 See Kades, "American Role."

39 See Constitution, chapter VI, arts. 76–82.

40 A more accurate translation of this provision would read, "Judges shall exercise their authority [or function] independently in accordance with their conscience and shall be bound by this constitution and the laws."

41 Materials on House of Councilors Judiciary Committee, *Saikō Saibansho no ikensho* [Supreme Court opinion letter], May 20, 1949, *Hōsō jihō* 1, no. 5 (1949): 71–72. See also N. Kumamoto, "Contemporary Reflections on Judicial Independence in Japan," in S. Shetreet and J. Deschênes, eds., *Judicial Independence: The Contemporary Debate* (Dordrecht, 1985), 239.

42 Itō v. Sakarauchi, Minister of Agriculture and Forestry, *Hanrei jihō* (No. 712) 24 (Sapporo Dist. Ct., Sept. 7, 1973), rev'd by the Sapporo High Court, *Gyōsai reishū* 27 (No. 8) 1175 (Sapporo High Ct., Aug. 5, 1976), appeal dismissed by the Supreme Court, 36 *Minshū* 36 (no. 9) 1679 (Sup. Ct., 1st P.B., Sept. 9, 1982). All three decisions are translated in Beer and Itoh, *Constitutional Case Law, 1970 through 1990*, 83–130. See H. Itoh, *The Japanese Supreme Court* (New York, 1989), 266–67.

43 Y. Taniguchi, "Japan," in Shetreet and Deschênes, *Judicial Independence*, 210.

44 Ramseyer and Rosenbluth, *Japan's Political Marketplace*, 164–70.

45 S. Miyazawa, "Administrative Control of Japanese Judges" (paper presented at the Joint Annual Meeting of the Law and Society Association and the ISA Research Committee on the Sociology of Law, Amsterdam, The Netherlands, June 25–29, 1991).

46 See, for example, observations on the Italian experience in F. Spotts and T. Wieser, *Italy: A Difficult Democracy* (Cambridge, 1986), 158–61, quoted in J. H. Merryman, D. Clark, and J. Haley, *The Civil Law*

Tradition: Europe, Latin America, and East Asia (Charlottesville, 1995), 578–81.

47 Japanese public opinion polls consistently find significantly higher levels of public trust in the courts than in any other major Japanese institution, including universities, labor unions, the national railways, and large business enterprises. The Diet ranks last by large margins. See, for example, National Yomiuri Poll nos. 447 (June 1983) and 348 (June 1989).

48 K. Tokoro, "Saiban no minshu-teki tōsei to dokuritsu," [Democratic control and independence of the courts], Hōshakai gakkai, *Saibankan-ron* [Study of judges] (*Hōshakaigaku*, no. 26) (Tokyo, 1973).

49 *Saibansho hō* (Law no. 59, 1947).

50 Mainichi Shinbun Shakaibu [Mainichi newspaper social affairs bureau], ed., *Kenshō-Saikō saibansho: Hōfuku no mukō de* [Verification-Supreme Court: Putting on the judicial robes] (Tokyo, 1991), 263–65, 266.

51 Ibid., 265.

52 Hattori, "Judicial Administration," 82–83.

53 Ibid., 81.

54 A total of 587 new career judges were appointed between 1947 and 1955, of whom at least 166 were Tokyo graduates, followed by 89 Kyoto, 98 Chuo, 14 Tohoku, 10 Kyushu, and 10 Waseda graduates. The almanac does not list the university from which 177 entering judges graduated, about 30 percent of the total for this period (*Zensaibankan keireki sokan* [Judges' almanac], 16–212).

55 Between 1956 and 1960, 65 of 392 new assistant judges were Kyoto graduates. Sixty-two were Chuo graduates as compared to only 82 listed Tokyo graduates. (120 had no listed university affiliation.) There were only 7 Tohoku graduates and 11 Waseda graduates (ibid.).

56 Of the eighty-eight judicial appointments, at least thirteen were graduates of Chuo, five Waseda, three Tohoku, two Hokkaido, and one each from the national universities of Nagoya and Kyushu, one from Osaka Prefectural University, and one each from International Christian University, Kansai Gakuin, Keio, and Meiji, all of which are private universities. The university affiliations of twenty-six are unlisted (ibid.).

57 Ibid., 126–55. The percentages for 1971 to 1975 were 25 percent Tokyo, 15 percent Chuo, 11 percent Kyoto; for 1976 to 1980: 21 percent Tokyo, 13 percent Kyoto, 10 percent Chuo; for 1981 to 1985, 32 percent Tokyo, 8 percent Kyoto, 7 percent Chuo, and for the first time ahead of all but Tokyo graduates, Waseda with 13 percent (ibid., 156–99).

Chapter 6: Community Confirmed

1 D. Foote, "Judicial Creation of Norms in Japanese Labor Law: Activism in the Service of—Stability?" *UCLA Law Review* 43 (1996): 635, 687.

2 Compare J. Embree, *Suye Mura: A Japanese Village*, 8th ed. (Chicago, 1969), 171, and H. Ooms, *Tokugawa Village Practice* (Berkeley, 1996), 216.

3 Ooms, *Tokugawa Village Practice*, 216–21.

4 See *Mori v. Japan*, Keiroku 17:1520 (Gr. Ct. Cass., 2d Crim. Dept., September 5, 1911); *Inamura v. Japan*, Keiroku 19:147 (Gr. Ct. Cass., 1st Crim. Dept., Jan. 31, 1913); *Fukuda v. Japan*, Keiroku 26:912 (Gr. Ct. Cass., 1st Crim. Dept., Dec. 10, 1920); *Nakayama v. Japan*, Keishū 7:533 (Gr. Ct. Cass., 1st Crim. Dept., Aug. 3, 1928); *Kamitani v. Japan*, Keishū 13:213 (Gr. Ct., Cass., 1st Crim. Dept., Mar. 5, 1934); *Suzuki v. Japan*, Hōritsu shinbun 8, no. 4442 (Gr. Ct., Cass., 3d Crim. Dept., April 28, 1939).

5 *Keihanshō* 86:10835 (Gr. Ct. Cass., 1st Crim. Dept., Dec. 10, 1920), 86:10836, translation in W. Sebald, *The Criminal Code of Japan* (Kobe and London, 1936), 174.

6 *Nagata v. Japan*, Kōsai keishū 7:217 (Fukuoka High Ct., Mar. 31, 1954); *Sanno v. Japan*, Kōsai keishū 10:602 (Osaka High Ct., Sept. 13, 1957).

7 *Matsumoto v. Japan*, Kōsai keishū 5:1832 (Nagoya High Ct., Sept. 24, 1953).

8 *Minroku* 7:47 (Gr. Ct. Cass., June 20, 1901).

9 M. Aoyama, "Wagakuni ni okeru kenri ran'yō riron no hatten" [Development of the theory of abuse of rights in Japan], in *Kenri no ran'yō*, (Tokyo, 1965), 1:19–20, translated in J. Haley and D. Henderson, *Law and the Legal Process in Japan* (Seattle, 1987), 2:633–49.

10 M. Ramseyer, *Good Law, Odd Markets* (Cambridge, 1996), 80–108.

11 See K. Steiner, "Postwar Changes in the Japanese Civil Code," *Washington Law Review* 25 (1950): 286–312; S. Wagatsuma, Democratization of the Family Relation in Japan," *Washington Law Review* 25 (1950): 405–26.

12 See M. Glendon, *The Transformation of Family Law: State, Law, and Family in the United States and Western Europe* (Chicago, 1989).

13 See Civil Code, art. 880, prior to amendments of law no. 222, 1947.

14 R. Ishii, *Meiji bunka shi* [History of Meiji culture] (Tokyo, 1954), 2:614; translated into English by W. Chambliss as *Japanese Culture in the Meiji Era*, (Tokyo, 1958), 18:673–74.

15 Civil Code, art. 770 (1)(v).

16 T. Bryant, "Marital Dissolution in Japan: Legal Obstacles and Their Impact," *Law in Japan: An Annual* 17 (1984): 74.

17 Ibid.

18 Ibid., 77.

19 Ibid., 76.

20 R. Dore, *City Life in Japan: A Study of a Tokyo Ward*, 3d ed. (Berkeley, 1971), 157–58.

21 E. Vogel, *Japan's New Middle Class* (Berkeley, 1967), 181–93.

22 *Minshū* 41:1423 (Sup. Ct., G.B., Sept. 2, 1987). In order to protect the parties' privacy, the fictitious family name Kōno is used with various given names (for example, Ichirō, Tarō, and Haruo for men and Hanako and Natsuko for women) in most Japanese official reports and periodicals as the Japanese equivalent of John and Jane Doe.

23 T. Bryant, "'Responsible' Husbands, 'Recalcitrant' Wives, Retributive Judges: Judicial Management of Contested Divorce in Japan," *Journal of Japanese Studies* 18, no. 2 (Summer 1992): 413–14.

24 Ibid., 414 (translation by Frank Upham).

25 *Kōno v. Kōno, Hanrei jihō*, no. 1256:28 (Sup. Ct., 3d P.B., Nov. 24, 1987), no. 1268:3 (Sup. Ct., 2d P.B., February 12, 1988), no. 1293:94 (Sup. Ct., 1st P.B., April 7, 1988); *Imanishi v. Imanishi, Saibanshū minji* 157:457 (Sup. Ct., 1st P.B., September 7, 1989).

26 *1989 Saikō saibansho hanrei kaisetsu, minji hen* [Supreme Court commentary on precedents, civil cases, 1989] (Tokyo, 1990), 585; Bryant, "Contested Divorce," 421.

27 *Sawada v. Sawada, Hanrei taimuzu*, no. 745:113 (Sup. Ct., 1st P.B., November 8, 1990).

28 See Bryant, "Contested Divorce," 422–23; *Hanrei taimuzu*, comment, 113.

29 *Kōno v. Kōno, Kasai geppō* 46, no. 9:40 (Sup. Ct., 3d P.B., Nov. 2, 1994).

30 See Bryant, "Marital Dissolution," 77.

31 Ibid., 86–90.

32 Ibid., 86.

33 T. Bryant, "Family Law Models, Family Dispute Resolution, and Family Law in Japan," (paper presented at the International Conference in Asian and Comparative Law, University of Washington, School of Law, Seattle, Wash., August 3, 1996).

34 See *Burgerliches Gesetzbuch* (BGB), as amended through January 1,

1992, secs. 620, 621, 622; *Code Civil*, art. 1780, as amended by the Labor Code (*Code du Travail*) of 1973.

35 See, for example, G. Garancsy, *Labour Law Relation and Its Termination in Hungarian Law* (Budapest, 1973).

36 See M. Glendon and E. Lev, "Changes in the Bonding of the Employment Relationship: An Essay on the New Property," *Boston College Law Review* 20 (1979): 457, 466.

37 In the United States some courts as well as legislatures have begun to modify the strict application of the "at will" doctrine. California courts have been at the forefront since the California Supreme Court decision in *Tameny v. Atlantic Richfield Company*, 27 Cal. 3d 167, 164 Cal. Rptr. 839, 610 P.2d 1330 (1980). See I. Szaszy, *International Labour Law* (Leyden, 1968), 312–25.

38 *Rōdō kijun hō* [Labor Standards Law] (Law no. 49, 1947), art. 20.

39 Foote, "Judicial Creation of Norms," 638.

40 See *X v. Shikoku Haiden* (Matsuyama Dist. Ct., Feb. 8, 1951); *Tsubaki v. Japan, Rōminshū* 4 (no. 1): 50, 78 (Ōtsu Dist. Ct., Mar. 11, 1953), cited in Foote, "Judicial Creation of Norms," 641.

41 See cases cited in Foote, "Judicial Creation of Norms," 642 n. 22, 643.

42 Ibid., 647–50.

43 *Ishikawa v. Nihon Shokuen Seizō K.K., Minshū* 29:456 (Sup. Ct., 2d P.B., Apr. 25, 1975).

44 *Shioda v. Kōchi Broadcasting Co., Rōdō hanrei*, no. 268:17 (Sup. Ct., 2d P.B., Jan. 31, 1977).

45 Foote, "Judicial Creation of Norms," 651–65.

46 *Takano v. Mitsubishi Jushi K.K., Minshū* 27:1536 (Sup. Ct., G.B., Dec. 12, 1973).

47 *Tōkyō Shibaura Denki K.K. v. Maeda, Minshū* 28:927 (Sup. Ct., 1st P.B., July 22, 1974).

48 *Dainippon Insatsu K.K. v. Takemoto, Minshū* 33:582 (Sup. Ct., 2d P.B., July 20, 1979).

49 Foote, "Judicial Creation of Norms," 648–49.

50 See, for example, R. Yamakawa, "The Role of the Employment Contract in Japan," in L. Betten, ed., *The Employment Contract in Transforming Labour Relations* (The Hague: 1995), 105–28; Foote, "Judicial Creation of Norms," 665–70.

51 *Shūshoku Bus v. Yoshikawa, Minshū* 22:3459 (Sup. Ct., G.B., Dec. 25, 1968).

52 See K. Sugeno, *Japanese Labor Law*, trans. L. Kanowitz (Seattle, 1992), 98–100.

53 *Hōsō jihō* 48, no. 8 (1996): 108, 111.

54 *Kurihashi v. Nippon Denki K.K., Rōminshū* 19:1111 (Tokyo Dist. Ct., Aug. 31, 1968), cited in Foote, "Judicial Creation of Norms," 668.

55 *Yoshida v. Tōa Paint K.K., Rōdō hanrei* 6 (Sup. Ct., 2d P. B., July 14, 1986).

56 *Reigenji v. Sano, Hōritsu shinbun* 24, no. 804 (Tokyo Dist. Ct., July 3, 1912).

57 *Fudosan tōko hō* [Immovable Registration Law] (Law no. 24, 1899).

58 For detailed accounts in Japan of the history leading to the enactment of the Building Protection Law and the Land and House Lease Laws, see Sawano Yukihiko, *Shakuchi shakuya hō no keizai-teki kiso* [Economic foundations of the land lease and house lease laws] (Tokyo, 1988), 157–63; Y. Watanabe, *Tochi-tatemono no hōritsu seido* [Legal institutions of land and buildings] (Tokyo, 1960), vol. 1.

59 *Tatemono hōgō ni kansuru hōritsu* [Law concerning the Protection of Buildings] (Law no. 40, 1909).

60 Nihon Teikoku Shihōshō [Ministry of Justice of the Empire of Japan], *Minji tōkei nenpō* [Annual report of civil law statistics], no. 45 (1919): 41; no. 48 (1922): 30.

61 T. Hozumi, "Hōritsu kōi no 'kaishaku' no kōzō to kinō, 2" [Structure and function of the 'interpretation' of juristic acts, pt. 2], *Hōgaku kyōkai zasshi* 78, no. 1 (1961): 27–71; translated by author in *Law in Japan: An Annual* 5 (1972): 132–64.

62 Ibid. (trans.), 156.

63 *X v. Y, Saikinhan* 69 (Tokyo Ct. App., June 25, 1909).

64 *Horikoshi v. Masumura, Minroku* 26:1247 (Gr. Ct. Cass., 1st Civ. Dept., Sept. 10, 1920).

65 *Shakuchi hō* [Land Lease Law] (Law no. 49, 1921); *Shakuya hō* [House Lease Law] (Law no. 50, 1921).

66 *Shakuchi shakuya hō* [Land Lease and House Lease Law] (Law no. 90, 1991).

67 For a fuller description of the new law and its background, see J. Haley, "Japan's New House and Land Lease law," in J. Haley and K. Yamamura, eds., *Land Issues in Japan: A Policy Failure?* (Seattle, 1992), 149–73. Much of this section is based on this article.

68 The classic studies are T. Kawashima, "The Legal Consciousness of Contract," trans. C. Stevens, *Law in Japan: An Annual* 7 (1970): 1–21,

and S. Macauley, "Non-Contractual Relations in Business: A Preliminary Study," *American Sociological Review* 28 (1963): 55–69. See also,
T. Nakamura, "The Relational Contract and Japanese Legal Consciousness," in V. Kasuda-Smick, ed., *United States/Japan Commercial Law
and Trade* (Dobbs Ferry, 1990), 696–705. Recently completed is one of
the most comprehensive empirical studies yet to be undertaken. A group
of scholars under the leadership of Tokyo University Professor Takeshi
Uchida and the auspices of the Center for Global Partnership Project on
Civil Responsibility conducted extensive surveys and interviews in Japan
with supplementary interviews in the United States. Their findings, currently in press, confirm the noted similarities in contract practices in
the United States and Japan.

69 This, of course, is Kawashima's principal point. Kawashima, "Legal Consciousness of Contract," 20–21.

70 Haley, "Relational Contracting: Does Community Count?" in H. Baum,
ed., *Japan: Economic Success and Legal System* (Berlin, 1996), chap. 5.

71 See *Okamoto v. Ashida, Hōritsu shinbun* 12, no. 3462 (Gr. Ct. Cass., 4th
Civ. Dept., Sept. 17, 1932).

72 R. Dore, *Flexible Rigidities: Industrial Policy and Structural Adjustment in the Japanese Economy, 1970–1980* (Stanford, 1986), 248.

73 M. Tilton, *Restrained Trade: Cartels in Japan's Basic Materials Industries* (Ithaca, 1996).

74 See R. Dore, "Goodwill and the Spirit of Market Capitalism," *British
Journal of Sociology* 34, no. 4 (1983): 459–82; M. Smitka, "Contracting
Without Contracts: How the Japanese Manage Organizational Transactions," in S. Sitkin and R. Bies, eds., *The Legalistic Organization* (Thousand Oaks, Calif., 1994).

75 Smitka, "Contracting Without Contracts," 100.

76 See R. Ellickson, *Order Without Law: How Neighbors Settle Disputes*
(Cambridge, Mass., 1991).

77 One of the most recent and thorough empirical studies was undertaken
under the leadership of Professor Takashi Uchida, under the auspices of
the Center for Global Partnership Legal Responsibility Research Project.

78 *Hōgaku* 11:1183 (Gr. Ct. Cass., Feb. 1942).

79 *Hanrei jihō* 25, no. 286 (Tokyo Dist. Ct., Dec. 13. 1961).

80 *Kakyū minshū* 12:2434 (Osaka Dist. Ct., October 12, 1961).

81 *Minshū* 25:1472 (Sup. Ct., 1st P.B., Dec. 16, 1971).

82 *Hokkaidō Ford Tractor K.K. v. Minoru Sangyō K.K., Hanrei jihō* 76, no.
1258 (Sapporo High Ct., Sept. 30, 1987).

83 C. Milhaupt, "A Relational Theory of Japanese Corporate Governance: Contract, Culture, and the Rule of Law," *Harvard International Law Journal* 37 (1996): 41–42. *Nihon Jetto K.K. v. Biwako Ginkō, Kin'yū hōmu jijō* 34, no. 1280 (Osaka Dist. Ct., Oct. 12, 1990).

Chapter 7: The Sense of Society

1 *Shinagawa v. Kurobe Railway Co., Minshū* 14:1965 (Gr. Ct. Cass., 3d Civ. Dept., Oct. 5, 1935), translated in H. Tanaka, *The Japanese Legal System: Cases and Materials* (Tokyo, 1976), 119–20.

2 *Minshū* 14:1796. The most common are *shakai gainen* [notions of society], *shakai tsūnen* [commonly accepted standards of society], and *shakai-teki jijō* [social attitudes or feelings].

3 D. Foote, "Judicial Creation of Norms in Japanese Labor Law: Activism in the Service of—Stability?" *UCLA Law Review* 43 (1996): 679.

4 See Constitution, art. 76(3).

5 See M. Aoyama, "Wagakuni ni okeru kenri ran'yō riron no hatten" [Development of the theory of abuse of rights in Japan], in *Kenri no ran'yō* (Tokyo, 1965), 1:9, translated in J. Haley and D. Henderson, *Law and the Legal Process in Japan* (Seattle, 1987), 541.

6 Ibid., 1:14.

7 See E. Makino, *Gendai no bunka to hōritsu* [Contemporary culture and the laws], 5th ed. (Tokyo, 1921), 1.

8 *Minroku* 11:1702 (Gr. Ct. Cass., 2d Civ. Dept., Dec. 20, 1905).

9 See, for example, *Kasuga v. Miyabara, Minroku* 5:1 (Gr. Ct., Cass., 2d Civ. Dept., Feb. 1, 1899); *Yoshida v. Inagaki, Minroku* 11:1326 (Gr. Ct. Cass., 2d Civ. Dept., Oct. 11, 1905).

10 *Mori v. Mega, Minroku* 23:14 (Gr. Ct. Cass., 2d Civ. Dept., Jan. 22, 1917).

11 *Japan v. Shimizu, Minroku* 25:356 (Gr. Ct. Cass., 2d Civ. Dept., Mar. 3, 1919).

12 *Minroku* 25:362–63.

13 *Osaka Alkali K.K. v. Tonomura, Minroku* 22:2474 (Gr. Ct. Cass., 1st Civ. Dept., Dec. 22, 1916).

14 See K. Sono and Y. Fujioka, "The Role of the Abuse of Right Doctrine in Japan," *Louisiana Law Review* 35 (1975): 1050.

15 See, for example, V. Bolgár, "Abuse of Rights in France, Germany and Switzerland: A Survey of a Recent Chapter in Legal Doctrine," *Louisiana Law Review* 35 (1975): 1015–57; J. Cueto-Rua, "Abuse of Rights,"

Louisiana Law Review 35 (1975): 965-1013; and J. Perillo, "Abuse of Rights: A Pervasive Legal Concept," *Pacific Law Journal* 27 (1995): 37–97.

16 Ghent, November 20, 1950, cited in Bolgár, "Abuse of Rights," 1022–23.

17 Lyon, April 18, 1856, D.P. 1856.2.199, cited in Cueto-Rio, "Abuse of Rights," 966.

18 *Hōritsu shinbun* 12, no. 4301 (Gr. Ct. Cass., 2d Civ. Dept., June 28, 1938), 14.

19 T. Uchida, "Gendai keiyaku hō no arata na tenkai to ippan jōko" [New directions in contemporary contract law and the general clauses], *NBL*, no. 516 (1993): 22, 28 n. 1. This article is the third in a series of four in which Takeshi Uchida traces the use of the good faith principle in contracts. The other articles and a concluding series of comments by leading civil code scholars appear in *NBL*, no. 514:6–11 (part 1); no. 515:13–21 (part 2); no. 517:32–40 (part 4); and no. 518:26–32 (part 5, comments). See also *Chūshaku minpō* [Civil code commentary], vol. 1, *Sōsoku* [General provisions], ed. T. Taniguchi (Tokyo, 1964), 69.

20 *Mukaiyama v. Yoshikawa, Minroku* 26:1947 (Gr. Ct. Cass., 3d Civ. Dept., December 18, 1920), 1950.

21 Uchida, "Gendai keiyaku," 28 n. 3. See, for example, O. Ishizaka, *Nihon Minpō* [Japanese civil law], 9th ed. (Tokyo, 1920), 1:374–79. The earliest copy of Ishizaka's treatise available to Uchida was the seventh edition, published in 1915. It is not clear whether the first edition, published in 1911, also contained the reference. The 1920 edition includes several pages, as indicated, devoted to an explication of the principle.

22 See, for example, J. E. de Becker, *The Principles and Practices of the Civil Code of Japan* (London, 1921).

23 See, for example, K. Ume, *Minpō yōgi* [Civil code essentials], 29th ed., 5 vols. (Tokyo, 1908).

24 E. Makino, "Hōritsu ni okeru gutai-teki datōsei" [The concrete relevance of laws], *Hōgaku shirin* 24, no. 10 (1922); reprinted in Makino, *Hōritsu ni okeru gutai-teki datōsei* (Tokyo, 1925), 1–101.

25 H. Hatoyama, "Saiken hō ni okeru shingi seijitsu no gensoku" [Good faith principle in the law of obligations] *Hōgaku kyōkai zasshi* 42, no. 1 (1924): 1–20; no. 2:82–105; no. 5:34–53; no. 7:26–44; no. 8:45–72. Cf. Uchida, "Gendai keiyaku," 29 fn 6.

26 Law no. 222, 1947.

27 Uchida, "Gendai keiyaku," 22.

28 T. Ogamino, "Shingisoku to kenri ran'yō ni kansuru saikōsai hanrei

sōran" [Review of Supreme Court decisions concerning the good faith principle and abuse of rights], *Hanrei taimuzu*, 1986, no. 568:38–41; no. 569:28–32; no. 570:24–29; no. 571:20–24; no. 572:35–38; no.574:22–26; no. 575:18–22; no. 576:21–23; no. 577:29–32; no. 578:28–32. Ogamino lists fifty Supreme Court cases reviewed, but he counts the Supreme Court First Petty Bench Judgment of March 1, 1980, twice because the principles were argued with respect to separate issues.

29　*Kudō v. Japan, Minshū* 29:143 (Sup. Ct., 3d P.B., Feb. 25, 1975) [state liability based on good faith principle]; *Komata v. Japan, Minshū* 35:56 (Sup. Ct., 3d P. B., Feb. 16, 1981) [plaintiff failed to prove state did not take adequate safety precautions]; *Takano v. Japan, Minshū* 37:477 (Sup. Ct., 2d P. B., May 27, 1983) [plaintiff failed to prove state did not take adequate safety precautions].

30　*K.K. Hayama Green Town v. Zushi Shinyō Kumiai, Kin'yū hōmu jijō*, no. 893:43 (Sup. Ct., 1st P. B., Mar. 1, 1979) [no abuse of right found]; *K.K. Umemoto Shōkō v. Miura Shinyō Kinko, Kin'yū hōmu jijō*, no. 989:47 (Sup. Ct., 2d P. B., Nov. 13, 1981) [no abuse of right found].

31　*Ogitani v. Ogitani, Minshū* 30:554 (Sup. Ct., 3d P.B., May 25, 1976) [abuse of right precludes defense].

32　*Obori v. Naito, Hanrei jihō*, no. 851:176 (Sup. Ct., 1st P.B., Mar. 31, 1977) [good faith principle defendant in action for damages responsible for impossibility of performance of lease]; *X v. Y, Kin'yū hōmu jijō*, no. 824:43 (Sup. Ct., 1st P.B., Mar. 31, 1977) [in separate case decided on same day, third party purchaser action for vacation of land by unregistered ground tenant held to constitute abuse of right]; *Kawaguchi v. Asano, Hanrei jihō*, no. 661:41 (Sup. Ct., 3d P.B., Nov. 9, 1971) [action for return of land barred by good faith and constituted an abuse of right]; *Ochi v. Amano, Hanrei jihō*, no. 674:69 (Sup. Ct., June 15, 1972) [action for eviction abuse of right and violation of good faith]; *Mori v. Shōwa Sekiyu, Minshū* 27:1192 (Sup. Ct., 2d P.B., Oct. 12, 1978) [good faith principle precludes termination of lease upon bankruptcy of tenant]; *Shimamura v. Makabe, Hanrei jihō*, no. 852:60 (Sup. Ct., 3d P.B., Mar. 15, 1972) [claim that ground lease not renewable because the buildings no longer existed barred by good faith principle]; *Onuki v. Serizawa, Hanrei jihō*, no. 914:54 (Sup. Ct., 1st P.B., Nov. 30, 1978) [violation of good faith principle and abuse of right to cancel lease for nonpayment of portion of rent increase permitted under rent control regulations]; *Satō v. Yasui, Minshū* 35:1289 (Sup. Ct., 2d P.B., Dec. 4, 1981) [abuse of right to seek vacation of land subject to ground lease upon denial of administrative designation of land for use as rental property]; *Uenaka v. Kojima, Hanrei jihō,* no. 1095:102 (Sup. Ct., 1st P.B. Mar. 14, 1983) [action for eviction from building and vacation of land barred by good faith principle]; *Akizawa v. Tajiri, Hanrei jihō,* no. 659:55 (Sup. Ct., 1st P.B., Jan. 20, 1972) [cancellation of lease violation of good faith principle]; *Furuhashi v. Aisan Shōkō K.K., Hanrei jihō,* no. 1086:92 (Sup. Ct., 3d P.B., Oct. 19, 1982) [abuse of right precluded claim for damages in case involving claim of unlawful possession].

33 *Hoizumi v. Konō, Hanrei jihō,* no. 1022:55 (Sup. Ct., 2d P.B., Oct. 30, 1981) [Lawsuit brought by successor of interest in land to have registration of transfer of ownership invalidated violated good faith principle]; *Atosato Iryō Kōgyō K.K. v. Hokkai Iryō Kōgyō K.K. , Minshū* 25:1472 (Sup. Ct., 1st P.B., Dec. 16, 1971), discussed in chapter 6.

34 *Kōno v. Kōno, Hanrei jihō,* no. 894:65 (Sup. Ct., 2d P.B., April 14, 1978) [Action to nullify false registration of parentage of child not violation of good faith therefore not abuse of right].

35 *Takano v. Mitsubishi Jushi K.K., Minshū* 27:1536 (Sup. Ct., G.B., Dec. 12, 1973), discussed in chapter 6.

36 *Amazaki Nissan Jidōsha K.K. v. Kageyama, Minshū* 29:193 (Sup. Ct., 2d P.B., Feb. 28, 1975) [Action to repossess automobile constitutes an abuse of right]; *X v. Y, Kin'yū hōmu jijō,* no. 835:33 (Sup. Ct., 1st P.B., Mar. 31, 1977) [Action to repossess automobile constitutes abuse of right]; *Nagano Toyota Jidōsha K.K. v. Iguchi, Hanrei jihō,* no. 1070:26 (Sup. Ct., 2d P.B., Dec. 17, 1982) [Action to repossess automobile constitutes abuse of right]; *Manzoku K.K. v. Nissan Sunny Gunma Hanbai K.K., Hanrei jihō,* no. 1018:77 (Sup. Ct., 3d P.B., July 14, 1981) [Action to prepossess automobile does not constitute abuse of right]; *Ishigaki v. Sendai Isuzu Motors K.K., Hanrei jihō,* no. 792:31 (Sup. Ct., 1st P.B., July 17, 1975) [Right of purchaser to offset costs of repairs against dealer].

37 *Nihon Chikudo Kaihatsu K.K. v. K.K. Hotel New Japan, Minshū* 27:1240 (Sup. Ct., 2d P.B., Oct. 26, 1973) [Claim that juridical status of new and old companies differs constitutes a violation of good faith]; *Ryōkoku Kigyō K.K. v. Chō, Minshū* 28:1605 (Sup. Ct., 1st P.B., Nov. 14, 1974) [Claim that breach invalidated contract for joint representative directors violated principle of good faith]; *X v. Y, Kin'yū jijō,* no. 780:33 (Sup. Ct., 1st P.B., Dec. 25, 1975) [Claim that transaction benefiting the director of another corporation invalid against good faith principle]; *Kyōtō Shiyaku Inryōkai v. Nippon Inryōdan, Minshū* 30:306 (Sup. Ct., 2d P.B., April 23, 1976) [Claim that *ultra vires* sale of assets by foundation invalid in vio-

lation of good faith principle]; *Kyūshōgō Ibaraki Sekitan K.K. v. Miru,
Minshū* 30:689 (Sup. Ct., 1st P.B., July 8, 1976) [Claim by employee
against employer for damages arising out of motor vehicle accident allowed under good faith principle].

38 *X v. Y, Kin'yū hōmu jijō*, no. 679:35 (Sup. Ct., 1st P.B., Mar. 1, 1980)
[Claim against guarantor under ongoing guarantee as well as special
agreement an abuse of right]; *Shikoku Trust Meishi K.K. v. Fukuda,
Minshū* 27:1391 (Sup. Ct., 2d P.B., Nov. 16, 1973) [Claim against issuer
of promissory note constitutes abuse of right]; *Nakano v. Nakamura,
Minshū* 36:1113 (Sup. Ct., 1st P.B., July 15, 1983) [Endorser of note unable in good faith to avoid liability]; *Murakami v. Miyaura Kōgyō K.K.,
Hanrei jihō*, no. 1053:168 (Sup. Ct., 3d P.B., July 20, 1982) [Abuse of
right for holder to seek payment against issuer of promissory note where
underlying obligation paid in full but note not delivered]; *Kinoshita
Mokuzai Kōgyō K.K. v. Uemura, Minshū* 27:890 (Sup. Ct., 2d P.B.,
July 20, 1978) [In action for payment under promissory note contradictory denial of facts in separate lawsuit does not constitute a violation of
good faith].

39 *X v. Y, Hanrei jihō*, no. 816:48 (Sup. Ct., 3d P.B., Mar. 23, 1976) [Change
of claim in contract dispute held to violate good faith principle]; *Eno-
mura v. Mitsuyoshi, Minshū* 30:799 (Sup. Ct., 1st P.B., Sept. 30, 1976)
[New lawsuit with change of cause of action of prior lawsuit violation of
good faith]; *X v. Y, Kin'yū-shōji hanrei*, no. 557:39 (Sup. Ct., Mar. 24,
1977) [Contradiction of claims in two lawsuits violation of good faith];
Y.K. Kenkō Yakuhin v. Sanenari, Minshū 32:888 (Sup. Ct., 1st P.B.,
July 10, 1978) [Lawsuit for confirmation of invalidity of shareholder
resolution constitutes abuse of process]; *Tōkyō Kaijō Kaji Hoken K.K. v.
Royal Interocean Lines* (Sup. Ct., 3d P.B., Nov. 28, 1975) [Choice of court
clause in bill of lading not violation of public policy]; *Kōno v. Kōno,
Hanrei jihō*, no. 1105:48 (Sup. Ct., 1st P.B., July 19, 1984) [Suit for transfer of registration of land ownership based on cancellation of donation
brought by losing party in prior lawsuit over registration based on denial
of donation not in violation of good faith].

40 *K.K. Kaneshō v. Suzuki, Hanrei jihō*, no. 868:26 (Sup. Ct., 1st P.B., Sept.
22, 1977).

41 *Fuji Kōgyō K.K. v. Kita-Kyūshū City, Hanrei jihō*, no. 1010:43 (Sup. Ct.,
3d P.B., June 16, 1981) [Good faith principle does not prevent enforcement of option to purchase land despite substantial increase in market
value]; *Neyagawa City v. Noya, Hanrei jihō*, no. 1123:85 (Sup. Ct., 3d

P.B., Dec. 6, 1983) [Municipality not liable for damages for misleading statements during negotiations over municipality's purchase of private land]; *Mitamura v. Suzuki, Minshū* 26:1067 (Sup. Ct., 3d P.B., June 27, 1972) [Right to sunlight]; *Lee v. Japan, Hanrei jihō,* no. 1060:76 (Sup. Ct., 2d P.B., Oct. 15, 1982) [Denial of claim for funds deposited in military postal savings account in Taiwan prior to World War II]; *Mitsui Fudō Shōsan K.K., Minshū* 28:1331 (Sup. Ct., 1st P.B., Sept. 26, 1974) [Good faith imposition of duty of owner of ship damaged in collision to pay for repairs]; *Ikeda v. Kadotani, Hanrei jihō,* no. 1137:51 (Sup. Ct., 3d P.B., Sept. 18, 1984) [Duty to negotiate in good faith].

42 *Minshū* 20:702 (Sup. Ct., G.B., April 20, 1966).

43 See M. Burrill, "Good Faith and the Abuse of Right: How Japanese Courts Try to Achieve Fairness in Treating Suits Barred by a Limitations Period" (LL.M. research paper, University of Washington, School of Law, Seattle, June 1986).

44 *Moriguchi v. Okada, Hanrei jihō,* no. 594 (Sup. Ct., 3d P.B., April 21, 1970).

45 *Yamanaka v. Nakajima, Hanrei taimuzu,* no. 464:108 (Tokyo Dist. Ct., Jan. 26, 1982).

46 *Kudō v. Shōa Parts Industries K.K., Hanrei jihō,* no. 882:78 (Sapporo Dist. Ct, Oct. 18, 1977); *Ogitani v. Ogitani, Minshū* 30:554 (Sup. Ct., 3d P.B., May 25, 1976); *Shimane Electrical Industries v. K.K. Tajima Bank, Hanrei jihō,* no. 656:65 (Hiroshima High Ct., Nov. 22, 1971).

47 *Kensetsu jijun hō* [Building Standards Law] (Law no. 201, 1950).

48 *Mitamura v. Suzuki, Minshū* 26:1067, 1069 (Sup. Ct., 3d P.B., June 27, 1972).

49 See, e.g., *Tsubaki v. Keihanshin Kyūkō Dentetsu K.K., Hanrei jihō,* no. 592:41 (Kobe Dist. Ct., Itami Br., Feb. 5, 1970).

50 Sono and Fujioka, "Abuse of Right," 1049–55.

51 *Hanrei Taimuzu,* no. 224:250 (Osaka Dist. Ct., April 26, 1968).

52 S. Kawakami, "Precontractual Liability: Japan," in *Japanese Reports for the XIIIth International Congress of Comparative Law, Montreal, August 19–24, 1990* (Tokyo, 1991), 44–66. See also E. Hondius, ed., *Reports to the XIIIth Congress of the International Academy of Comparative Law* (The Hague, 1990), 205–21.

53 *Tahira K.K. v. Tahara, Hanrei jihō,* no. 1082:47 (Sup. Ct., 3d P.B., April 19, 1983); *Ikeda v. Kadoya, Hanrei Taimuzu,* no. 542:200 (Sup. Ct., 3d P.B., Sept. 18, 1984).

54 Uchida, "Gendai keiyaku," 24.

55 See J. Haley, "Sheathing the Sword of Justice in Japan: An Essay on Law without Sanctions," *Journal of Japanese Studies* 8, no. 2 (1982): 265–81.

56 *Ota v. Koji, Minroku* 19:327 (Gr. Ct. Cass., 2d Civ. Dept., May 12, 1913); S. Wagatsuma, *Hanrei kommentaaru* [Commentary of precedents] (Tokyo, 1965), 4:85.

57 *Ueda v. Matsuda, Minroku* 10:1453 (Gr. Ct. Cass., 1st Civ. Dept., Nov. 15, 1904).

58 *Gotō G.K. v. Shibuya, Hōritsu shinbun*, no. 4655:13 (Korea App. Ch., Dec. 3, 1940).

59 *Hōritsu shinbun*, no. 827:24 (Hakodate Dt., Ct., Oct. 9, 1912).

60 *Kakyū minshū* 2:146 (Nara Dt. Ct., Feb. 6, 1951).

61 See Wagatsuma, *Hanrei kommentaaru*, 4:83.

62 H. Suekawa, "Fuka kōryoku," in *Minji hōgaku jiten* [Civil law dictionary] (Tokyo, 1960), 1705.

63 Civil Code, articles 274, 275, 348, 419, 609, and 610; Commercial Code, articles 576, 594, 741, 756, 761, 782, 799, 821, 832, and 825.

64 *Minroku* 16:807 (Gr. Ct., Cass., 2d P.B., Nov. 25, 1910).

65 *Minroku* 12:1358 (Gr. Ct. Cass., 2d P.B., Oct. 29, 1906).

66 T. Sawada, *Subsequent Conduct and Supervening Events: A Study of Two Selected Problems in Contract Jurisprudence* (Tokyo and Ann Arbor, Mich., 1968); K. Igarashi and L. Reike, "Impossibility and Frustration in Sales Contracts," *Washington Law Review* 42 (1967): 445–62.

67 M. Katsumoto, *Minpō ni okeru jijō henkō no gensoku* [Changed circumstances doctrine in Civil Law] (Tokyo, 1926), 992.

68 *Minshū* 23:613 (Gr. Ct. Cass., 4th Civ. Dept., Dec. 6, 1944).

69 *Nakasato v. Takano, Minroku* 26:1343 (Gr. Ct. Cass., 1st Civ. Dept., Sept. 24. 1920).

70 *Minshū* 5:36 (Sup. Ct., 2d P.B., Feb. 6, 1951).

71 *Minshū* 8:234 (Sup. Ct., 1st P.B., Jan. 28, 1954).

72 *Minshū* 8:448 (Sup. Ct., 2d P.B., Feb. 12, 1954).

73 See also M. Katsumoto, "Business Stringencies of Enterprises and the Principle of Change of Circumstances," *NBL*, no. 55 (1974): 6.

74 *Minshū* 9:2027 (Sup. Ct., 3d P.B., Dec. 20, 1955).

75 See, for example, *Iwanari v. Kurihara, Minshū* 10:342 (Sup. Ct., 2d P.B., April 6, 1956).

76 See, for example, *Oba v. Endo, Kakyū minshū* 9:666 (Sendai High Ct., April 14, 1958) [setting an original resale price of 520 yen at the tax assessment of 64,070 yen or the fair market value of 324,000 yen]; *Ideguchi v. Ishikawa, Kakyū minshū* 3:791 (Nagasaki Dist. Ct., June 9, 1942).

Chapter 8: Between the Individual and the State

1 See C. Kades "The American Role in Revising Japan's Imperial Constitution," *Political Science Quarterly* 104 (1989): 215–47.

2 See A. Ōtsuka, "Welfare Rights," in P. Luney and K. Takahashi, eds., *Japanese Constitutional Law* (Tokyo, 1993), 270–87.

3 *Minshū* 30:223 (Sup. Ct., G.B., April 4, 1976); *Kōshoku senkyō hō* (Law no. 100, 1950).

4 *Kanao v. Hiroshima Prefecture Election Commission*, Minshū 39:1100 (Sup. Ct., G.B., July 17, 1985), translated in L. Beer and H. Itoh, *The Constitutional Case Law of Japan, 1970 through 1990* (Seattle, 1996), 394–405. In 1983 the Court had affirmed the 1976 decision in *Kurokawa* in dismissing a constitutional challenge to the 1977 House of Councillors election. *Shimizu v. Osaka Prefecture Election Commission, Minshū* 37:345 (Sup. Ct., G.B., April 27, 1983), translated in Beer and Itoh, *Constitutional Case Law, 1970 through 1990*, 375–94.

5 *Keishū* 16:1593 (Sup. Ct., G.B., Nov. 28, 1962), translated in H. Itoh and L. Beer, *The Constitutional Case Law of Japan: Selected Supreme Court Decisions, 1961–1970* (Seattle, 1978), 58–73.

6 Some Japanese scholars argue that *Nakamura* did not hold the statutory provision unconstitutional but instead merely held that lack of notice under the provision constituted a denial of due process. See, e.g., N. Ashibe, "Japan: Human Rights and Judicial Power," in L. Beer, ed., *Constitutional Systems in Late Twentieth Century Asia* (Seattle, 1992), 224–69, 229.

7 *Keishū* 27:265 (Sup. Ct., G.B., April 4, 1973), translated in Beer and Itoh, *Constitutional Case Law, 1970 through 1990*, 143–70.

8 *Sumiyoshi K.K. v. Governor, Hiroshima Prefecture, Minshū* 29:572 (Sup. Ct., G.B., April 30, 1975), translated in Beer and Itoh, *Constitutional Case Law, 1970 through 1990*, 188–99.

9 *Minshū* 41:408 (Sup. Ct., G.B., April 22, 1987), translated in Beer and Itoh, *Constitutional Case Law, 1970 through 1990*, 327–45.

10 *Shinrin hō* (Law no. 161, 1959), art. 186; Civil Code, art. 256(1).

11 *Koshiyama v. Tokyo Metropolitan Election Commission, Minshū* 18:270 (Sup. Ct., G.B., Feb. 5, 1964), translated in Itoh and Beer, *Constitutional Case Law, 1961–1970*, 53–57.

12 *Japan v. Yamato, Keishū* 4:2037 (Sup. Ct., G.B., Oct. 11, 1950), translated in J. Maki, *Court and Constitution in Japan: Selected Supreme Court Decisions, 1948–1960* (Seattle, 1964), 129–55; quote, 131–32.

13 *Keishū* 4:2126 (Sup. Ct., G.B., Oct. 25, 1950).

14 *Shimizu v. Japan, Keishū* 9:89 (Sup. Ct., G.B., Jan. 26, 1955), translated in Maki, *Court and Constitution,* 293–97.

15 *Keishū* 26:586 (Sup. Ct., G.B., Nov. 22, 1972), translated in Beer and Itoh, *Constitutional Case Law, 1970 through 1990,* 183–88.

16 Ashibe, "Human Rights," 240–41.

17 See, for example, *Itō v. Minister of Agriculture and Forestry, Minshū* 36:1679 (Sup. Ct., 1st P.B., Sept. 9, 1982); *Ishizuka v. Japan, Minshū* 43:385 (Sup. Ct., 3d P.B., June 20, 1989). Both decisions and related cases translated in Beer and Itoh, *Constitutional Case Law, 1970 through 1990,* 83–141.

18 T. Kasuya, "Constitutional Transformation and the Ninth Article of the Japanese Constitution," *Law in Japan: An Annual* 18 (1986): 1–26.

19 See, for example, Y. Higuchi, *Shiho no sekkyokusei to shokyokusei* [The active and passive aspects of justice], 5th ed. (Tokyo, 1988), 92–126.

20 For a recent Tokyo High Court decision requiring a separation of prosecutorial and judicial functions in administrative proceedings, see *Toshiba Chemical K.K. v. Fair Trade Commission, Kōtō reishū* 47:17 (Tokyo High Ct., Feb. 25, 1994).

21 See D. Foote, "From Japan's Death Row to Freedom," *Pacific Rim Law & Policy Journal* 1 (1992): 11–103.

22 *Japan v. Koyama, Keishū* 11:997 (Sup. Ct., G.B., Mar. 13, 1957), translated in Maki, *Court and Constitution,* 3–37.

23 Maki, *Court and Constitution,* 9.

24 *Ishii v. Japan, Keishū* 23:1239 (Sup. Ct., G.B., Oct. 15, 1969), translated in Itoh and Beer, *Constitutional Case Law, 1961–1970,* 183–217.

25 See, for example, *Sato v. Japan, Keishū* 34:433 (Sup. Ct., G.B., Nov. 28, 1980), translated in Beer and Itoh, *Constitutional Case Law, 1970 through 1990,* 469–78.

26 E. Reischauer, *The Japanese* (Cambridge, Mass., 1982), 213.

27 K. van Wolferen, *The Enigma of Japanese Power* (New York, 1989), 9.

28 J. Sklar, *Legalism: Law, Morals and Political Trials* (Cambridge, Mass., 1986).

29 C. Gluck, *Japan's Modern Myth: Ideology in the Late Meiji Period* (Princeton, 1985), 138–43. See also H. Hardacre, *Shinto and the State, 1868–1988* (Princeton, 1989).

30 K. Inoue, *MacArthur's Japanese Constitution: A Linguistic and Cultural Study of its Making* (Chicago, 1991), 122.

31 Sato Tatsuo, October 22, 1945, quoted in Inoue, *Constitution,* 128.

32 *Minshū* 31:533 (Sup. Ct., G.B., July 13, 1977), translated in Beer and Itoh, *Constitutional Case Law, 1970 through 1990,* 478–91. For an excellent study of all but the most recent constitutional decisions involving freedom of religion, see D. O'Brien, *To Dream of Dreams: Religious Freedom and Constitutional Politics in Postwar Japan* (Honolulu, 1996).

33 *Chihō jichi hō* [Local Autonomy Law] (Law no. 67, 1947).

34 *Gyōsai reishū* 18:246 (Tsu Dist. Ct., Mar. 16, 1967).

35 *Gyōsai reishū* 22:680 (Nagoya High Ct., May 14, 1971).

36 *Kamisaka v. Mayor, Minoo City, Minshū* 47:1687 (Sup. Ct., 3d P.B., February 16, 1993).

37 E. Peterson, "The Minoo Chukonhi and Memorial Services Lawsuits: 'Carrots' and Remembrance" (Essay of Distinction in Japanese Studies, Jackson School of International Studies, May 26, 1995). I am indebted to Ms. Peterson for much of the historical background of the *Minoo Chūkonhi* cases.

38 *Kamisaka v. Nakai, Mayor of Minoo City, Hanrei jihō,* no. 1036:20 (Osaka Dist. Ct., March 24, 1982); *Kamisaka v. Nakai, Mayor of Minoo City, Hanrei jihō,* no. 1068:27 (Osaka Dist. Ct., March 1, 1983).

39 *Kamisaka v. Nakai, Mayor of Minoo City, Gyōsai reishū* 39:997 (Osaka Dist. Ct., Oct. 15, 1988).

40 *Hanrei jihō,* no. 1454:41 (1993), 55.

41 See, for example, *Hiyashi v. Japan, Hanrei taimuzu,* no. 789:94 (Osaka High Ct., July 30, 1992), finding that "despite doubts," participation by Prime Minister Nakasone in Yasukuni Shrine ceremony in 1985 did not violate article 20.

42 See, for example, *Iinuma v. Ikeda, Hanrei jihō,* no. 1438:36 (Kyoto Dist. Ct., November 4, 1992), dismissing damage action against school officials for playing *kimi-ga-yō* as the national anthem.

43 *Anzai v. Shiraishi, Hanrei jihō,* no. 1601:47 (Sup. Ct., G.B., April 2, 1997).

44 *Hanrei jihō,* no. 1419:38 (Takamatsu High Ct, May 12, 1992), reversing the March 17, 1989, judgment of Matsuyama District Court.

45 *Japan v. Nakaya, Minshū* 42:277 (Sup. Ct., G.B., June 1, 1988), translated in Beer and Itoh, *Constitutional Case Law, 1970 through 1990,* 492–516.

46 N. Field, *In the Realm of a Dying Emperor* (New York, 1991), 109–10.

47 Ibid., 107.

48 See O'Brien, *To Dream of Dreams,* 142–78, 192–93.

49 *Nakaya v. Japan, Hanrei jihō,* no. 921:44 (Yamaguchi Dist. Ct., Mar. 22, 1979).

50 *Japan v. Nakaya, Hanrei jihō*, no. 1046:3 (Hiroshima High Ct., June 1, 1982).

51 See J. Braithwaite, *Crime, Shame and Reintegration* (Cambridge, 1989).

52 See O'Brien, *To Dream of Dreams*, 191.

Conclusion

1 The lectures were subsequently published in the *Yale Law Journal:* K. Hatoyama, "The Civil Code of Japan Compared With the French Civil Code," *Yale Law Journal* 11 (1901–2): 297–98.

2 See J. Haley, *Authority Without Power: Law and the Japanese Paradox* (New York and London, 1991), especially chapter 8.

3 See T. Inoue, "The Poverty of Rights-Blind Communality: Looking Through the Window of Japan," *Brigham Young University Law Review* (1993): 517–51; S. Miyazawa, "For the Liberal Transformation of Japanese Legal Culture: A Review of Recent Scholarship and Practice," *Kobe University Law Review* 29 (1995): 64.

4 Inoue, "Rights-Blind Communality," 545.

INDEX

The Spirit of the Laws

Alan Watson, General Editor

www.ingramcontent.com/pod-product-compliance
Lightning Source LLC
Chambersburg PA
CBHW021553210326
41599CB00010B/428